Modern Psychotherapies

A Comprehensive Christian Appraisal

Stanton L. Jones
Richard E. Butman

Volume 1 of 2

16
EasyRead Large

RHYW

Copyright Page from the Original Book

InterVarsity Press
P.O. Box 1400, Downers Grove, IL 60515-1426
World Wide Web: www.ivpress.com
E-mail: email@ivpress.com

InterVarsity Press® is the book-publishing division of InterVarsity Christian Fellowship/USA®, a movement of students and faculty active on campus at hundreds of universities, colleges and schools of nursing in the United States of America, and a member movement of the International Fellowship of Evangelical Students. For information about local and regional activities, write Public Relations Dept., InterVarsity Christian Fellowship/USA, 6400 Schroeder Rd., P.O. Box 7895, Madison, WI 53707-7895, or visit the IVCF website at <www.intervarsity.org>.

While all stories in this book are true, some names and identifying information in this book have been changed to protect the privacy of the individuals involved.

Design: Cindy Kiple
Images: Cargo/Getty Images

ISBN 978-0-8308-2852-4

Printed in the United States of America ∞

green press INITIATIVE *InterVarsity Press is committed to protecting the environment and to the responsible use of natural resources. As a member of Green Press Initiative we use recycled paper whenever possible. To learn more about the Green Press Initiative, visit <www.greenpressinitiative.org>.*

Library of Congress Cataloging-in-Publication Data

Jones, Stanton L.
Modern psychotherapies: a comprehensive Christian approach / Stanton L. Jones & Richard E. Butman; with contributions by Sally S. Canning . . . [et al.].
p. cm.
Includes bibliographical references and index.
ISBN 978-0-8308-2852-4 (casebound: alk. paper)
1. Psychotherapy—Religious aspects—Christianity. 2. Christianity—Psychology. 3. Pastoral psychology. I. Butman, Richard E., 1951- II. Title.
BV4012.J65 2011
261.5'15—dc23

2011023124

P 20 19 18 17 16 15 14 13 12 11 10 9 8 7 6 5 4 3 2 1
Y 28 27 26 25 24 23 22 21 20 19 18 17 16 15 14 13 12 11

TABLE OF CONTENTS

WITH CONTRIBUTIONS BY Sally Schwer Canning, Kelly Flanagan, Tracey Lee, Michael W. Mangis, Mark R. McMinn, Laura Miguélez, David Van Dyke, Michael J. Vogel, Robert Watson and Terri Watson

Our little systems have their day;
They have their day and cease to be:
They are but broken lights of Thee,
And Thou, O Lord, art more than they.

Alfred Tennyson,
"In Memoriam"

Twenty years ago, we dedicated the original version of this text to our children. We retain that dedication, noting that God has allowed each to grow into adulthood and has answered our prayers for their lives beyond what we could have ever dreamed.

To
Jenny, the gentle spirit;
Brandon, full of sensitive brightness;
and Lindsay, an effervescent sprite—
in hopes that you will each grow up to know the fullness of God's love.

And to
Ashley Elizabeth, aglow with wonder—
in hopes that you will continue to manifest God's grace
in the lives of those you touch.

ACKNOWLEDGMENTS

Reformed Christian thinkers often assert that in pursuing truth, we attempt to "think God's thoughts after him." We cannot be so confident to claim that we are presenting "God's thoughts" in this book, but it has been exciting to pursue that goal in this project. As we wrote, we were acutely aware of those who have been friends, conversation partners and mentors to us in some form or another along the paths of our development. In some sense, much of what might be good in all that follows is due to their influence—we have been thinking "their thoughts" as well as God's thoughts. What is inadequate in what follows is due to our own weaknesses.

Our acknowledgments in the original version of this book need to be retained, because the basic contours of our thinking as influenced by our friends and collaborators endures in this new, revised edition. Twenty years ago we thanked, and continue to thank, the following individuals: scholars C. Stephen Evans and Alan Tjeltveit, who read the first draft of the first manuscript in its entirety; colleague Michael Mangis, who did the initial draft of the "ContemporaryPsychodynamicPsychotherapies" chapter for us; colleagues Dennis Okholm, Frances J. White, Siang Yang Tan, Robert

Roberts, H. Newton Malony, Kirk Farnsworth, Don Bosch, Drew Loizeaux, Brian Van Dragt and Jon Peterson, who offered critiques of individual chapters at various stages of development; our first editors at InterVarsity Press, Michael Maudlin and Rodney Clapp; our secretaries at Wheaton College, Carol Blauwkamp and Geraldine Carlson; and several generations of research assistants including Joel Arp, Karen Crow Blankenship, Rose Buier, David Dodd, Michael Gillis, Kathy Hobson, Todd Keylock, Kathleen Lattea, Stephen Moroney, Grace Ann Robertson, Lauren Strickler, Trudy Walk, Elizabeth Watson, David Wilcox, Don Workman and Chris Zang. Our thanks go out yet again for the gracious hosting twenty years ago of our respective first sabbaticals: for Stan, to the recently deceased Don Browning and the faculty of the University of Chicago Divinity School, and for Rich to H. Newton Malony and the faculty, students and staff of the Graduate School of Psychology at Fuller Theological Seminary.

The passing of twenty years and the completion of a new revision of this volume offers a whole new array of persons and things for which to give thanks. At the broadest level, this book bears the imprint of the marvelous institution at which we work. As we write, the journal *First Things,* a forum for discussion of the impact of religion in the public sphere, in its November 2010 issue has just declared that "Wheaton College in Illinois is the single best place to go to college in America" (p.3). While there is certainly room to challenge their methodology, their rankings of the various colleges in America are based on the confluence of three major variables: academic seriousness, social healthiness, and spiritual and theological integrity and thoughtfulness. Their ideal college would be a place where students are mentored by quality faculty at the forefront of their disciplines, where the campus atmosphere encourages growth into responsibility and maturity rather than degeneration into debauchery, and where resources are offered to facilitate growth in Christlikeness. Such a college environment that is healthy for students is equally healthy for the professionals blessed to serve there. Such is Wheaton College.

Since the first version of this book was completed in 1990, dramatic changes have occurred in the study of psychology at Wheaton College. The department has doubled in size, moving from a department of six undergraduate faculty and three graduate faculty serving undergraduate majors and students pursuing a master's degree in clinical psychology to a department of seventeen individuals serving undergraduate and master's students but also

a cadre of students pursuing a doctorate in clinical psychology. The addition of so many capable faculty colleagues has multiplied the riches for conversation and reflection on what it means to be a Christian psychologist.

There have also been personal changes for the two of us. Rich moved long ago from the undergraduate faculty to the graduate faculty, focusing increasingly on the teaching of psychopathology and psychological assessment. Stan, after a too brief, one-year stint as the Rech Chair of Psychology and Christian Faith, moved in 1996 to his current role as provost of Wheaton College. While these transitions have continued to foster our reflections on matters of the relationship of psychology and Christian faith, neither one of our positions have allowed us to continue to teach the survey courses in Christian approaches to psychotherapy that formed the basis of our first version of this book.

Thus, this new revision has become a community project. As we began to consider revision of this book, it became abundantly clear that we needed to reach out for help to the extraordinary community of scholars around us who are teaching these different psychotherapy approaches to tap their rich integrated understandings of the various approaches. As is noted in the list of authorship on the table of contents, each colleague took one of our original chapters and revised and updated it. This eventually led to a substantial reorganization of the material of the book. We also added a new chapter on community psychology to broaden our understandings beyond the typical dyadic counselor-client relationship to see broader possibilities for constructive change using the tools of psychology. Our heartfelt thanks go out to our coauthors for their friendship, their expertise and their patience during the long revision process.

Portions of chapter one in the current volume are based on S.L. Jones (2010), "An Integration View," in E. Johnson (Ed.), *Psychology and Christianity: Five views* (2nd ed., pp.101-128), Downers Grove, IL: InterVarsity Press; used by permission. Portions of chapters five and six were originally based on S. Jones (1988), "A Religious Critique of Behavior Therapy," in W. Miller and J. Martin (Eds.), *Behavior therapy and religion* (pp.139-170), Newbury Park, CA: Sage; used by permission.

Handling the issue of gender in writing is an ever-troublesome matter. We have chosen to use inclusive terms wherever it did not torture the language to do so. In places where it was not stylistically pleasing to use neutered terms, we have attempted to alternate references to females and males. We were not compulsive in the process, so some unintentional inequities may remain, but we hope not.

Stan will be eternally grateful to Brenna, with profound gratitude for her support, love, patience and encouragement; without her this revised book would never have been completed. Thank you for being excellent in all that you do.

Rich would like to express his deep gratitude to both his immediate and extended families that have stood with him in the good times—and in the difficult and challenging times. Recently, this has included his graduate teaching assistants, Tamara Koch and Stalin George, and his clinical colleagues, Tim Brown, Alex Tsang, Sandy Johnston Kruse, Victor Argo, Terri Watson, William Struthers, Gary Burge, Don Kerns and Rob Ribbe. Finally, he wants to acknowledge the support of his mountaineering friends, who have faced together seemingly innumerable changes, losses and transitions over a span of nearly four decades.

COLLABORATORS

Sally Schwer Canning is associate professor of psychology at Wheaton College and a clinical psychologist at Lawndale Christian Health Center.

Kelly S. Flanagan is a child clinical psychologist, and assistant professor of psychology and Psy. D. program director at Wheaton College.

Tracy Lee is a clinical psychologist working in private practice in Columbus, Ohio, specializing in the area of psychological assessment.

Michael W. Mangis is a clinical psychologist and professor of psychology at Wheaton College.

Mark R. McMinn is a clinical psychologist and professor of psychology at George Fox University.

Laura C. Miguélez is an ordained deacon and works as an adjunct assistant professor of theology at Wheaton College.

David J. Van Dyke is a marriage and family therapist and an associate professor at Illinois School of Professional Psychology.

Michael J. Vogel is pursuing a doctoral degree in clinical psychology from George Fox University.

Robert A. Watson is a clinical psychologist who maintains a clinical and consulting practice in the Chicago area.

Terri S. Watson is a board certified clinical psychologist and an associate professor of psychology at Wheaton College.

INTRODUCTION

This book attempts to appraise each of the current major psychotherapy approaches or theories in the mental health field from the perspective of evangelical Christianity. It is a dialogue between the supposedly nonreligious therapeutic psychologies and the Christian religious and theological tradition. But it is a dialogue where one side of the conversation, that of the Christian faith, is presumed to have the ultimate standing as truth. Nevertheless, we presume that the various psychologies have much to teach us and may in fact lead us to see certain truths of the Christian tradition in a different light.

In 1977, I (Stan) was in the first year of graduate school and while struggling with issues of faith in the context of a highly secular program came across a book written in the 1950s relating Christian faith to the field of psychology. It was authored by one who was at that time one of the most eminent scholars in the field of clinical psychology, someone whose enduring legacy continues to this day. I wrote an enthusiastic letter to this scholar, asking if he had written more in this area. He graciously replied, saying that he was no longer a Christian; he was not sure where he stood religiously, but it was probably closest to Zen

Buddhism. But he also added that while he no longer had a personal commitment to the presuppositions from which he wrote in the 1950s, he nevertheless felt that the earlier book was logically sound; that is, the form and content of his analysis stood even though he no longer believed the foundations for what he wrote at that time. Unlike this scholar, we remain passionately committed to the truth of the Christian faith, but consistent with his answer, we seek to provide here a thoughtful analysis of the psychotherapy enterprise that will assist fellow believers in approaching psychotherapy from a distinctively Christian perspective, and which may also yield helpful reflections for nonbelievers on the philosophical and assumptive foundations of their approaches to helping persons change.

Because of our presumption of the truth of the orthodox Christian tradition, this book may be perceived as parochial by some, as it represents only one religious tradition. Our intended audience is students, pastors, mental health professionals, and interested and informed laypersons in the evangelical Christian tradition. But in line with the story of the previously mentioned scholar, we would argue that the form of our analysis stands even if one is not an evangelical Christian. Christians of other stripes, and perhaps even those of non-Christian faith traditions, will, we hope, find this book helpful in outlining the religious implications of the various psychotherapy traditions and in suggesting how religious faith might interact with and revise the way we think about personality and psychotherapy.

When we were writing the first edition of this book in the late 1980s, the "integration of psychology and Christianity" movement was just gaining momentum. In the decade of the 1980s, very few Christian institutions of higher learning had graduate programs in applied psychology, and only two had doctoral programs in clinical psychology (Fuller Theological Seminary and Rosemead School of Psychology at Biola University). At the same time, signs of openness were only beginning in the field of psychology to consideration of religious and spiritual factors affecting the field, and indications of continuing hostility toward religious faith among many in the mental health fields were remarkable.

How things have changed! The integration movement has continued to grow in its volume, complexity and breadth (this is more thoroughly developed in chap.1). Notably, movements critical of the idea of integration such as the biblical counseling movement have continued to hold sway in certain parts of the conservative Christian church. At the same time, a vibrant movement to endorse a distinct "Christian psychology" approach is prospering, and the integration movement continues as well (all discussed ably in Johnson, 2010). Helpful anthologies tracing the development of these conversations have been published (Stevenson, Eck & Hill, 2007). Training programs in the mental health field have proliferated amazingly; by the mid-1990s, our own Wheaton College had initiated our doctoral program in clinical psychology, and now quite a number of Christian institutions of higher learning are host to doctoral training programs that embody Christian distinctiveness in various ways.

In the meantime, the conversation has changed in the mainstream, secular discipline. We are pleased to have played some role in this process. In 1994, Stan published a key article (Jones, 1994) in what is regarded as the "flagship journal of the American Psychological Association (APA)" (Stevenson et al., 2007, pp.94-95) arguing for a major shift in professional attitudes toward religion, specifically for a move to consider religion as a partner in constructive dialogue in both the scientific and professional practice dimensions of the discipline of psychology. Whether this article was crucial in what followed or not, its publication marked an opening for a different kind of engagement by the APA with spirituality and religion, namely, that "Prior to this article, the topic of religion (including integration) had been virtually ignored in APA publication materials. Since its publication, the APA has published a number of books and articles (in APA's own journals) stressing the centrality and predictive importance of religious faith in psychological functioning" (Stevenson et al., 2007, p.95; see for example Shafranske, 1996, and Miller & Delaney, 2005). In short, a good bit of the hostility and resistance to the role of religion and spirituality in life has been ameliorated, replaced by an unprecedented dialogue about the role of such factors in human well-being.

Even so, the degree and nature of this openness should not be overestimated or misunderstood. Our summary judgment is that there is much more openness to generic, humanistically grounded spirituality than there is to substantive religious faith, especially as that religious faith is grounded in formal creeds and ecclesiastical institutions. There is a growing trend in the field to view religious faith and spirituality as a natural human capacity that exists and persists because it serves basic human needs despite its ultimately illusory nature. A recent journalistic account (Azar, 2010) captures this well in its subtitle: "Religion may fill the human need for finding meaning, sparing us from existential angst while also supporting social organization, researchers say." The traditional Christian has every reason to believe that true religion does indeed serve basic human needs, and we would argue that it does so because it is ultimately grounded in a true account of reality; the secular psychology accounts, however, serve to subtly erode such understandings.

This resistance to more formalized versions of religious faith, at times seeming especially directed toward orthodox Christianity, is often subtle, but not always. At this writing, two different court cases, winding their way through the appeals courts, have resulted from graduate students who are traditionalist Christians with conservative moral views of sexuality (particularly homosexual conduct) being ejected from graduate training programs in counseling (i.e., counseling per se as defined by the American Counseling Association, and as differentiated from counseling psychology) for holding views deemed incompatible with and not acceptable in the counseling profession. Even though there is a good case to be made that scientific findings have done little to invalidate the moral concerns of traditional Christians (Jones & Yarhouse, 2000; Jones & Kwee, 2005), and despite the ostensible moral neutrality of the APA and the various other mental health professional organizations, there are signs of movement toward similar reactions against Christian moral stances (also shared by traditionalist Jews, Muslims and Buddhists) in the discipline of psychology (APA, 2009); these moves have been contested (Jones, Rosik, Williams & Byrd, 2010). These are just some of the signs of tension in the relationship between religion and psychology broadly construed. The seeming openness of the field to spirituality should not be engaged naively.

In each of the chapters, we cite recent literature that examines the particular issues and psychotherapies we are addressing. Often this literature will be from the growing and increasingly sophisticated integration literature; at other times it may reflect literature that is a part of the more generic spirituality dialogue of the broader field. In composing this book we and our coauthors have been able to build on the work of many able scholars, to whom we are each heavily indebted.

Before embarking on our study, we will briefly examine the nature of psychotherapy and counseling, since it is vital to have a general picture of the nature of what we are appraising before we focus on the details.

WHAT IS PSYCHOTHERAPY AND COUNSELING?

The topics we will examine in this book are germane to the concerns not just of professional psychologists, but to all mental health workers, pastoral counselors and pastors, and indeed to the concerns of informed laypeople who desire to be effective in their interpersonal ministries. But despite the number of people involved in this endeavor, defining psychotherapy and counseling is quite complicated.

The Problem of Diversity

Psychotherapy is a generic term that covers a wide variety of theories and techniques, all of which have articulate spokespersons and supporters and make claims of success. The varied theories and techniques are derived, for the most part, from clinical experience and reflection rather than deductively from scientific axioms or from systematic empirical research. This helps to explain the proliferation of therapy approaches. They emerge from each theorist's unique experiences of the type of people he or she has seen for counseling, the types of problems they manifest, the cultural context of the therapist, his or her assumptions about how people change, and the core beliefs that shape the therapist's life philosophy. This understandably leaves wide room for diverse approaches to people-helping.

There are an incredible array of approaches. Not only are there numerous major theories, but each seems to have a number of variations as well. Even twenty-five years ago, leading experts had identified 260 distinct schools of psychotherapy (Strupp & Binder, 1984); since then, many of these have drifted into obscurity only to be replaced by other unique approaches. Certainly, many of these approaches are kissing cousins rather than truly unique approaches.

Since many approaches to psychotherapy claim impressive results, it is difficult to evaluate critically the ultimate worth of a particular theory or technique. One must get the broad perspective when assessing the value of a specific system: Who is working with whom, under what conditions and assumptions, and on what particular problems and concerns? There is an ever-present danger of the overenthusiastic extrapolation of a theory or technique to client populations or problems for which it was never intended, or for which there is little or no reason to suggest its effectiveness. For example, the unquestionable effectiveness of behavior modification with many autistic children (Lovaas, 1987) has little bearing on its use with adults struggling with the meaning of life. Likewise, counselors should be appropriately humble in their pronouncements about their theories and techniques, though we don't know of a single counseling approach that hasn't in some form claimed to be the true and best way.

Defining Psychotherapy and Counseling

In light of all this diversity, it is not surprising that academicians, clinicians and researchers have found it difficult to agree on a specific definition of counseling and psychotherapy. As London (1964) noted, many find it easier to practice the art and science of people-helping than to describe it.

Still, across theories and techniques there appear to be some common features. In fact, many theoreticians and researchers today argue that these common factors influence, or even determine, the likelihood of a successful therapeutic outcome. Some approaches to understanding these common factors focus on the common techniques that all psychotherapists seem to use (though with differing frequencies). A classic work from thirty years ago (Garfield, 1980) concluded that most psychotherapy comprises varying mixtures of four basic interventions offered by the therapist or counselor: (1) offering reassurance and support, (2) desensitizing the client to distress, (3) encouraging adaptive functioning, and (4) offering understanding and insight. While clearly there are some intervention strategies that don't fit in any of these categories, this analysis still has some validity. Understanding these common features can be helpful as one tries to define counseling.

Another recent approach to the investigation of common-factors focuses is not on technique but on variables that seem to determine or shape the outcome of any counseling approach. As we will explore more in chapter eleven, McMinn and Campbell (2007) interpret the best meta-analytic empirical research on psychotherapy to indicate that the key variables that influence positive outcome include specific psychotherapeutic techniques, but more importantly expectancy effects (the degree of hopefulness and optimism versus pessimism of the client), the quality of the relationship between the counselor and client, and the degree of contextual or situational support (or lack thereof, or even stressfulness and aversiveness) in the person's immediate environment.

We would describe individual counseling or psychotherapy as a dyadic (two-way) interaction between a client who is distressed, and perhaps confused and frightened, and a professional helper whose helping skills are recognized and accepted by the client. The two engage in an ongoing, private, collaborative encounter that is structured as to time, place and overall purpose in a way that informal friendships are not. The relationship is likely to rely heavily on verbal communication of the client's thoughts, feelings, attitudes and behaviors. The client comes to believe in and develop hope from what happens in therapy, in part because the therapist appears to have a theory for understanding and explaining the client's distress as well as having intervention techniques for reducing it. In a supportive atmosphere with an empathetic and caring therapist, the client begins to disclose and reevaluate feelings and behavior patterns, to understand and accept previously rejected aspects of herself, to take risks, to become more open and honest about herself, to learn new methods of living with self and others, and to gain new satisfactions from life. With the client having less need for the psychotherapy, the process is usually terminated by mutual consent with the therapist (adapted from Frank, 1961; Garfield, 1980; and particularly Goldenberg, 1983, pp.172ff.). While this definition assumes that the client is an individual, increasingly practitioners of psychotherapy are open to the client being a couple, a family, a group or a larger system.

Given that counseling and psychotherapy is so intensely personal and yet is regarded as a professional rather than personal relationship, how is psychotherapy and counseling different from friendship? As is commonly observed, a lot of good counseling goes on over cups of coffee, in the barber shop or over a backyard fence; perhaps a lot more than goes on during any given day in the offices of psychotherapists (Matarazzo & Wiens, 1972). There are some important differences, though. Ideally, the therapist is able to avoid undue emotional involvement with the client so as to be more objective, allowing the client to more freely communicate his thoughts and feelings (Copans & Singer, 1978). The therapist's personal qualities and the environment she creates encourage risk taking and facilitate the acquisition of skills and sensitivities that will foster the development of health and wholeness. Perhaps the most important distinction between psychotherapy and friendship is that the former is by definition a one-way relationship emotionally and psychologically, and it is the client who is supposed to derive good from the interchange. The growth and healing of the therapist is not the purpose of this limited and purposeful relationship (Korchin, 1976). Friendships, on the other hand, are ideally mutually beneficial emotionally and psychologically, and are not structured intentionally for the benefit of only one of the parties involved. It is obvious, though, that we cannot say that psychotherapists derive no benefit from the therapeutic relationship, as financial, professional and social benefits certainly can and do accrue to the psychotherapist who is effective.

Are Psychotherapy and Counseling Different?

An important and often hotly debated question that is no more settled today than it was thirty years ago is how psychotherapy and counseling are to be differentiated (McLemore, 1974). The traditional distinction promulgated by doctoral-level practitioners has been that counseling is done by less comprehensively and intensively trained professionals (e.g., pastors, school guidance counselors) and by paraprofessionals (lay counselors or mental health volunteers). It is done with less seriously disturbed groups of persons, such as those struggling with decisions of what career to pursue, whether or not to get married and so forth. Counseling has often been regarded as relying heavily on the giving of wise advice as a major mode of intervention.

Historically, psychotherapy was thought to be more appropriate for "deeper" problems and was most often done by more highly trained or certified therapists. The focus was on significant personality change rather than adjustment to situational and life problems. It is sometimes said that psychotherapy attempts significantly to change the personality of clients, often paying less attention to specific current life problems, while counseling works within existing personality structures to help people adjust to the current demands on them.

Although some authors still prefer to make a distinction between counseling and psychotherapy, we have chosen to use the terms interchangeably in this text for two main reasons. The first is that clinical and counseling psychology, which were once substantially different disciplines and arose out of different historical roots, have grown closer together over the last several decades. The distinctions between the two subdisciplines were hard to make out twenty-five years ago (see Altmaier, 1985) and are even harder today. Notably, among the doctoral-level faculty in our own clinical psychology faculty at Wheaton College are a number of respected colleagues whose doctorates are in counseling psychology.

Perhaps more importantly, we will not make the distinctions here because the very same theories are utilized as guides for the change process by psychotherapists and counselors.

Survey textbooks for counseling theories and methods, and for psychotherapy theories and methods, contain almost identical content. While there can be different emphases in books to the two professional populations, the basic theories are not different.

STRUCTURE OF THE BOOK

Our perspective in this book is decidedly psychological and spiritual. In taking this perspective we do not wish to minimize the clear importance of the biological/physical perspective on mental health, nor of the sociological/sociocultural perspective (Yarhouse, Butman & McRay, 2005). But our focus will be on the current interactional psychotherapies. We believe that a careful critique of these approaches is important for the Christian world today.

We also believe that psychologists do not have the final word in understanding humanness, suffering and growth. If anything, psychologists have been saying too much and the populace has been listening too much. It is no wonder that many today describe psychologists as the "secular priests" of our age. We believe that the centrality of religious reflection must be reasserted, as well as the value of philosophical, artistic, literary and other facets of our human ways of knowing.

Psychotherapy has assumed a position of high visibility and importance in many sectors of our American society. Our goal is to come to a new understanding of this field in order that we might more effectively participate in the work that God is doing in and through his church. The needs of contemporary society are creating new and potentially challenging roles for Christians who desire to minister in the name of Christ to a hurting world. We believe strongly that a greater awareness and knowledge of both the assets and liabilities of the major psychotherapy approaches can contribute in a significant way to the larger mission and work of the church.

As we mention in our acknowledgments, the most significant change in this book, as we move from the first edition to the second, is our indebtedness to numerous coauthors who have worked to create new versions of each chapter in this book. We believe the diverse perspectives that these coauthors bring added new richness and vitality to our work.

This book is structured in three parts. In the two introductory chapters we have outlined a summary of our view of what it means to relate or integrate the Christian faith with a field like psychology or psychotherapy theory. Chapter one discusses this process in general terms and deals with some important and frequently expressed objections (at least in conservative circles) to such an approach. Since an examination of psychotherapy from a Christian perspective must proceed from a foundational Christian understanding of persons, chapter two focuses specifically on the broad strokes of our Christian view of persons. Having clarified our method and the Christian view of persons, we then proceed into the heart of our appraisal.

Chapters three through ten cover a variety of approaches to psychotherapy. The four major paradigms in the field today are the psychodynamic, the cognitive-behavioral, the humanistic, and the family approaches; in a real sense, we devote two chapters to each of these four major paradigms. The most important representatives of each of these traditions are examined from our Christian perspective. Each chapter will begin with a summary presentation of each model; the interested reader can get a more exhaustive presentation of these approaches by consulting the volumes suggested for further reading at the end of this introduction and at the end of each chapter.

The book will conclude with an examination of how one can profitably draw from more than one approach in elaborating one's approach to counseling (chap.11) and a discussion of what it means to be a Christian counselor (chap.12). Our main premise in these concluding chapters is that there are many ways to counsel Christianly. But it is not and cannot be the case that "anything goes." We hope that our suggestions in these concluding chapters will help the process of putting it all together for the reader.

This volume is offered in fervent hope that it will instigate and support the rigorous development of thoroughly Christian mental health professionals who will manifest and embody biblical truth as they serve those in need of quality mental health services.

FOR FURTHER READING

Browning, D.S., & Cooper, T.D. (2004). *Religious thought and the modern psychologies* (2nd ed.). Minneapolis, MN: Fortress.

Corey, G. (2009). *Theory and practice of counseling and psychotherapy* (8th ed.). Belmont, CA: Thomson/Brooks Cole.

Corey, M.S., & Corey, G. (2011). *Becoming a helper* (6th ed.). Belmont, CA: Brooks/Cole.

Corsini, R. (2008). *Current psychotherapies* (8th ed.). Belmont, CA: Brooks/Cole. Some of the many accessible textbooks providing broad overviews of the current theories and practices in psychotherapy and counseling.

Johnson, E.F. (Ed.). (2010). *Psychology and Christianity: Five views* (2nd ed.). Downers Grove, IL: InterVarsity Press. The best "one-stop shop" to read about the dialogue over how Christian faith and psychology can relate.

McMinn, M., & Campbell, C. (2007). *Integrative psychotherapy: Toward a comprehensive Christian approach.* Downers Grove, IL: IVP Academic.

Tan, S.Y. (2011). *Counseling and psychotherapy: A Christian perspective.* Grand Rapids, MI: Baker Academic. Representative samples of the kinds of rigorous Christian engagement available in reflecting on psychotherapy.

REFERENCES

Altmaier, K. (1985). Counseling psychology. In D. Benner (Ed.), *Baker encyclopedia of psychology* (pp.252-254). Grand Rapids, MI: Baker.

APA Task Force on Appropriate Therapeutic Responses to Sexual Orientation. (2009). Report of the Task Force on Appropriate Therapeutic Responses to Sexual Orientation.

Retrieved from www.apa.org/pi/lgbt/resources/therapeutic-response.pdf.

Azar, B. (2010, December). A reason to believe. *APA Monitor on Psychology, 41* (11), 52-55.

Copans, S., & Singer, T. (1978). *Who's the patient here?* New York, NY: Oxford University Press.

Corey, G. (2009). *Theory and practice of counseling and psychotherapy* (8th ed.). Belmont, CA: Thomson/Brooks Cole.

Corey, M.S., & Corey, G. (2011). *Becoming a helper.* (6th ed.). Belmont, CA: Brooks/Cole.

Corsini, R. (2008). *Current psychotherapies* (8th ed.). Belmont, CA: Brooks/Cole.

Frank, J. (1961). *Persuasion and healing.* Baltimore, MD: Johns Hopkins University Press.

Frank, J. (1973). *Persuasion and healing.* (Rev. ed.). Baltimore, MD: Johns Hopkins University Press.

Garfield, S. (1980). *Psychotherapy: An eclectic approach.* New York, NY: Wiley-Interscience.

Goldenberg, D. (1983). *Contemporary clinical psychology* (2nd ed.). Monterey, CA: Brooks/Cole.

Johnson, E.F. (Ed.). (2010). *Psychology and Christianity: Five views* (2nd ed.). Downers Grove, IL: InterVarsity Press.

Jones, S.L. (1994). A constructive relationship for religion with the science and profession of psychology: Perhaps the boldest model yet. *American Psychologist, 49* (3), 184-199.

Jones, S., & Kwee, A.W. (2005). Scientific research, homosexuality, and the church's moral debate: An update. *Journal of Psychology and Christianity, 24* (4), 304-316.

Jones, S., Rosik, C.H., Williams, R.N., & Byrd, A.D. (2010). A scientific, conceptual, and ethical critique of the Report of the APA Task Force on Sexual Orientation. *The General Psychologist, 45* (2), 7-18.

Jones, S., & Yarhouse, M. (2000). Homosexuality: The use of scientific research in the church's moral debate. Downers Grove, IL: InterVarsity Press.

Korchin, S. (1976). *Modern clinical psychology.* New York, NY: Basic Books.

London, P. (1964). *The modes and morals of psychotherapy.* Washington, DC: Hemisphere.

London, P. (1986). *The modes and morals of psychotherapy* (2nd ed.). Washington, DC: Hemisphere.

Lovaas, O. (1987). Behavioral treatment and normal educational and intellectual functioning in young autistic children. *Journal of Consulting and Clinical Psychology, 55* (1), 3-9.

McLemore, C.W. (1974). *Clergyman's psychological handbook.* Grand Rapids, MI: Eerdmans.

Matarazzo, J., & Wiens, A. (1972). *The interview: Research on its anatomy and structure.* Chicago, IL: Aldine.

McMinn, M., & Campbell, C. (2007). *Integrative psychotherapy: Toward a comprehensive Christian approach.* Downers Grove, IL: IVP Academic.

Miller, W.R., & Delaney, H.D. (Eds.). (2005). *Human nature, motivation, and change: Judeo-Christian perspectives on psychology.* Washington, DC: American Psychological Association.

Shafranske, E. (Ed.). (1996). *Religion and the clinical practice of psychology.* Washington, DC: American Psychological Association.

Stevenson, D.H., Eck, B.E., & Hill, P.C. (Eds.). (2007). *Psychology and Christianity integration: Seminal works that shaped the movement.* Batavia, IL: Christian Association for Psychological Studies.

Strupp, H., & Binder, D. (1984). *Psychotherapy in a new key.* New York, NY: Basic Books.

Yarhouse, M., Butman, R., & McRay (2005). *Modern psychopathologies: A comprehensive Christian appraisal.* Downers Grove, IL: InterVarsity Press.

1

THE INTEGRATION OF PSYCHOLOGY AND CHRISTIANITY

Stanton L. Jones and Richard E. Butman

***

Christian counselors and psychotherapists are vitally concerned with understanding the human condition, fostering human flourishing and alleviating human suffering. Our field has arisen in a time when it is painfully obvious that improving our standard of living and our physical health does not guarantee anyone a sense of personal well-being. Far too many people are in emotional, mental or spiritual pain.

Out of a desire to improve the human condition and alleviate suffering, many Christians today are interested in the mental health fields. There is a strong desire to enrich Christian ministry by drawing upon the resources of the evolving field of psychology and its related disciplines. What thoughtful pastor or counselor would not want to use all available knowledge and techniques to make his or her people-helping as effective as possible?

But there is also considerable ambivalence about and outright opposition to drawing upon the strengths of psychology among some conservative Christians. Some describe the field of psychotherapy as "satanic" or "completely secularized" and "unredeemable." While in graduate school, one of us (Stan) spoke to Jay Adams, the founding father of "Biblical Counseling." I asked if he had any words of guidance for Christians studying psychology, to which Adams responded, in essence, "Drop out of graduate school. If you want to serve God as a counselor, you can only do so by going to seminary, studying the Word of God rather than the words of men, and becoming a pastor."

Neither one of us took Dr. Adams's advice. We have, however, tried to maintain our foundational commitments to Jesus Christ in our work as psychologists. This book is the fruit of the working out of that goal. It covers a significant aspect of what we believe it means to be a Christian psychologist, mental health professional, counselor or psychotherapist.

This book is about thinking Christianly about contemporary approaches to psychotherapy and counseling. We strongly believe that it is not enough simply to pray for clients, or to refrain from discouraging their spiritual sensitivities, or to have high ethical standards while the Christian psychotherapist otherwise uses the methods and practices of theories and methods derived from secular sources. Every theory or method of people-helping carries with it a system of beliefs, a way of seeing or understanding people: who they are, why they experience what they do, how they can change and what they should be aiming for in life. As Browning and Cooper (2004) put it, psychological science (and particularly the applied psychologies) "cannot avoid a metaphysical and ethical horizon" (p.xiv). These theoretical suppositions may or may not conflict with direct assertions of the Christian faith or with more indirect implications of the faith. *It is because we feel that these theories of psychotherapy have often been either summarily dismissed or uncritically embraced by Christians that we have attempted to provide a balanced appraisal of these views from a Christian perspective.*

In this first chapter we want to set our foundations by grappling with the core of how a religious faith should interact with the seemingly "secular" and "scientific" field of psychotherapy. Since this task is often called "the integration of psychology and Christianity" or of "psychology and theology," the core of this chapter is a discussion of what *integration* means. We approach this in two stages, discussing first the general stance of the Christian toward "secular knowledge," then moving to the more specific issue of our stance toward "psychological knowledge and science." We will then briefly discuss criticisms from various directions of the integration movement and conclude with a discussion of the specific integration methodology we will use to appraise or critique the various approaches to psychotherapy.

HOW DOES CHRISTIANITY RELATE TO "SECULAR KNOWLEDGE"?

Being a Christian is easy when faith is contained in a "spiritual" corner of one's life. But the living God has a mind of his own. Not being content with such limits, he often breaks out into the rest of our lives and lays claim to territory we had not yet thought about deeding over to him.

Often he first lays claim to our moral lives, with the result that we discover that being a Christian entails confronting and struggling with our selfishness, jealousy, anger, pettiness or rebelliousness. This often has implications for our vocational lives, such as when we must curtail unethical practices or when we must reassess the values that have energized us for years.

But God can lay claim to our thought lives as well. Do we need to think differently about politics, science, art, philosophy and indeed all areas of life as a result of our faith? Indeed we do. The claims of the gospel are all-inclusive, spanning every dimension of our private and public lives, because Christ has been declared the Lord of all (Col 1:15-20).

What does it mean for sincere Christians to relate their religious beliefs and faith to an area not overtly or obviously religious or theological? There is a distinctive Christian position on the nature of God and of salvation, but is there a correct Christian position on literary criticism, on thermodynamics, on the nature of human memory, on the fundamental motivations of human personality or on the nature of depression? Answering this general question on the relation of faith and scholarship or science has absorbed the energies of many Christian thinkers over the centuries.

This is not a new question. Thanks to the work of faithful believers over at least three millennia, we have abundant examples to follow in answering this question, examples that are too little known among Christian students today. Let's begin with the Old Testament's description of the "wise man" or "sage."

Derek Tidball (1986) points out that in ancient Jewish society, before the coming of Christ, there were three types of "pastors": priests, prophets and wise men. "The objective of the wise men was to provide down-to-earth counsel about the ordinary affairs of life" (Tidball, 1986, p.43); thus, it seems to us that there are many parallels between the wise man role in ancient Jewish life and the role mental health professionals serve in contemporary American life. Tidball suggests that the wise men did not often provide their counsel according to explicit divine revelation; they were grappling with practical matters which simply were not a preoccupation of God's revelatory energies. In other words, they dealt with matters for which no simple recourse to "the Bible says X" was possible. "Their approach was to consider, with steady logic, the truth which was hidden within human nature and creation in order to discover the regularities which could form the basis of their lives and counsel" (Tidball, 1986, p.43). The provision of such wisdom is a prime duty of the Christian psychotherapist, for whom it is vital to remember, as did these wise men, that true wisdom begins with "the fear of the Lord" (Prov 1:7).

Tidball seems to suggest that there are two primary elements of the wise man's or sage's methodology: grounding their approach in God's word in the Scriptures, and then searching in human experience with "steady logic" for enduring truth. In a recent volume Coe and Hall (2010a, b) also urged that Christian psychology be founded on following the model of the sage, and, like Tidball, seem to suggest the same two methodological elements. On this basis Coe and Hall argue that "the Old Testament sage's psychology is not an act of integration; rather, it is one single, though complex, act of doing a science or psychology" (2010b, p.155). Unfortunately, Coe and Hall are simply wrong that the work of the sage is not an act of integration in nature, and their specific citation of Proverbs 24 as a prototype of the work of the sage is helpful in establishing why.

Coe and Hall seem bothered that the integrationist turns to and engages secular sources of wisdom to expand our knowledge, striving to make sense of such secular knowledge within our deeper Christian intellectual commitments. But it turns out that this is *exactly* what the Old Testament sage or wise man did. In addition to being grounded in God's Word and using steady logic about what we observe of human nature, the very Old Testament sages that wrote Proverbs and Ecclesiastes did what we are here calling integration.

The author of Ecclesiastes, thought by many scholars to be King Solomon, calls himself

"Qoheleth," which can be translated teacher, preacher or sage.[1] And in explaining his own methodology, he writes "He pondered and searched out and set in order many proverbs. The Teacher [i.e., Qo-heleth] searched to find just the right words, and what he wrote was upright and true" (Eccles 12:9-10). Just how far-reaching was that search for proverbs by Qoheleth? Quite extensive, it turns out. Proverbs 24, as well as Proverbs 31 and other passages in these two wisdom books, are heavily influenced by pagan wisdom literature. As I argued elsewhere (Jones, 2011), it turns out that the sages who wrote the Old Testament wisdom literature were well grounded in the Hebrew Scriptures and skilled in steady logic, but also facile in the pagan, secular literature of the day. The sages who composed Proverbs were discerning editors and compilers, integrationists who appropriated good ideas from secular literature, adapted them and built on them.

Recognition that Proverbs 24 is just such a passage is so widespread that it has made its way into the notations of prominent evangelical study Bibles. The *English Standard Version Study Bible* notes that Proverbs 22:17– 24:22

---

1 Treier (forthcoming) argues compellingly that the best translation of Qoheleth is Sage.

or "The Thirty Sayings of 'The Wise'" reflects "an awareness of the Egyptian wisdom text, *The Instruction of Amenemope,* dated to about 1250B.C. Clearly [the sage/author] did not slavishly copy *Amenemope,* but there are many affinities in content" (p.1173; see also the *New International Version Archeological Study Bible).* Far from slavishly copying, theologian Daniel Treier argues that the sage/author always adapted what he drew from secular literature to godly purposes: "the most important features for interpreting particular proverbs [drawn from pagan sources] concern their recontextualization within or relation to the fear of Yhwh, Israel's God" (forthcoming, p.113 in ms.; see also Waltke, 2004, 2005). So we have evidence already in the Old Testament of the value of appropriating secular wisdom to God's purposes, if that work is done with due diligence to remain faithful to God's revealed Word.

Let us now move into the New Testament era, the era of the church. Among conservative Christians today, many assume that a "Bible only" stance of antagonism toward "secular knowledge" is what has marked "real Christians" for two millennia. Often unwittingly, they adopt a posture mimicking one of the most prolific early church fathers, Tertullian (C.A.D.160-220), who wrote (taking "Athens" as a metaphor for secular Greek philosophical wisdom and

"Jerusalem" for the wisdom of the Bible as directly inspired by God):

> What indeed does Athens have to do with Jerusalem? What concord is there between the [philosophical] Academy and the Church? What between heretics and Christians? ... Away with all attempts to produce a mottled Christianity of Stoic, Platonic, and dialectic composition! We want no curious disputation after possessing Christ Jesus, no inquisition after enjoying the Gospel! With our faith, we desire no other belief. For this is our palmary faith, that there is nothing which we ought to believe besides. (in Geehan, 1971, p.vi)

Sadly, Christians who adopt such a stance are unaware that Tertullian was himself a brilliant product of a broad, humanistic education in the very Academy he mocks in this quote, and that he drew capably and well on that broad background in service of the gospel as he wrote apologetics and theological works. In this quote he was engaging in a bit of preacherly hyperbole to make a particular point; the quote in isolation considerably exaggerates his true position on the value of secular knowledge.

It is more important to note that the early church never systematically embraced any such repudiation of secular knowledge. Indeed, engagement with secular knowledge has always been important to the church. Philosopher Arthur Holmes's *Building the Christian Academy* (2001) gives an exceptionally readable introduction to this fascinating history. Holmes discusses how the earliest Christian liberal arts academy was established in Alexandria, Egypt, in the third century. The term *liberal arts* in the ancient world had nothing to do with today's political liberalism. It was an ancient Greek term by which they distinguished the type of technical education suitable for slaves, whose job was to do specific tasks, from the education suitable for *liberated* peoples—the free citizens of the state, whose role was to guide the civic order by their wisdom and breadth of learning. As opposed to technical education, the liberal arts centered on the *trivium* (the three arts of language—grammar, logic and rhetoric or persuasion) and the *quadrivium* (the four mathematical arts—arithmetic, geometry, astronomy and music). A liberal arts education was presumed applicable to everything; it ideally equipped the student to reflect deeply and critically on the current state of affairs, preparing the citizen to lead.

According to Holmes (2001), the first Christian liberal arts academy was established almost eighteen centuries ago for four reasons, reasons as relevant today as then: (1) to interact with the best thinking of unbelievers for the sake of evangelism and apologetics to reach nonbelievers with the gospel, (2) to learn from non-Christian thought, since clearly nonbelievers can think rigorously and well, and it would be arrogant of Christians to think that they have nothing to learn from non-Christian thought, (3) to worship and honor God, who is truth in himself and the source and the author of everything, by thinking broadly and well, and (4) to provide a holistic education of both mind and character, fostering growth both in intellect and in personal maturation, out of recognition that we are unitary beings whose minds are interconnected with our hearts and souls.

Holmes (2001) summarizes some of the high points of the Christian academy over the ensuing centuries. He mentions the great monasteries of the medieval period, where monks that loved God and loved knowledge preserved learning through the Dark Ages. There were direct connections between such monasteries and the establishment of the first great universities at Bologna, Paris, Oxford and Cambridge, universities that began as training schools for clergy, yet were comprehensive in their curricula; the founders of these institutions originally saw learning as an outgrowth of sincere Christian faith and a liberal arts education as necessarily done in the context of Christian reflection on the subject matter.

Theologian Don Browning (2010) recently sketched one particularly pivotal moment in the church's engagement with secular knowledge. For centuries the great thinkers of the church had focused on the writings of Plato for their dialogue with secular thought, but one millennium ago in Spain and Sicily, the medieval intellectual world was shaken and revitalized by the rediscovery of the texts of Aristotle. These texts had been lost in the Christian world but preserved in the Islamic world, and as these two worlds collided in Spain and Sicily, the texts of Aristotle became the focus of an intellectual dialogue among Islamic, Jewish and Christian scholars. This rich dialogue spurred forward the explosive progress of science and the humanities in the following centuries. The work of Thomas Aquinas, whom many consider the greatest mind ever to work in the Christian tradition, is clearly indebted to the fruits of this religious dialogue.

Returning to Holmes (2001), his next focus for discussion of the Christian academy is on the heroes of the Protestant Reformation, whose indebtedness to their engagement with secular learning is remarkable. John Calvin, for example, is often described today as a theologian, but in truth he was educated in the humanities (liberal arts) and specifically in the field of law. So also Jonathan Edwards, whom many regard as the most capable scholar America has ever produced, was deeply shaped by his liberal arts education.

In the following two centuries Christianity in general and Protestantism in particular fostered the development of modern science by (1) providing a theological foundation for an embrace of physical reality as good and worthy of study, (2) emboldening the search for universal laws by construing the physical world as the engineering of a universal law-giver who had left imprinted on the world the traces of his rational mind, (3) inspiring empirical research by emphasizing God's free will in creating, such that the structure of the world could not be deduced by the armchair philosopher but had to be discovered by the empirical researcher, and (4) providing personal motives for scientists such as improving the world to bring glory to God or helping to provide rational evidence for God's existence (Brooke, 1991). In this early period of what is often called modernism, faith was not seen as antagonistic to science, rationality or knowledge at all, and so it was common for great figures in science such as Francis Bacon, Nicholas Copernicus, Galileo Galelei, Blaise Paschal, Isaac Newton and many others to be devout Christians of various sorts while standing as dominant figures in their scientific fields.

But it is in the 1800s and 1900s that we begin to see why it makes sense to talk about "integration," because during this period faith and learning became disintegrated and fragmented from each other. In the late modern period the intellectual movement called the Enlightenment drove a deep wedge between faith and reason. For very complicated reasons, religion, tradition and authority came to be seen as the enemy of knowledge (Toulmin, 1990). What emerged over time was a view that "facts" were produced by logic or by empirical science, whereas religion was ultimately about values, ethics or about some other undeniable, ethereal aspect of human experience that had nothing to do with the world of facts (Johnson, 2010b; Jones, 2010). Increasingly, faith was seen as the enemy of knowledge, ushering in our situation today where so many of the "new atheists," such as Richard Dawkins, trumpet science as the antithesis of religious faith. And these developments have had a profound impact on educational institutions as well; whereas the original mentality in the great universities of the world was that theology was the "queen of the sciences," today, religion has been driven from, or to the periphery at, most of the universities, and these schools are often experienced by Christians as communities of great hostility toward orthodox faith (e.g., Marsden, 1994).

HOW DOES CHRISTIANITY RELATE TO SECULAR PSYCHOLOGY? THE INTEGRATION VIEW

It is in this intellectual context that contemporary psychology has come to maturity (or what passes for maturity). As Jones (1994), Johnson (2010b) and many others have discussed, almost every movement in psychology has had a facet of antagonism toward, dismissal of or the impulse to explain away religious faith in general and often Christianity in particular. The psychologies of Sigmund Freud, B.F. Skinner, Carl Rogers and others are often explicit (and contemptuous) in their dismissal of Christianity, and thus appropriation of what is of value from these approaches takes great care and discernment.

Even though Christians ought to approach the topic of psychology believing in and celebrating the unity of all knowledge in Christ, the practical reality we encounter is a field of knowledge that has become disintegrated and fragmented. Vast swaths of the discipline of psychology contain implicit or explicit commitments antagonistic to Christian faith, as the chapters that follow in this book will illustrate. The task of the integrationist in this present circumstance is to bring back together that which God intended as a seamless whole but which in present reality lies fragmented.

We use this term *integration* even though we regard it as problematic. The word implies that things that don't naturally mix must willfully be brought into connection, to be integrated. This is surely not the vision of faith and scholarship that we are advocating, as we believe that faith and scholarship naturally and inevitably interrelate.

We will not often refer to the integration of psychology and *theology* (i.e., the academic discipline), because this implies that the goal is the fusing together of what are and should properly be two distinct conceptual disciplines. Surely integration is misguided if it is directed at creating a new academic discipline, such as "psychotheology" or "theopsychology."

There are a number of different approaches to understanding the integration of Christian faith with the discipline of psychology.[2] Indeed, a plethora of articles and books have been dedicated to sorting and resorting these approaches. Years ago Jones (1986) characterized the main three approaches to integration as (1) *ethical integration,* the focus on the application of faith-based moral principles to the *practice* of science (including, in this case, the professions of psychotherapy); (2) *perspectival integration,* the view that scientific and religious views of any aspect of reality are independent, with the result that scientific/psy-

---

2 Much of the discussion of these issues of integration has been influenced by recent developments in the philosophy of science. We wish to acknowledge immediately that the field of psychotherapy does not conform in all ways to the common meaning of the term science. In other words, we are not treating the terms science, psychology and psychotherapy as equivalent. But we would argue, on the other hand, that the most central issues in relating religious faith to a putatively nonreligious area of scholarship have been illuminated by discussions of the hardest case, that of science, since science is supposedly the human activity with the least to do with other ways of human knowing. What we are after in this section are the lessons that have been learned about the general character of integration from the dialogue about relating faith to science generally and the scientific discipline of psychology in particular. These lessons will form the context for our specific discussion of psychotherapy.

chological views and religious understandings complement but don't really affect each other (e.g., Jeeves, 1976; this view has come to be called the levels-of-explanation view); and (3) *humanizer or Christianizer of science integration,* an approach that involves the explicit incorporation of religiously based beliefs as the control beliefs that shape the perceptions of acts, theories and methods in social science (e.g., Evans, 1977, 1989; or Van Leeuwen, 1985). Let us use this same grid to understand the basic layout of the discussion of the relationship of psychology and Christianity today, but broaden the final category of humanizer or Christianizer approaches into two groups as follows.

- *Ethical integration.* Practitioners of variations of the ethical approach have found particular expression recently among Anabaptist Christians. For instance, out of their basic theological commitments, Jacobsen and Jacobsen (2004) suggest that the primary goal of the Christian scholar should be to "strike up the friendships [with secular scholars] that might lead to mutual respect and cooperation" (p.24). Relationships become the primary ethical imperative for the Christian scholar. Any approach to scholarship that is not first premised on an imperative of cooperation, in this view, is suspect. These authors emphasize the contours of friendship over truth claims of Christian faith, arguing that "Christian scholars will probably need to develop a range of new, less grandiose ways of relating faith and learning that are more attuned to contemporary scholarly practices" (p.28). They seem to prioritize cooperation and acceptance, and to be averse to conflict with the secular academy.

Another Anabaptist ethical work is the proposal of Dueck and Reimer (2009) for a "peaceable psychology." While much more open than the Jacobsens to conflict with the secular academy (indeed, they are adamant in their criticisms of the field of psychology), Dueck and Reimer are not at all prone to propose that we seek out approaches to Christian scholarship that conform to secular standards. Indeed, they call Christians to construct a distinctive psychology, both theoretical and therapeutic, that is driven by its allegiance to Christ in its being marked by ethical commitments to peacemaking and reconciliation. Their approach clearly is driven by its ethical dimension.

The levels-of-explanation and Christianizer approaches are well on display in Johnson (2010a), who in *Psychology and Christianity: Five Views* portrays the levels-of-explanation view and two variants of the humanizer or Christianizer of science approach, namely (1) integration, and (2) Christian psychology (in three variations).

- *Levels-of-explanation.* Myers (2010) defends the levels-of-explanation view, arguing that scientific and religious views of any aspect of reality are to some degree independent. Myers is particularly motivated to defend the integrity of science as a unique and successful method to develop knowledge. Myers argues first that much of religious discourse—the teachings of Scripture and of theology—is less about empirical reality (the particular domain of science) and more about the values, purposes, morality, meanings and significance of our experiences. Where the teachings of Scripture and of theology touch on the world of facts, those teachings are simply too vague, imprecise or inconsistent to substantively guide science. The result is that scientific/psychological views and religious understandings complement but don't really affect each other. We will jump over the integration view, returning to it later.
- *Christian psychology.* Three examples of Christian psychology approaches are presented: Roberts and Watson (2010) present what they term the Christian psychology view, Coe and Hall (2010a) the transformational psychology view, and Powlison (2010) the

biblical counseling view. What marks these views in common is their claim that the unique resources of the Christian tradition, including the Scriptures themselves and the great theological resources of the church, including the pastoral and psychological works of many of the great thinkers of the church, can provide some definitive starting points for shaping and determining our fundamental starting points in constructing an approach to psychology such that we can develop a (emphasis on the singular) distinctive Christian approach to psychology. The biblical counseling approach (Powlison, 2010) is marked by yet further independence from secular psychology in comparison to the other Christian psychology views, such that while academic psychology might be of some intellectual value, in the applied world of counseling for hurting persons resources from the psychological disciplines are deemed as having almost no value whatsoever in favor of the sufficient resources that can be gleaned from the Bible itself.

- *Integration approach.* So how is the integration view different? What defines it? Jones (2010) argues that what is right about the levels-of-explanation view is its high valuing of science properly conducted and the knowledge that we obtain from it. What is right about the Christian psychology and biblical counseling approaches is their high valuing of the truth we obtain about the human condition from the Scriptures and the Christian tradition, and also their insistence that these truths from Christian sources should shape the contours of our understandings of persons and thus influence how we do psychological science and how we practice the mental health professions.

Further details about concerns an integrationist has with the other views can be found in the specific responses Jones wrote to each in the Johnson (2010a) volume. But at the broadest level the integration view contrasts with the levels-of-explanation view in arguing that even how we conduct and interpret science will be shaped by our Christian convictions. Christians must ask then whether they can absorb unfiltered the products of secular scientific inquiry, and further ask if Christian understandings of the person might lead us to ask different questions, develop different hypotheses, utilize different methods of inquiry and start from different fundamental convictions than unbelieving scientists.

More subtle to grasp are the differences between the integration view and the Christian psychology approaches. These other views argue for a specific approach that emerges as "the" Christian approach to understanding persons, "the" Christian approach to psychology, whereas the integration view posits that the result of our Christian engagement will be a family of views that share a sibling resemblance to each other based in their common commitments to biblically grounded truths. We are tempted to argue that the very structure of the Five Views book (Johnson, 2010a) proves our point, in that the three Christian psychology approaches each claim to be "the" Christian approach, and yet each of the three disagree in fundamental ways with each other! What better proof could we produce than while Christian truth can and should guide us, and will be determinative of many aspects of our thought, that nevertheless our best hope should be for a family of views, all shaped by their grounding in Christian truth? The integrationist would argue that rather than *the* view, our aspiration should be to have a civil and progressive conversation with each other, our fellow Christians, about how to progressively sharpen our understanding of persons, a conversation that includes not just theological elements but the fruits of solid scientific study as well!

The heart of the integration approach is a commitment to thinking biblically about our subject matter. Greidanus (1982) argues rightly that the task of the Christian scholar is "to study reality in the light of biblical revelation" (p.147). Because the claims of the gospel are all-inclusive, and the gospel should penetrate to the core of all who claim the name Christian, the task of integration is that of being distinctively Christian in an appropriate and responsible fashion in one's scholarly pursuits. Specifically, Jones (2010) offers the following definition of the task of integration:

> Integration of Christianity and psychology (or any area of "secular thought") is our living out—in this particular area—of the Lordship of Christ over all of existence by our giving his special revelation—God's true Word—its appropriate place of authority in determining our fundamental beliefs about and practices toward all of reality and toward our academic subject matter in particular. (p.102)

So how do we approach this task?

Destructive and Constructive Modes of Integration

The work of integration is open-ended and dialogical. The work begins with a determined but humble embrace of Christian perspectives on our subject matter, in this case of human personality and character. Grounded in Christian truth, we nevertheless recognize that even our understandings of biblical truth are subject to our finiteness and sinfulness as human beings, and thus are potentially correctable by knowledge from any source, including the findings of science. Just as we know that Jesus' pronouncement that "You are the salt of the earth" (Mt 5:13) does not mean that we are literally made of salt because our rational capacities grounded in our experiences of reality recognize this exclamation as a metaphor rather than a scientific pronouncement, so also, for instance, the expanding findings of science challenge us to sort through what is metaphorical and theological as opposed to scientific in the first chapter of Genesis. So also the scientific fruits of studying psychology may help us to discern better what Scripture is teaching about humanity.

But the reverse is also true. Our commitments to biblical truth demand that we sort bad science, or anti-Christian philosophy masquerading as science, from good science. When classic Freudian psychology posits that humans are fundamentally irrational and driven by libidinal and death-seeking motivations, or radical behaviorism claims humans are nothing but material creatures shaped by learned associations, it is our commitment to Christian truths that will lead us to challenge such pronouncements.

Integration can be performed with either an essentially destructive or constructive stance toward relating the Christian faith to the life of the mind, with very different results. Many of the classic opponents of integration (such as Adams, 1979; Bobgan & Bobgan, 1979, 1987; Kilpatrick, 1985) assume a destructive stance toward non-Christian thought in psychology, feeling this is the only viable option. They approach the study of psychotherapy theories with the assumption that each therapy model is a vision of human nature that is in direct competition with the Christian faith. Thus the approach must be deconstructed, disproved by finding critical flaws in it so that it can be rejected. This certainly appeared to be the main method of Adams (1970) in *Competent to Counsel,* where he dismissed the theories of Freud and Rogers after showing that the assumptions on which they are built were in places incompatible with Christian faith.

This destructive mode of functioning is vital, in many ways, for Christians today. There are times when the best response of the Christian is to "demolish arguments and every pretension that sets itself up against the knowledge of God" (2 Cor 10:5). But we contend that the appropriate time for such apologetic efforts is when the views actually are raised up against God. In other words, when the views of humanist Carl Rogers, for instance, are presented as ultimately satisfying answers to the major questions of life, the right Christian response is to point out critical flaws in the approach and to reject his views. This is what we appreciate about the critics of psychotherapy—they take matters of faith so seriously that they are zealous to protect it from distortion or perversion. Surely it is right and good to have such a concern.

But there is a constructive side of relating Christian faith to human scholarship that is unrecognized by the critics of psychotherapy (from Stoker, 1971). A believer who strives to stand upon a distinctive commitment to the truths of the living Christian faith and build an understanding of persons that is true, broad and more complete can validly engage in a constructive dialogue with the psychotherapy theories. The Bible, although containing God-inspired revelation that is infallible and authoritative, is nevertheless of limited scope (i.e., Scripture doesn't cover everything). Thus it is not unfaithful to search out how to reasonably expand our understanding beyond what God chose to reveal in the Bible.

In discussing the value of secular learning to the Christian thinker earlier, we were already laying a foundation for this approach. Christian intellectuals have long sought to build beyond the basic structure of the fundamental truths of Scripture to answer questions only tangentially addressed in the Bible. Christian theologians engage in this sort of constructive interaction when they gain enlightenment from secular philosophers for resolving nagging theological problems (e.g., Allen, 1985). In fact, Christian theologians sometimes even derive benefit from the study of other religions! The late Anglican bishop and theologian Stephen Neill (1984) summarized a respect-worthy position on this matter: "The Christian faith may learn much from other faiths; but it is universal in its claims; in the end Christ must be acknowledged as Lord of all" (p.284). We can profitably learn from other thought systems that are not explicitly Christian if we retain the distinctiveness of our faith commitments to Christ in the process.

Yet, even this constructive approach should embody some elements of the more critical spirit of the destructive approach. While appropriating what is good in a particular theory, we must also discern the erroneous baggage it carries. Christians who get naively excited about some superficial compatibilities of a psychotherapy theory with the faith and turn off their critical faculties can be led astray. Christians examining the psychotherapy theories with a constructive motive (as we will try to do) should retain an attitude of careful, constructive criticism, and should note problems encountered in order not to fall prey to error. But neither should they summarily dismiss an entire system because of the problems encountered.

In summary, if our goal is, for instance, to show how Skinnerian behaviorism is an inadequate life philosophy, then our stance must be destructive, showing how the Skinnerian metaphysical system is an impoverished and unsatisfying materialistic deception. But if our task is a constructive one of building the truest distinctively Christian view of psychotherapy possible, or even the more modest but positive applied goal of developing the most effective method to alter the self-destructive behavior of a severely autistic child, we would look at and learn from Skinnerian behaviorism after taking a firm stand on the foundation of the orthodox Christian faith and tradition. This would be especially the case if God had given us a burden for a population where behavioral methods have been shown to be effective.

The Two Stages of Constructive Integration

There are two stages in constructively integrating Christian scholarship with secular thought. The first is critical evaluation, where we engage in a dialogue with secular thought to find what may be of value in models that are not easily and obviously compatible with a Christian stance. This phase is essentially one of sorting through the approaches of others to retain the good and discharge the bad. We must recognize, however, that the end product of this phase alone will be a rather disjointed conglomeration of useful insights and helpful tidbits that hardly form a powerful and cohesive system of thought.

Critical evaluation needs to be followed up with the second stage, theory building. After Christian scholars have discerned the advantages of secular models with which they have interacted in the critical evaluation phase, they need to develop new and different theories to incorporate these insights. They need to propose new hypotheses and theories for scholarly examination, ones that bear the imprint of the Christian presuppositions. We would contend that good integrators must not only review research but do research as well. This implies active involvement in the process of doing science, informed by enlightened notions of philosophy of science (Evans, 1989; Jones, 1994, 1996). Good integrators must be committed to evaluation and assessment of their endeavors. Currently, the community of Christian psychologists demonstrates only modest strength in this area, though there are some promising signs of growth (Jones, 2010).

Our hope is that readers of this volume will contribute to the theory-building enterprise from a Christian presuppositional base. This is critical because, as we will argue in chapter twelve, the work of the mental health field significantly overlaps with the healing and reconciling work of the church. It is vital that Christian scholars develop thoroughly Christian approaches to counseling. The work of the church has suffered from those who promote either hastily baptized versions of secular models or superficial renderings of "biblical" models.

While developing a tested family of Christian psychotherapy approaches is our dream, we know that this book represents only the first stage, the critical evaluation phase, of constructive scholarship. We do not offer a powerful new theory but hope to encourage the development of thoroughly Christian thinking by offering a critique of existing secular theories.

In other words, we believe the place to start is to appraise the thinking of the secular theorists who have gone before us. We believe that carefully listening to them from the perspective of the Christian tradition is an essential first step.

We anticipate that a thoughtful reader will find this book inadequate, in that we will end with finding none of the approaches adequate for understanding human nature, while pointing out many benefits of most of the approaches. We challenge such a thoughtful reader to join in the dialogue of developing the comprehensive Christian approach that we all so need!

The Dangers of Integration

The process of integration is complicated in part because in many areas, and especially in psychology, adequate scholarship requires interacting with scientific theories and clinical models that are questionable from a Christian standpoint. We believe that the field of psychology in general and psychotherapy in particular can be a slippery path for Christians to walk. Why do we regard the study and practice of psychotherapy as a different and riskier endeavor compared to other areas such as forestry, dentistry or physics?

First, many of the major proponents of secular approaches to psychotherapy were (or are) non-Christian thinkers, with many having large axes to grind against religion generally and Christianity in particular. In this field of study, one inevitably encounters direct and indirect jabs against the Christian faith. Some of the major psychotherapy systems have been set up as competing life views that are religious in scope and content. Research has shown that psychologists as a group tend to be socially and politically more liberal and less traditionally religious than the general population (Lovinger, 1984, chap.1). Thus it is not uncommon to have the type of encounter one of us had when he began his graduate studies: In the opening moments of the first class, the professor gave a five-minute diatribe against Christianity! And as Jones (1994) argued, psychology has often been overtly imperialistic toward religious faith, stretching to claim that it has explained and hence explained away religious experience. We concur with Dueck and Reimer (2010) when, with reference to secular psychology, they argue that "Secularity and Christianity are not only two traditions, they are *competing* social projects with different cultural aims and practices" (p.84).

More often the antagonism against Christianity is subtle, demonstrated more in the silence about religion in psychology texts, papers and classes than in open antagonism. Kirkpatrick and Spilka (1989), for instance, have documented the almost total neglect of religion as a meaningful human phenomenon in major psychology texts. We are convinced that this conspiracy of silence about things spiritual can be more deadly than open antagonism. Christians are seduced into lowering their guard and being lulled into a secular mindset where faith is neither good nor bad, true nor false, but simply irrelevant. (This has not always been the case. In the first half century of American psychology—1880-1930—religion was a major area of investigation for the field [Spilka, Hood & Gorsuch, 1985].)

Second, we believe that psychology in general and psychotherapy in particular are especially prone to subtle errors or departures from truth. As theologian Emil Brunner (1946) suggested, sin biases and distorts not only our moral behavior but also our thoughts (this is called the noetic effect of sin by theologians). Brunner went on to argue that sin would have a more subtle and profoundly disturbing effect on belief the closer one gets to the "center of existence," where one is struggling with the core truths of human life. Proportionally, the further one is away from this core, the less the influence sin has on thought. Thus when one is studying the nocturnal migration behavior of the notch-winged red-bellied thrush (if there is such a species), one is not grappling with quite the same core issues that one encounters in grappling with the central motivations and needs of human life.

The closer one gets to this core of existence, the further one gets from the facts or data of experience and the more one depends on speculation. Data can be seen as a restraint on speculation (being held accountable to clear and irrefutable facts); in the absence of such close restraint, when the scholar is attempting to propose a grand theory of personality and therapy, one may be freer to drift from the facts into pure speculation and hence error. We are not, however, arguing that science can only function with pure facts or that Christians should only deal with pure facts; actually, contemporary philosophers of science have shown that there really is no such thing as a pure fact. All facts rest in a web of interpretation of some kind; it is simply the case that some human assertions are more interpretation than others (see Wolterstorff, 1984).

Third, as we will develop more fully in our last two chapters, we believe that there are some very seductive elements of the profession of psychotherapy that can ensnare the immature or unwise Christian. Psychotherapists take great pride in being in a "people-helping" profession and, in most circles, are accorded respect for their skills and professional activities. One can subtly begin to believe that helping people on an interpersonal dimension is all there is to caring for others. It is all too easy to become enamored of the powerful position one occupies in relation to one's clients and to the financial rewards possible in the field (though these have been greatly exaggerated), which can open the door to great error.

We have offered these points as what we feel are realistic warnings about some dangers of the task of integration. Critics of integration go beyond these warnings to voice concerns they claim render the entire task of integration illegitimate. We will summarize their core concerns, showing that every concern has a kernel of truth but has been exaggerated beyond reasonable and biblical bounds.

CRITICISMS OF THE WORK OF INTEGRATION

Criticism of the integration approach is abundant, and we should always listen to our critics with care. We will summarize and respond briefly to three major sets of criticism: that integration is unscientific, unbiblical and hyper-rationalistic.

Integration Is Unscientific

The late Harvard scientist and intellectual Stephen Jay Gould (1999) offered a provocative and terse argument for why science and religious belief should never interact with each other. His argument is embedded entirely within his opening definitions: "Science tries to document the factual character of the natural world, and to develop theories that coordinate and explain these facts. Religion, on the other hand, operates in the equally important, but utterly different, realm of human purposes, meanings, and values" (p.4). If these definitions are true, then indeed science and religious belief should never interact.

But if these definitions are flawed, as indeed they are, then the argument falls apart. Science, it turns out, is not best understood as comprising exclusively facts woven into theories. Rather, it is now broadly acknowledged that even the most basic empirical observations do not occur in a contextless void. Humans make even the most basic observations from the context of preunderstandings of reality that influence what we see. For this reason it is now commonly said that all facts are "theory laden" or, as we argued earlier, that facts always reside in a web of belief. And scientific judgments about theories are never a mechanical, syllogistic process but rather are human judgments that are indeed rational, but inclusive of aesthetic and value-laden aspects of judgment.

On the other hand, Christianity (we will leave others to deal with generic religion) is not merely about "purposes, meanings, and values." Christianity is in part about purposes, meanings and values, but these are in turn based on the claim that God has revealed himself in history and acted in history in ways that are every bit as factual as anything else humans can claim as facts. If God really said that murder is immoral, then the declaration "murder is immoral" is as fundamental a fact of the universe as $E=MC^2$. And claims that Christ turned water to wine and rose from the grave after dying are claims about the real state of affairs of the universe, about facts, not merely about values.

Putting these together, if science is much more complicated than Gould's (1999) simplistic description, and if Christianity is about real events and universal truths about reality, then there is room—indeed an obligation—to examine how science and Christian faith interact. For more on these complicated issues, see Jones (1994, 2010) and Wolterstorff (1984).

Briefly, we must examine an additional concern about integration and science, expressed this time by conservative Christians rather than secular scientists. This is the claim that while Christians indeed should pay attention to good science, to facts, that this does not justify engagement with bad science. Psychology, they argue, and particularly psychotherapy, is bad science. Surely the vain speculations and philosophies of mere humans (2 Cor 10:5) do not merit a place in our beliefs alongside God's Word (Bobgan and Bobgan, 1987, pp.29-30).

In response, let us first address an implicit claim in the argument. We deny the fundamental premise that Christians can only derive knowledge from two sources of facts, authoritative revelation or science. Revelation merits the most fundamental place among human ways of knowing, and science also merits a place as well. Properly understood, all human routes to knowledge deserve an appropriate place in the cognitive life of the believer. Authority (including revelation), experience, intuition and reason—the four commonly described ways of knowing—all have legitimate roles to play (Foster & Ledbetter, 1987). On the basis of the foregoing, then, we reject the simplistic assertion that Christians need heed only authoritative revelation and science. If only life were that simple!

Is psychology "bad science"? This argument is usually pressed quoting historian and philosopher of psychology Sigmund Koch saying that "psychology cannot be a coherent science" (Koch, 1981, p.262). This statement is taken to mean that psychological research is incoherent. What Koch was actually arguing, however, is that psychology covers too broad a span of reality (from the neurons of insects to the psychology of human communities) to ever have one model of scientific methodology govern all areas of study. Thus if the requirement for coherence as a science is a uniform methodology, then psychology will never be a coherent science. We must use different methods to study neurons and multiple personalities.

Koch further argues that some scientists would have a rigid, restricted list of methods for what counts as science, but that psychology can never be captive to such a list. Koch argued that investigators in some areas of study should properly distance themselves from the rigidly empirical methods traditionally associated with hard science, such as physics and chemistry, if these investigators are to do justice to their areas of study. In these areas, psychologists may properly use methods traditionally associated with history, anthropology or even literary scholarship in their pursuit of truth. In other words, being "nonscientific" in some areas of psychology is a virtue to Koch. Psychology is an amazingly broad discipline that cannot be easily defined by one model of science and suffers from confusion and lack of clarity regarding standards for properly scientific methodology (see Koch & Leary, 1985).

Psychology is not necessarily bad science. Christians should carefully look at any way of knowing that helps us better understand the human condition, even if that way of knowing does not conform to some narrow definition of "good science." On the other hand, we must acknowledge that some areas of psychotherapy (and some of what passes for theology) are neither good science nor good reasoning, good intuition nor anything else; they are rather examples of slipshod argumentation and speculation.

Integration Is Unbiblical

There are two core variations of the "integration is unbiblical" argument that traditionally have been advanced. They are:

1. The assertion that the Bible declares itself (in passages such as 2 Tim 3:16-17; 2 Pet 1:4; 3:14-18) to be sufficient to meet all human needs. Thus, to argue that one should study anything other than the Bible (such as psychol-

ogy) in order to better meet human needs is tantamount to declaring the holy Scriptures to be inadequate to equip the servant of God and also to rejecting God's own claims for his revelation (Bobgan & Bobgan, 1987, p.11; Adams, 1979, p.46).

2. The belief that "the Bible's position is that all counsel that is not revelational (biblical), or based upon God's revelation, is Satanic" (Adams, 1979, p.4; see also Bobgan & Bobgan, 1987, p.32). Thus to decide to listen to and learn from a non-Christian in an area where God has revealed his will (i.e., in psychology) is to "walk in the counsel of the wicked" (Ps 1:1).

In response, first, we affirm the sufficiency of the Bible. At the same time, we must remember that it is God, not the Bible itself, who is declared to be all-sufficient, to provide all that pertains unto life (2 Pet 1:4; 3:14-18). Christians should courageously claim and proclaim whatever authority and power that the Scriptures declare for themselves—no less and no more.

Second Timothy 3:16-17 teaches that Scripture is inspired (God-breathed), but is not declared to be the only and all-sufficient source for every bit of knowledge that will ever be needed by anyone for any purpose related to human need. Rather, it is called "useful." We do not look to Scripture for guidance for theoretical physics or surgery; nor should we for distinguishing schizophrenia from autism.

Paul teaches that Scripture is essential to the forming of our character, which, if shaped and molded by God's living Word, can prepare us for beginning any good work, though the accomplishment of that good work may also depend on the mastery of other key skills. Thus, though the Bible is an essential foundation for a Christian approach to psychotherapy, it is not an all-sufficient guide for the discipline of counseling. The Bible is inspired and precious, but it is a revelation of limited scope, the main concern of which is its presentation of God's redemptive plan for his people and of the great doctrines of the faith. The Bible doesn't claim to reveal everything that human beings might want to know.

Second, all truth is from above (Jas 1:17). Correspondingly, Satan is the father of lies, ranging from out-and-out fabrications to lies that are subtle twists and perversions of the truth. In addition, humanity is fallible, fallen and finite. Thus our theologies, our confessional heritages, our Bible teachings (not the Bible itself) and our prayers are filled with subtle and sometimes blatant falsehoods and imperfections. We are not right in all that we believe, though by God's grace through the Holy Spirit and the influence of the body of Christ, we are guided into sufficient truth to be able to actually relate to God and understand something of his nature, and to even be able to proclaim our faith as the truth.

The flip side is that Christians are not the sole possessors of truth. Just as the rain falls on the just and the unjust, so too does truth, by the process that theologians call God's common grace. Romans 1 speaks of God even revealing central truths about his nature to unbelievers (Rom 1:19). John Calvin, that great figure in the Protestant Reformation, stated it well when he said, "The human mind, however much fallen and perverted from its original integrity, is still adorned and invested with admirable gifts from its Creator.... We will be careful ... not to reject or condemn truth wherever it appears" *(Institutes of the Christian Religion,* 2.2.15).

Thus, God's counsel is not always synonymous with the counsel of a Christian, and Satan's counsel is not synonymous with the counsel of a non-Christian. Rather, we should identify God's counsel with the truth, and Satan's counsel with falsehood. Sometimes a so-called secular approach to understanding a given topic may be nearer the truth than the distorted understanding of a particular Christian person. If we understand God's counsel to be truth, we will be committed to pursuing truth wherever we find it. And we may sometimes find it in the careful and insightful writings of unbelievers. (For more on responding to this general criticism, see Jones, 2001.)

Integration Is Hyper-Rationalistic

In a postmodern context, some scholars emphasize the personal. Jacobsen and Jacobsen (2004) criticize the integration approach as overly rationalistic, attributing this to a bias toward Reformed (Calvinistic) theology. They question whether "faith supplies the believer with a full-blown Christian worldview" and then ask a series of rhetorical questions:

> Is Christian revelation personal or propositional? Does revelation supply us with a complete vision of the world, or is revelation more piecemeal, offering important clues about the origins, meaning, and purpose of the universe but never spelling things out in fine detail? Do Christians possess extrafactual knowledge about the world, or is the addition of Christian revelation primarily a matter of values and attitude? (p.28)

Their rhetorical questions risk serving as a pretext for the dismissal of a controlling function of special revelation over the cognitive life of the Christian scholar. Take two key assertions they seem to make—that to focus on the rational is a Reformed theological bias, and that one must decide between knowledge as personal or propositional. We can challenge both questions at the same time by turning to the non-Reformed theologian Pope John Paul II, who said, in *Fides et Ratio,* "What is distinctive in the biblical text is the conviction that there is a profound and indissoluble unity between the knowledge of reason and the knowledge of faith" (II.16.4). Further, "Belief is often humanly richer than mere evidence, because it involves an interpersonal relationship and brings into play not only a person's capacity to know but also the deeper capacity to entrust oneself to others, to enter into a relationship with them which is intimate and enduring" (III.32.1). John Paul II sees the interpersonal *enriching* the knowing process and not counterposed against it; he sees the human capacity to know cognitively as complementary to the capacity to know interpersonally. It is not "personal or propositional," rather, it is personal *and* propositional.

The Jacobsens have created a straw man. A worldview may not be a "complete vision of the world" and yet still be worthwhile, just as a map can be an imperfect and incomplete representation of reality yet still be good enough to guide us. Knowledge from the Bible that is partial can nevertheless be knowledge secure enough to serve to organize our thoughts. The issue is whether we have a word from God that has relevance for our work as scholars. Integrationists agree that revelation does not constitute our disciplines; Scripture does not exhaust what humans know or can know. But if God has spoken and acted, and if his spoken or enacted Word has relevance for our area of academic study, what could possibly be our rationale for ignoring that Word?

METHODOLOGY FOR CHRISTIAN APPRAISAL

To evaluate models of counseling and psychotherapy, we must think clearly about our theological commitments, our views of humanity and our moral standards. While we must be careful about being overly dogmatic and rigid, good evaluation is brutally honest about the realities of the human condition in all their tragic complexities.

The following are the major guidelines we intend to pursue in critiquing the theories in this book.[3]

Philosophical Assumptions

We begin each chapter looking carefully at the philosophical assumptions or presuppositions that ground each approach to counseling. Ideas about human character and personality do not arise in a vacuum. As Browning and Cooper (2004) say, "the modern psychologies

---

3 Our colleague Robert C. Roberts at Wheaton has derived independently criteria for the evaluation of therapy systems that are similar to our own. Roberts (1985, 1987) has argued for what he calls the "virtues approach to integration." He starts the examination of an approach to psychotherapy by looking at the virtues that the approach strives to cultivate. This is similar to our criterion of a model's vision of ideal humanness or wholeness. Roberts argues in turn that each virtue is embedded in a network of assumptions that he calls the "grammar" of the virtue (alluding to the way that verbal ideas are nested in linguistic grammar systems). Minimally, this grammar system includes a concept of human nature (similar to our criterion of the view of personality), an explanation for the failure to achieve virtue (a theory of abnormality), and some ideas for how change toward the development of the virtues of the system can be facilitated (prescriptions for change).

function within larger contexts of meaning about the way the world is" (p.87). The approaches vary widely in terms of how explicitly they articulate their philosophical assumptions. Behaviorism has been an easy target for Christian critique over the years because Skinner was so transparent about his assumptions (see chap.5). The originators of some other approaches have not been so explicit, resulting in the need for careful work in unearthing their presuppositions.

No common philosophy unifies the many diverse and varied approaches. Each has a different view of reality, truth, purpose, personhood and the like. These assumptions and presuppositions are of crucial importance for the Christian academician, clinician or researcher, as these convictions directly or indirectly affect every phase of science and of the people-helping process. Theory significantly affects practice, whether or not this relationship is acknowledged.

A distinctively Christian approach to counseling and psychotherapy will have theological and philosophical underpinnings compatible with Christian faith. It will look at the task of the psychotherapist from both eternal and temporal perspectives and will fully acknowledge the reality of the supernatural. Sin and the consequences of the Fall will be taken seriously, as well as the reality of supernatural evil.

Model of Personality

We must also examine the personality theory or model of humanity on which an approach is built. Every theory must build on an understanding of what defines human character and action. These approaches vary widely in terms of their understandings of human motivations, personality structure and core characteristics. As Tjeltveit (1989) says, "Models of human beings—explicit or implicit, complex or simple, internally consistent or inconsistent, ... open to change or static—shape society, the actions of every human being, and every individual's worldview.... [They are] part of every psychotherapy session" (p.1).

Our understandings of persons and personhood must be grounded in the words of Scripture, but also in Christian experience in the context of our confessional communities and the historic teachings of the church. The purpose of Scripture is to present a record of God's redemptive dealings with persons throughout history, to present a plan of salvation and discipleship, and to provide us with the knowledge necessary to guide us into productive life. The Scriptures were never intended to be a textbook of all psychological conditions and disorders, although they should anchor and condition our metaphysical and ontological assertions about persons and provide a practical foundation for moral guidance.

We begin by asking if each theory of personality is compatible with Christian truth. Is it clear yet comprehensive? Does it do justice to what is known about human behavior and experience, and does it reflect diverse gender, socioeconomic and sociocultural contexts? Is the personality theory concerned with all dimensions of human behavior and experience—cognitive, affective, interpersonal, spiritual, physical and behavioral? Is the theory elegant and parsimonious, given the complexity of the subject? Does it generate serious research and study? Does it directly inform clinical practice and theory? In short, is the theory valuable at multiple levels of inquiry (i.e., theory, research and practice)?

Model of Abnormality

We will look with care at each theory's understanding of human abnormality. To discuss a theory of personality is usually to presume that one also understands deviations from normal personality development. To suggest how one can change human action is to presume that one has some understanding as to the processes that explain how it came to need changing in the first place.

How compatible is the view of abnormality with the Christian faith? Are the core concepts like human accountability, responsibility and sinfulness compatible with the model? Is faith itself classified as pathological? Are the Christian virtues viewed as abnormal? Is there a balance between personal causation of distress ("because of my sins") and systemic causation of distress ("because I live in a fallen world")?

Model of Health

Every theory has an explicit or implicit vision of human wholeness which complements its view of abnormality. To discuss the change one intends to engender in the client's life is to presume a direction that one is going to move in, a goal one is moving toward. Even theoreticians who are aiming to be value neutral by saying that they are just trying to decrease pain are working from an implicit hypothesis that minimizing pain is part of human wholeness.

The goals and views of normalcy within a particular psychotherapy tradition should be closely examined. What does the theory propose the truly healthy individual will be like? What are the explicit and implicit notions of maturity, wellness, wholeness or health being advocated? Methods of therapy are often intimately intertwined with the theory of normalcy of the approach. For instance, a therapist may use emotional catharsis ("discharge") techniques because the therapist's view of normalcy includes emotional expressiveness as one of the criteria for health. Further, unless theorists or therapists are clear about where they are headed, therapy tends to become directionless and unfocused. Goals for change should be explicit and communicated to clients at the beginning of therapy.

Model of Psychotherapy

We need to look at the prescribed methods of change to gauge their essential credibility. Some proposed change methods are quite similar to intuitive or lay understandings of the process of growth, while others can be so radically different as to require substantial support merely to make them look credible. Do the counseling processes and techniques provide real resources for healing? Are the techniques proposed ethical and moral?

As Tan (1987) has observed, a distinctively Christian approach to people-helping will emphasize the primacy of warm, empathic and genuine relationships, stressing the relevance of *agape* love. Such compassion should extend to the clinician's personal and professional relationships with others. A distinctively Christian approach will take the role of the Holy Spirit seriously, as well as the many spiritual resources available to the Christian counselor (see chapters eleven and twelve). Large contextual factors like familial, societal, religious and cultural influences will not be minimized, and appropriate community and church resources will be mobilized when necessary. We have to be more than pragmatists (using whatever works), being sure to employ techniques that are consistent with biblical truth and with the wisdom and discernment of the confessional community.

Demonstrated Effectiveness

Finally, as a matter of Christian stewardship, it behooves us to look not merely at the five more conceptual criteria already listed, but also at what the scientific research says about the effectiveness of a particular approach. There has been a huge movement within clinical psychology over the last two decades toward what are widely called "empirically validated treatments." The research literature on psychotherapy and counseling is vast and yet deserves the serious consideration of the Christian would-be people-helper. A full-fledged literature review of effectiveness studies for every approach is beyond the scope of the present volume, but we will try at least to provide the reader with a summary of the state of the empirical literature for each major approach today.

CONCLUSION

The business of evaluating psychotherapy theories is complex, and healthy (but not paranoiac) caution is in order. What at first may seem like clear compatibilities between faith and a particular theory can hide radical incompatibilities. On the other hand, superficial incompatibilities can distract the Christian professional from perceiving deep and striking areas of compatibility between the faith and the theory. Only sustained, lucid analysis in the context of a thoughtful community of faith can save us from errors on either side. It is our prayer that this volume, which emerges from the discussions and interactions of our particular Christian intellectual community, will advance that cause.

FOR FURTHER READING

Browning, D.S., & Cooper, T.D. (2004). *Religious thought and the modern psychologies* (2nd ed.). Minneapolis, MN: Fortress.

Though written from a self-described liberal Christian perspective and requiring much theological sophistication to fully digest, the first of these valuable works explores the religious implications of many of the major therapy systems we will examine in this book, and the second the broad contours of Christian engagement with the world of ideas.

Browning, D.S. (2010). *Reviving Christian humanism: A new conversation on spirituality, theology and psychology.* Minneapolis, MN: Fortress.

The best "one-stop shop" to read about the debate over how Christian faith and psychology can relate.

Johnson, E.F. (Ed.). (2010a). *Psychology and Christianity: Five views* (2nd ed.). Downers Grove, IL: InterVarsity Press.

A massive and challenging overview of the status of psychology as a discipline. Probably not readable by the nonpsychologist, it has inadequate coverage of applied psychology, especially the area of psychotherapy.

Koch, S., & Leary, D. (Eds.). (1985). *A century of psychology as science.* New York, NY: McGraw-Hill.

This and Shafranske are two of the more fascinating compilations of articles discussing religion and psychology published by the American Psychological Association, indicating burgeoning interest in this topic.

Miller, W.R., & Delaney, H.D. (Eds.). (2005). *Judeo-Christian perspectives on psychology: Human nature, motivation, and change.* Washington, DC: American Psychological Association.

Shafranske, E. (Ed.). (1996). *Religion and the clinical practice of psychology.* Washington, DC: American Psychological Association.

This volume honoring the fiftieth anniversary of the Christian Association for Psychological Studies contains, as the title indicates, a plethora of key historic articles in the movement of integration.

Stevenson, D.H., Eck, B.E., & Hill, P.C. (Eds.). (2007). *Psychology and Christianity integration: Seminal works that shaped the movement.* Batavia, IL: Christian Association for Psychological Studies, Inc.

A classic, readable and intriguing discussion of contemporary philosophy of science from a Christian perspective.

Wolterstorff, N. (1984). *Reason within the bounds of religion* (2nd ed.). Grand Rapids, MI: Eerdmans.

REFERENCES

Adams, J. (1970). *Competent to counsel.* Grand Rapids, MI: Baker.

Adams, J. (1979). *More than redemption: A theology of Christian counseling.* Phillipsburg, NJ: Presbyterian & Reformed.

Allen, D. (1985). *Philosophy for understanding theology.* Atlanta, GA: John Knox Press.

Bobgan, M., & Bobgan, D. (1979). *The psychological way/The spiritual way.* Minneapolis, MN: Bethany Fellowship.

Bobgan, M., & Bobgan, D. (1987). *Psychoheresy: The psychological seduction of Christianity.* Santa Barbara, CA: Eastgate.

Brooke, J.H. (1991). *Science and religion: Some historical perspectives.* Cambridge: Cambridge University Press.

Browning, D.S. (2010). *Reviving Christian humanism: A new conversation on spirituality, theology and psychology.* Minneapolis, MN: Fortress.

Browning, D.S., & Cooper, T.D. (2004). *Religious thought and the modern psychologies* (2nd ed.). Minneapolis, MN: Fortress.

Brunner, E. (1946). *Revelation and reason* (O. Wyon, Trans.). Philadelphia, PA: Westminster Press. (Original work published 1938).

Coe, J.H., & Hall, T.W. (2010a). A transformational psychology view. In E. Johnson (Ed.), *Psychology and Christianity: Five views* (2nd ed., pp.199-226). Downers Grove, IL: InterVarsity Press.

Coe, J.H., & Hall, T.W. (2010b). *Psychology in the Spirit: Contours of a transformational psychology.* Downers Grove, IL: InterVarsity Press.

Dueck, A., & Reimer, K. (2009). *A peaceable psychology: Christian therapy in a world of many cultures.* Grand Rapids, MI: Brazos.

Evans, C.S. (1977). *Preserving the person.* Grand Rapids, MI: Baker.

Evans, C.S. (1989). *Wisdom and humanness in psychology.* Grand Rapids, MI: Baker.

Foster, J., & Ledbetter, M. (1987). Christian anti-psychology and the scientific method. *Journal of Psychology and Theology, 15,* 10-18.

Geehan, E. (Ed.). (1971). *Jerusalem and Athens.* Phillipsburg, NJ: Presbyterian & Reformed.

Gould, S.J. (1999). *Rocks of ages: Science and religion in the fullness of life.* New York, NY: Ballantine.

Greidanus, S. (1982). The use of the Bible in Christian scholarship. *Christian Scholar's Review, 11,* 138-147.

Holmes, A.F. (2001). *Building the Christian academy.* Grand Rapids, MI: Eerdmans.

Jacobsen, D., & Jacobsen, R. (2004). *Scholarship and Christian faith: Enlarging the conversation.* New York, NY: Oxford University Press.

Jeeves, M. (1976). *Psychology and Christianity: The view both ways.* Downers Grove, IL: InterVarsity Press.

John Paul II. (1998). *Fides et ratio: On the relationship between faith and reason.* Retrieved from www.catholic-pages.com/documents/fides_et_ratio.pdf.

Johnson, E.F. (Ed.). (2010a). *Psychology and Christianity: Five views* (2nd ed.). Downers Grove, IL: InterVarsity Press.

Johnson, E.F. (2010b). A brief history of Christians in psychology. In E. Johnson (Ed.), *Psychology and Christianity: Five views* (2nd ed., pp.9-47). Downers Grove, IL: InterVarsity Press.

Jones, S. (1986). Relating the Christian faith to psychology. In S. Jones (Ed.), *Psychology and the Christian faith* (pp.15-34). Grand Rapids, MI: Baker.

Jones, S.L. (1994). A constructive relationship for religion with the science and profession of psychology: Perhaps the boldest model yet. *American Psychologist, 49* (3), 184-199.

Jones, S.L. (1996). Reflections on the nature and future of the Christian psychologies. *Journal of Psychology and Christianity, 15* (2), 133-142.

Jones, S. (2001). An apologetic apologia for the integration of psychology and theology. In T.R. Phillips & M.R. McMinn (Eds.), *The care of the soul: Exploring the intersection of psychology and theology* (pp.62-77). Downers Grove, IL: InterVarsity Press.

Jones, S.L. (2010). An integration view. In E. Johnson (Ed.), *Psychology and Christianity: Five views* (2nd ed., pp.101-128). Downers Grove, IL: InterVarsity Press.

Jones, S.L. (2011). Psychology and Christianity in 3-D. *Christian Scholar's Review, 40* (3), 267-81.

Kilpatrick, W. (1985). *The emperor's new clothes: The naked truth about the new psychology.* Westchester, IL: Crossway.

Kirkpatrick, L., & Spilka, B. (1989, August). *Treatment of religion in psychology texts.* Paper presented at the annual Convention of the American Psychological Association, New Orleans, LA.

Koch, S. (1981). The nature and limits of psychological knowledge. *American Psychologist, 36,* 257-269.

Koch, S., & Leary, D. (Eds.). (1985). *A century of psychology as science.* New York, NY: McGraw-Hill.

Lovinger, R. (1984). *Working with religious issues in therapy.* New York, NY: Jason Aronson.

Marsden, G.M. (1994). *The soul of the American university: From Protestant establishment to established nonbelief.* New York, NY: Oxford University Press.

Myers, D.G. (2010). A levels-of-explanation view. In E. Johnson (Ed.), *Psychology and*

Christianity: Five views (2nd ed., pp.49-78). Downers Grove, IL: InterVarsity Press.

Neill, S. (1984). *Christian faith and other faiths.* Downers Grove, IL: InterVarsity Press.

Powlison, D. (2010). A biblical counseling view. In E. Johnson (Ed.), *Psychology and Christianity: Five views* (2nd ed., pp.245-273). Downers Grove, IL: Inter-Varsity Press.

Roberts, R.C. (1985). Carl Rogers and Christian virtues. *Journal of Psychology and Theology, 13* (4), 263-273.

Roberts, R.C. (1987). Psychotherapeutic virtues and the grammar of faith. *Journal of Psychology and Theology, 15* (3), 191-204.

Roberts, R.C., & Watson, P.J. (2010). A Christian psychology view. In E. Johnson (Ed.), *Psychology and Christianity: Five views* (2nd ed., pp.149-178). Downers Grove, IL: InterVarsity Press.

Spilka, B., Hood, R., & Gorsuch, R. (1985). *The psychology of religion: An empirical approach.* Englewood Cliffs, NJ: Prentice-Hall.

Stoker, H. (1971). Reconnoitering the theory of knowledge of Professor Dr. Cornelius Van Til. In E. Geehan (Ed.), *Jerusalem and Athens* (pp.25-70). Phillipsburg, NJ: Presbyterian & Reformed.

Tan, S.Y. (1987). Intrapersonal integration: The servant's spirituality. *Journal of Psychology and Christianity, 6,* 34-39.

Tidball, D. (1986). *Skillful shepherds: An introduction to pastoral theology.* Grand Rapids, MI: Zondervan.

Tjeltveit, A. (1989). The ubiquity of models of human beings in psychotherapy: The need for rigorous reflection. *Psychotherapy, 26,* 1-10.

Toulmin, S. (1990). *Cosmopolis: The hidden agenda of modernity.* Chicago, IL: University of Chicago Press.

Treier, D.J. (forthcoming). *Brazos theological commentary on the Bible: Proverbs and Ecclesiastes.* Grand Rapids, MI: Baker/Brazos.

Van Leeuwen, M. (1985). *The person in psychology.* Grand Rapids, MI: Eerdmans.

Waltke, B.K. (2004). *The book of Proverbs chapters 1–15.* Grand Rapids, MI: Eerdmans.

Waltke, B.K. (2005). *The book of Proverbs chapters 15–31.* Grand Rapids, MI: Eerdmans.

Wolterstorff, N. (1984). *Reason within the bounds of religion* (2nd ed.). Grand Rapids, MI: Eerdmans.

2

A CHRISTIAN VIEW OF PERSONS

Stanton L. Jones, Laura Miguélez and Richard E. Butman

***

Our task is to critically evaluate the major secular psychotherapy theories in light of Christian revelation and faith. But what is "the" Christian view, particularly of human beings, by which we are going to grade the secular psychotherapy approaches? Is there a Christian personality theory hidden in the pages of the Bible?

The purpose of this chapter is to highlight what we believe the Christian Scriptures assert about human beings, as these beliefs will be the backdrop or plumb line against which all else will be evaluated. It is our contention that the Scriptures and Christian theology do not teach a theory of personality as understood by contemporary psychology. We are grounding our position in the Reformed understanding of the perspicuity (clarity) of Scripture, namely, that the Bible is clear in its central message of salvation and holiness and capable of being understood by any literate person. Scripture teaches us the way to eternal fellowship with the Creator-Father-God, and everything we need to know about ourselves and our predicament to obtain salvation and to grow as persons. It records God's redemptive dealings with his people throughout the ages. But it teaches us less than we need to know (or less than it would be edifying to know) to understand why individual persons have the characteristics they do (for instance, why a particular person struggles with obsessive tendencies or another is blessed with incredible strength of character). Scripture also teaches us less than we need to know to help many individuals move beyond the pain and confusion they feel.

What the Scripture does teach about persons lacks the specificity and precision necessary for qualifying either as a formal scientific theory of personality or as a clinically useful heuristic model for understanding personality functioning. ("The general judgment of theologians has been that the Bible gives us no scientific teaching on man, no anthropology, which should or could concur with scientific anthropological research on man" [Berkouwer, 1962, p.194]). Even in ancient times, pastoral theologians found it necessary to develop models for understanding personality that were built on but went beyond scriptural revelation in order to develop guidelines for pastoral care. In doing this, Christian pastoral thinkers have frequently turned to contemporary nonreligious scholarship about dimensions of personhood to construct more complete models of ministry (Clebsch & Jaekle, 1975; Oden, 1984). While some seem to regard this as heresy (e.g., Adams, 1979), as discussed in the previous chapter, we regard this as a strength as long as the distinctives of the Christian faith are preserved and given preeminence.

But if we are not searching for a personality theory, what in the Scriptures can we reasonably expect to find? In brief, we believe that our foray into theological and biblical anthropology will give us the essential foundation for a more true and more complete understanding of persons by giving us "control beliefs" (Wolterstorff, 1984) or presuppositions. These control beliefs are the "givens," the foundational assumptions that control or shape all other thought. We can then use these control beliefs to build a theory of personality with greater Christian distinctiveness.

Before embarking on this task, we would endorse a number of basic hermeneutical principles (from Greidanus, 1982) that undergird orthodox biblical interpretation.

First, since God is the Creator, there can be no ultimate conflict between knowledge from special revelation (God's specific self-disclosure, especially in Christ and Scripture by means of the Holy Spirit) and general revelation (God's self-disclosure in creation or nature). There can be and often has been, however, conflict between interpretations of special revelation and interpretations about the facts of the created order. In such cases of conflict, our interpretation of either special or general revelation, or possibly both, can be wrong.

Second, "the Bible is the Word of God addressed to the heart of man" (Greidanus, 1982, p.140). Hence a sincere submission to the Lord who speaks through the Scriptures and is revealed in them by his Holy Spirit enables us to see reality, however imperfectly, from God's perspective, the only proper perspective. Special revelation is specific, and that is why Calvin suggested that the Scriptures can function as spectacles that correct our vision of God's creation when sin has distorted our understanding.

Third, the Bible is a historical book recording God's interactions first of all with a particular people in their culture at a certain time and for particular occasions and purposes. Thus the biblical message to us today cannot be understood properly without understanding its historical and cultural context. With a proper appreciation of these factors, we can confidently expect that we will hear God's voice speak to us through his words to ancient peoples.

Fourth, the Bible was written using phenomenological language, including commonly accepted concepts of the day. In other words, historical and scientific matters were addressed in terms of how they appeared to the authors. Care must be taken not to apply twenty-first-century standards of exactness and science to these ancient texts. For example, when Scripture speaks of the sun standing still (Josh 10:13), this is not a scientific statement but a descriptive one in much the same way as people today speak of the sun "rising."

Similarly, many of the verses often cited as teaching formal psychological concepts cannot responsibly be interpreted scientifically because they were meant as descriptions. The folk psychology in the verses is merely a vehicle by which to teach the main point of the verse. For instance, Paul's use of "spirit, soul and body" (1 Thess 5:23) connotes the whole person, every aspect of the believer, and does not necessarily mean that Paul was authoritatively teaching a tripartite (three-part) view of personhood (see further discussion of this matter later in this chapter). The danger here is expecting from Scripture something God did not intend to provide.

Fifth, biblical passages must be understood in light of the author's intention or meaning, and in the light of the totality of the biblical revelation. It is especially important to remember the Reformers' judgment that Scripture is to interpret Scripture. Since God is the source of all of Scripture, obscure or unclear biblical passages should be interpreted in light of clearer, more unequivocal passages, and deference must be given to the cumulative weight of many passages over one seemingly clear text if there is apparent conflict.

Our overview of humanity derives from Augustine's classic understanding, articulated in his *Enchiridion* (CXVIII; 1961), of humanity's four stages of the Christian life: (1) Prefallen humanity was created *posse non peccare* (able not to sin). (2) Fallen humanity became *non posse non peccare* (not able not to sin) and thus were slaves to sin. (3) Redeemed humanity, by the Holy Spirit's regeneration and the work of God's grace in Christ, are once again *posse non peccare.* (4) Glorified humanity will one day be *non posse peccare* (not able to sin).

HUMANITY IN ITS CREATED STATE: POSSE NON PECCARE

Intelligibility, Meaning and Value

"In the beginning God created the heavens and the earth" (Gen 1:1). Historically, the Christian doctrine of creation *ex nihilo* (creation from or out of nothing) is derived from the first chapter of the Bible. Though some scholars today view these opening verses as referring to God's organizing the created order rather than his creating ex nihilo, most evangelical scholars continue to accept this doctrine based on statements elsewhere in Scripture (Ps 33:6; Heb 11:3). Consequently, God's creating *ex nihilo* has assumed a place of priority in all the historic creeds (e.g., the Apostles' Creed: "I believe in God, the Father Almighty, Maker of heaven and earth") and doctrine.

The first biblical information we have about humanity occurs later in the creation story, where we find, "Then God said, 'Let us make man in our image, in our likeness'" (Gen 1:26). Humanity and the entire created order were made by the purposeful actions of the sovereign God of the universe. Far from being the chance products of blind causal forces with lives that are thereby unintelligible and meaningless, we were created intentionally. Our understanding of ourselves begins here. Our basic identity will remain confused until we see ourselves as part of God's creation.

In his book *Maker of Heaven and Earth,* theologian Langdon Gilkey (1985) examines the myriad implications of this central Christian doctrine. Prominent among these implications is the notion that being created, rather than having simply come to exist by naturalistic processes operating without purpose or meaning, is the foundation of intelligibility and meaning for our lives. Our lives are intelligible precisely because we can have faith that our existence is the result of the actions of an all-knowing, intelligent God. Our lives have meaning because God meant or intended for us to be. His plan or purpose remains sovereign throughout history.

In addition to having meaning, we accrue value in at least three ways. First, being the creation of the all-perfect Lord imputes value to us in the same way that all creation has value; we are the work of the Lord, and all of God's works have value. It would be contempt toward God to suggest that any of his creations are without value (as is said in our vernacular, "God doesn't make junk"). Second, we have special value in that we are the only aspect of creation specifically said to be created in God's image. Finally, and getting a bit ahead of ourselves, we have value because God chose to send his Son in complete human form, a high priest who is able to sympathize with our weaknesses, and who in every respect has been tempted as we are, yet without sin (Heb 4:15), to live, suffer, die and rise again for us and our salvation. Surely, God would not waste the life of his dear Son on beings that are without value. We gained value through the acts of the incarnation, the life, suffering, death and resurrection of Jesus Christ. Thus God's mighty works both give us value and reveal that we had and have value. These realities form the basis for our psychological perception of value.

As one final implication of being created, we should note that if we were made by God out of nothing, then we are different from and separate from God, though we are continually dependent on him as the ultimate ground of our very being. As Gilkey (1985, pp.58ff.) has noted, it is an undeniable implication of Eastern monism (the doctrine that the universe is of one indivisible essence; everything is God) and pantheism (God is everything) that humans are part of God and thus finiteness (being less than God) and individuality (being a creature separate from others, including God) are illusory and evil.

For Christians, separateness from God and others is real and good. We belong in relationship to God and others, but this relatedness is not meant to consume and destroy our separateness. Union with God is a theme of Scripture, but nowhere are we taught that we cease being ourselves in the process of this union. As in marriage, two persons become one without the loss of their personal identities; so it is with our union with God. An image of heaven as a time when we will merge and become one with the Godhead, losing our individuality in the process, is a perversion of the Christian view of heaven; this distortion stems from the influence of non-Christian Eastern religions pervasive in Western understandings of spirituality today.

The Image of God

The scriptural teaching that human beings are made in the image of God (the *imago Dei)* is utterly foundational to a Christian understanding of persons, but there is ambiguity about what this doctrine means. A number of authors (e.g., Beck & Demarest, 2005) have classified views of the *imago Dei* in three basic categories: substantive, functional and relational.

The substantive understandings of the *imago Dei* focus on what we *are.* Since only humans are noted in Genesis as made in the *imago Dei* (Gen 1:26; cf. 1:20), this view proposes that what makes humans distinctive is what we are made of or possess, whether that is a substance (such as spirit) or a capacity (such as reason, understood to be a function of the spirit), distinct from the rest of the created order. According to classic Reformed teaching, humans image God in their capacity for *rationality* and *morality:* the possession of a spirit or soul is how people image God in their very being.

The functional understandings of the *imago Dei* focus on what we *do.* Humans are understood to be made in God's image because we relate to the rest of the created order in a way that represents or reflects God. One common example is the argument that in obedience to God's command to humanity to exercise "dominion" over creation as God's stewards and representatives (Gen 1:28), we mirror God's dominion over the entire cosmos.

Drawing from the statement in Genesis that God made humans male and female (Gen 1:27), the relational understanding of the *imago Dei* focuses on our *unique relationship to God:* "to be in the image of God is to be related to God in the way that other creatures are not, and so related to the other creatures differently from the way in which they are related to one another" (Gunton, 2002, p.42). This relational understanding is also extended to include our ability to relate to others, whether in marriage (Barth understood the image as being most exemplified in our male and femaleness) or relationships within society (Brunner's position).

Our point here is that even for this most central of doctrines about what it means to be a human being, ambiguity remains about the exact meaning of this key concept. A spiritual component or dimension is what, ultimately, distinguishes the uniqueness of human creation. Unlike plants and animals, which are created "according to their kinds" (Gen 1:12, 25), God's image is imprinted on human beings. We are not created after our own kind, but are made in God's kind! And the reader can probably see that all three views—the substantive, functional and relational—interact. Just picking out one strand of each view, one could argue that we are rational because we are God's children, that God made us rational so we could exercise dominion and be in relationship with him, and that we are fully rational only when we are in relationship with him and doing the dominion work he set for us to do. Dominion and relating are part of the total picture, but the reason humans are able to exercise dominion and have relationships with God and one another is precisely because they are made in God's image.

Reducing the *imago Dei* to either being rational or exercising dominion or relating limits the image only to those who are healthy and able to exercise it and excludes certain people. For example, an infant is made in God's image though she has limited rational powers and is unable to exercise dominion; an autistic child is made in God's image even though he may be unable to relate fully to those in his environment.

Thus, to be made in the image of God is to bear his imprint on our very spirit, or soul. A scriptural understanding of human flourishing indicates that we fulfill our human created purpose best when we love and serve the Lord God with all our heart, soul, mind and strength (Deut 6:5; Mt 22:37), love others (Lev 19:18; Mt 22:39)—as per the relational view—*and* care for the created order in which God has placed us—as per the functional view.

Compound Beings

Scripture presents us with some challenges in understanding the basic constituent elements of human nature, the substance(s) of which we are made. The basic options boil down to three: monism, dichotism and trichotism (see Beck & Demarest, 2005, pp.119-141). Monists believe that humans are made of one substance, with some believing we are exclusively physical beings and others some form of spirit. Dichotomists believe we are composed of two substances—our physical bodies and some type of nonphysical soul/spirit. Trichotomists believe that soul and spirit are different substances, distinct from the physical and from each other, so that we are rightly understood to be composed of three substances.

There are good arguments, grounded in Scripture and in human rationality, for each of the positions, with the dichotomist position being the most widely held in church history. When we add in other passages that speak of four elements (heart, soul, mind, strength [Mk 12:30]), or note the flexibility with which Scripture often speaks about psychological phenomena (invoking psychological functions of the heart, bowels, kidneys and so forth), we are driven to be cautious in advancing dogmatic, scientifically precise formulations of biblical teachings about our constituent elements.

Historically, the trichotomist position has based its understanding on Scriptures such as 1 Thessalonians 5:23 and Hebrews 4:12, which speak of our "spirit, soul and body." Irenaeus (as well as the Scofield Bible notes) reflects this trichotomist view. The dichotomist position draws its support from passages such as

Matthew 10:28 and James 2:26, which speak of the possible separation of soul (or spirit) from body. Another key body of texts that undergird this position point to an intermediate state, a state of provisional happiness (or judgment) until Christ returns. Jesus' statement to the thief on the cross in Luke 23:43 ("today you will be with me in paradise") seems to indicate an immediacy to the thief's presence with Christ. So too Paul's statements in Philippians 1:22-23 ("I desire to depart and be with Christ") and 2 Corinthians 5:6 ("as we are at home in the body we are away from the Lord"—and vice versa) suggest that though at the time of death we die physically, we nonetheless live spiritually to God in Christ who is the Giver of eternal life to those who believe in him (Jn 11:26).

More recently, at least three developments have caused some evangelicals to adopt a monistic view of the human person. First, science has confirmed an intense and close interconnection between physical and psychological aspects of humanness, supporting the idea that people are truly purely material beings. For example, the findings that electrical stimulation to certain parts of the brain may elicit emotional reactions, memories or movements suggest profound physicality of our most "purely" cognitive experiences. Dichotomists such as Cooper (2000) and others counter by noting that by God's design our bodies and souls/spirits are so intertwined that both are naturally affected when one is strongly affected. Neural stimulation may elicit reactions, but so also subjects instructed to think about certain things are noted to create patterns of brain activity that represent clear changes from their preintervention state. The fact that the two aspects of our humanity—the physical/brain and the mental/psychological—are highly correlated does not mean the mental collapses into the physical.

A second argument in favor of monism criticizes the idea of the immortality of the soul as nothing but an adoption of the Greek view rather than a scriptural understanding of resurrection. These monists note, with some merit, that the traditional Christian view does not attribute to the human soul the attribute of immortality on its own strength or by its very nature. That is, while Plato may have believed that souls are simply things that have and will exist eternally, Christians have believed instead that souls come to exist in the womb, live out their course of life on this earth and then have everlasting life either as beings resurrected for heavenly communion with God or hellish judgment. Dualists like Cooper respond that this is exactly the traditional view of immortality: the soul's immortality has traditionally been understood as ongoing existence beyond physical life based on our coming resurrection, our physical rising from death at Christ's return or parousia.

Third, Green (1998) and other monists reinterpret Paul's statements about "being absent from the body is to be present with the Lord" in an eschatological sense, as if these statements refer only to the end of the ages. This position requires a rereading of Scripture that many regard as too imaginative; for instance, requiring Christ's assurance to the thief that he would be with him that day in paradise as presupposing a "soul sleep" between the moment of death and the thief's eventual resurrection.

Three important facets of this matter deserve special emphasis. First, though our position is that the biblical data best support a bipartite view, the biblical emphasis is always on the unity of the person. As McDonald (1982) says, persons are "constituted of a unity of these two entities" (p.78), and hence it is not true that one aspect (the soul-spirit or the body) is the real person and the other part an add-on. We are embodied soul-beings. This is why we prefer the term *bipartite* rather than *dichotomous* for this view, since the latter term might imply that the two elements are fundamentally opposed and irreducibly separate and noninteracting (Hoekema [1986] uses "psycho-somatic unity" and Cooper [2000] "holistic dualism" to make the same point). The former term, however, implies that while the two elements are distinguishable in the human person, full human identity is vested in the union of the two aspects. We can never say, "That was my body that did that, not my spirit," or vice versa.

Often, biblical words for the various aspects of our being are used to refer to the whole person from a certain perspective. Nevertheless, there is a center to our persons, and the biblical term *heart* (Mt 15:18; Lk 16:15; Acts 14:17; 2 Cor 5: 12) is most consistently used to describe this core of what psychologists and philosophers often call our self. The scriptural emphasis on "heart" teaches us the importance of understanding ourselves as a unity.

Second, this recognition of two distinct essences cannot be used to make a hard differentiation in value between the two essences (as when many Christians are exposed to teachings emphasizing soul over body). In spite of passages suggesting that our temporal existence is of lesser importance (e.g., Mt 10:28; 2 Cor 12:3), ultimately people are their bodies and soul-spirits in unity. The value of bodily existence is unquestionably assumed in the creation (God made us bodily beings), the incarnation (God became a bodily being), and in Christ's and our own bodily resurrection (through which we will remain bodily beings, albeit perfected bodies, for eternity). As McDonald (1982) said, "Thus does the biblical view of man represent him as consisting of two principles, the cosmic and the holy, which unite the individual into a free and personal oneness of being" (p.78).

Finally, one tendency that can be quickly noted among secular (and Christian) thinkers is that of exaggerating one end or the other of our compound natures (Evans, 1990). Some so emphasize or exaggerate the immaterial side of our being as to deify humanity and deny that we are inevitably conditioned by our physical existence. We will see this tendency among the humanistic psychologists (chaps. 7, 8). The other extreme is to emphasize or exaggerate our temporal existence so as to make us mere physical machines that are just another biological phenomenon caught up in the grand mechanistic universe. Behavioral and classical psychoanalytic thought make this mistake (chaps. 3, 5).

A Christian view of the person balances these diverse aspects of personhood, emphasizing our unity and respecting that we are at the same time embodied spirits and enspirited bodies, embodied souls and ensouled bodies. Over the last few decades something like this unified vision has been embraced in the secular discipline in the form of what has been called the biopsychosocial model (Engel, 1977). This model argues that psychological health outcomes (see Straub, 2006) are influenced by what are understood as the three primary dimensions of human existence: the biological (most often understood as the physiological dimension of the body studied by biologists), the psychological (understood as the psychological experiences such as consciousness, cognition and affect studied by psychologists) and the sociological (the relationships between humans and their interaction with culture studied by sociologists). The causal influence is presumed to go both upward and downward. Within psychology the biopsychosocial model seeks to avoid narrow understandings of human beings by requiring that they nearly always be understood as biological and psychological beings existing within nested social networks. This model might appear to be common sense to most because of its intuitive acknowledgment that people exist across these multiple dimensions, but there often is a bottom-up flavor to it. There are numerous examples of research into psychopathology using brain imaging studies or genetics findings that, despite reference to a biopsychosocial model, manifest a reductionistic approach to psychopathology. Such studies unilaterally explore the impact of biology on the "higher" psychological and social factors, but ignore the fact that this model also allows for a "downward" flow of causal influence as well. Research has shown clearly, for instance, that sociological stressors can exert negative influence on psychological states (such as depression) and also affect negatively immune functioning.

The development of the biopsychosocial model opens room for conversation about Christian understandings of the unity of persons, but there are limitations to the approach as well. Within the context of this model, religion is often treated as a social factor and spirituality is understood as a psychological process. Christian scholars must be cautious about the reductionism inherent in such a conceptualization: personal faith is more than mere psychology (it involves a living relationship with Christ), and our corporate Christian faith is more than mere sociology (it involves participation in the living body of Christ). Even so, the biopsychosocial understanding, complemented by fully developed Christian understandings of religious faith, give us a fuller understanding of what it means to be a unified human being. All of these dimensions of our personhood are crucial, and all have a causal influence on our lived experience. The influence can be "upward": brain damage or immunological issues may very well influence a person's ability to be empathetic or to feel close to God. The influence may be "downward": as the spiritual life of an individual grows and deepens, it can impact his or her social relationships, mental health, immunological status and even modify synapses in the brain. A fully developed biopsychosocial-spiritual model of persons would direct the Christian psychotherapist to assess the interrelationships of the multiple dimensions and systems that contribute to our personhood, ranging from the genetic to the spiritual. By understanding the reciprocal relationships between the various levels and how they constantly affect (or fail to affect) psychological problems, a more realistic and holistic view of pathology and recovery can be developed.

Human Agency

As we put together the diverse elements that we have uncovered so far concerning our essential natures, we begin to see an emerging pattern of humans as persons with capacities and qualities unique among the created order. One of the premier capacities of personhood merits special attention, that of responsibility, limited freedom or agency.

Evans (1977) put it well in saying that "human beings are first and foremost agents. Their lives do not merely consist of a string of happenings or events, but constitute a series of choices and decisions about what they will do" (p.144). C.S. Lewis (1963), in discussing this matter, said, "Yet, for us rational creatures, to be created also means 'to be made agents.' We have nothing that we have not received; but part of what we have received is the power of being something more than receptacles" (p.50).

One way Reformed doctrine views human agency is by understanding humans as "created persons" (Hoekema, 1986, p.5). We are "created" and therefore completely dependent on God for our being; but we are also "persons" with a sense of responsibility to God. To be a human being is to reflect God in our capacity to act responsibly, and to act responsibly may require some freedom but not perfect freedom.

It is not necessary to a Christian view of freedom to argue that a person always and in every instance reacts with complete and unbounded freedom. Some events in our lives may be so powerful as to cause us to react involuntarily, which may occur, for example, when a young woman sexually abused since childhood reacts with fear and revulsion when approached by an aggressive young man interested in a date. In such instances, she may have practically no freedom to respond as she might rationally choose. At other times, we may be characterized as having limited freedom, as when the abused woman has struggled with and reflected on her experience and can make some choices of thought and action as an adult that will at least partially reshape her responses to men. Finally, there may be some instances wherein people act with almost total freedom, when they have few powerful forces impinging on their choices and they freely choose their actions. A pastor whose marriage is relatively stable but who chooses to have an affair to experience the excitement of rebellion against "rules and regulations" might be such an example.

The Christian view of persons requires that people have some responsibility in life, not that we always act without influence or constraint. Precisely how this influence interacts with human responsibility and agency is a profound mystery. The fact that we are so profoundly influenced by God's providence, by our biological inheritance, our families, our communities, our cultures and by the idiosyncratic events that happen in the course of life only adds to the mystery.

Personhood

Our understanding of humanness is also affected by the continually changing attitudes toward sexuality, gender and race.

Sexuality. The Christian Scriptures present a positive and cohesive portrait of our sexuality (Jones & Hostler, 2005), teaching that:

1. Our physical bodies are good. God made us physical beings; we do not just *have* bodies, we *are* bodies though we are more than just bodies.

2. God made us sexual beings, male and female, and our sexuality is good.

3. We are made for relationship; in Genesis 2:15-24 we learn that even the perfect man—in the perfect environment and in perfect relationship with God—is insufficient by himself. God declares that it is not good that the man be alone; human beings are made for relationship with a complementary version of human being, a man for a woman and a woman for a man.

4. Humans are created capable of "becoming one flesh" through the joining of their bodies, and the resulting capacity for reproduction in marriage is blessed by God and a blessing from God.

5. Humanity rebelled against God and in the process broke God's beautiful gift of sexuality,

along with all of his other gifts to us. As a result, we are rebellious, broken, twisted.

6. God is at work redeeming our sexuality in two crucial ways: God has revealed his standards or rules for how we are to conduct our sexual lives (and his laws are for our own good [Deut 10:12-13]), and then he offers us a living relationship with him through the death and resurrection of his Son, Jesus Christ, so that we are actually capable of living our lives in a way that gives him pleasure and moves us toward the holiness he intended for us.

7. The Scriptures reveal to us that sexual intercourse has a meaning fixed and determined by God: it creates a one-flesh union between a man and a woman, a union that is to knit them together in a way that's supposed to remain permanent through life (and thus this teaching is the foundation for Jesus' condemnation of divorce in Matthew 19 and Paul's condemnation of sexual immorality in 1 Corinthians 6).

Gender. Storkey (2007) has noted the plethora of work done by evangelicals in the past quarter century investigating how gender engages with the breadth of Christian doctrine (Trinity, Christology, soteriology, personhood, eschatology, Godhead language). Out of this discussion (or at times, acrimonious debate) have emerged two primary schools, with many gradations in between: the complementarian view and the egalitarian view. The key divide is over ordination to official offices of the church and the issue of headship and authority in marriage. The debate is grounded in a strong commitment to scriptural authority on both sides. But fueling the debate is the complexity and at times mysteriousness of the scriptural witness on these matters. For example, the apostle Paul on the one hand commends Junia (a feminine proper name in Greek) as one of the apostles (Rom 16:7) and yet grounds his prohibition on women teaching in seemingly absolute terms in the creation account (1 Tim 2:12-14). Thus, the scriptural position is far from clear, despite strong statements from both schools.

Part of the importance of this discussion is that historically some Christians have grounded arguments against women's ordination or for male headship in assertions about women being the "weaker" or lesser sex, only to see these views subsequently used to mistreat women or deprive them of basic human rights and dignity. Fortunately, today the primary exponents of both the complementarian and egalitarian positions together affirm women as made fully in God's image, as equally given the dominion mandate to carry out alongside men, as re-deemed equally by Christ Jesus, and as indwelt fully by the Holy Spirit, the giver of all gifts. They are also united in recognizing increasingly that both the Old and New Testaments present views of women that were uniquely empowering, affirming and respectful in the context of their contemporary cultural contexts. Despite those who insist that Scripture is univocal on this issue, to avoid further division in the church over this matter the wisest course may be to hold one's position with humility given the lack of biblical consensus.

Race. The realities of globalization provide tremendous opportunities for realizing the promise made to Abraham that all nations would be blessed through him (Gen 12:3). The "Christian family" today is profoundly multiracial and multiethnic. For too long in the Western world, theology was viewed as being properly understood only through Western eyes, yet there is an increasing awareness today of careful and Christ-honoring theological work being done not only in North America and Britain/Europe, but also in Africa, Asia and Latin America. Though agreeing on the foundations of theological belief—the triune God, the authority of Scripture, the fallenness of humanity, salvation being provided through Jesus Christ—this intercultural conversation is helping Christians everywhere appreciate better what aspects of their "Christian" views derive from Scripture and which derive from culture. There is an increasing recognition that because all humans are made in the image of God and will one day, together, come and worship the Lord (Rev 15:4), we have much to learn from one another during the early earthly part of our sojourn as well.

Human Motivations in Creation

The Bible gives no direct message about the nature of human motivation, but that does not mean that we are left drifting on this important point. We find it highly instructive to study carefully the first two chapters of the Bible to see the tasks that the first persons were assigned in the beginning. If we believe that God created our first parents as a perfect match for the role they were intended to fill in the Garden, then perhaps part of the matching would be that we are motivated at a fundamental level to live out the tasks assigned to us.

As noted earlier, part of human flourishing calls us to image God in our roles of dominion and relating to God and others. In Genesis 1:26 we read that we were made to rule over all of creation. We were also made male and female, and in being blessed by God we were instructed to be "fruitful and increase in number" (Gen 1:28). God then repeated the instruction that we are to rule over all living things, plant and animal. In Genesis 2 the charge to rule reoccurs in the instruction to cultivate and keep the Garden of Eden (Gen 2:15). Further, Old Testament scholars point out the additional significance of Adam naming the animals, since naming was a function of authority in ancient times, signifying one who owns or controls. In the creation of Eve we learn that God himself uttered the words that "it is not good for the man to be alone" (Gen 2:18). We learn that it was God's creational intent to provide a partner for the man, one for whom he was to separate from his family, to whom he was to cleave and with whom he was to become one flesh (Gen 2:24).

Two themes emerge. The first is the theme of *responsible dominion.* Humans were meant to rule on God's behalf, in dependence on him. Our vocations, our callings, are a primary vehicle through which we rule. Even seemingly mundane work such as gardening is a manifestation of our capacity for exercising dominion. We are God's stewards in this world, and all persons are meant to live out their Godlikeness in exercising responsible dominion over their part of the created order. Our contention is that this command entails a human need for *purposeful activity in life, a need for meaningful work and the realization of purpose outside of ourselves.*

The second theme is that of *loving relatedness.* Though there are scholars who view the use of the plural pronoun in Genesis 1:26 (God said, "Let us make man in our image, in our likeness") as primarily reflecting the language of royal theology common to the ancient Near Eastern world, and thus as being a reference to those in God's court (such as angels), we stand with many others who view these plural statements as reflecting God's triune nature. God has always related to himself. This is what divine perfection means. He did not need to create us, for he already had triune fellowship, but he chose to create. And it is clear that we were created for fellowship with God. Like our Creator, human beings are intrinsically relational and social beings. God's greatest gift to us at the beginning was not the order of creation or the beauty of the Garden, but the fellowship of his own person and the capability to enter into that fellowship. The Scriptures talk about our relationship with him in terms of a covenant or marriage contract. As Paul so eloquently notes, "Christ loved the church and gave himself up for her, that he might sanctify her, having cleansed her by the washing of water with the word, so that he might present the church to himself in splendor, without spot or wrinkle or any such thing, that she might be holy and without blemish" (Eph 5:25-27 ESV). This is the Christian's individual and corporate destiny. Yet the web of relatedness intended by God reaches up not only to the sovereign Lord, but also out to our fellow believers in marriage by our capacity to become one with another who is separate and different from us. In this union we image God in having the capacity for procreation, a reflection of God's much more profound capacity for creativity and generativity. Having children anchors us in cross-generational relationships of loving acceptance and discipline. But we also image God more broadly by our relational capacity reflected in the rich possibilities of celibate friendship through which the individual, whether single or married, can live a life of love and sharing in the community of the people of God. Such relatedness with our Christian brothers and sisters is vital for all of the heavenly Father's children. Obviously, generating biological children is not the only means of our reproducing ourselves. Adoption and cross-generational ministry are among the many profound ways of passing on one's riches to the next generation.

It bears special emphasis in these times that a Christian view of persons will emphasize family as fundamental to what it means to be human, not the least of which includes our local communities of worship, our true family created by our brother Christ who has provided a means for us of becoming children of our heavenly Father by his indwelling Holy Spirit. Families are webs of relationships in which we are imbedded throughout life, for better or for worse, in much the same way that God who created us remains in relationship with us, his fallen and wayward people. And family is a profound metaphor for our interrelating in Christ. This creation mandate of relatedness suggests that a fundamental human motive will be the establishment and maintenance *of meaningful relationships characterized by intimacy and unity even while we celebrate our uniqueness.*

HUMANITY IN ITS FALLEN STATE: NON POSSE NON PECCARE

Though we were created for dominion and relatedness, we managed to corrupt both capacities in the Fall. We were given the task of accountable dominion over the earth and were given the freedom and the abilities to discharge those responsibilities, but there were limits to the dominion marked by God, and we violated those guidelines in prideful disobedience. Though created to be in loving relationship with the Father, we betrayed his faithfulness and love toward us with our rebellion and deceitfulness. We betrayed the loving Father who had only our good at heart. Created to be open and responsive to God, we became willful, accountable rebels against God, and as Hubbard (1979) said, "at that moment God's scepter of glory became his gavel of justice" (p.78).

This is seen as unpopular and harsh language in certain evangelical circles, but biblical realism takes sin seriously, and we must do the same. Fallen and under divine wrath, we became alienated from God. As a further result, we became disoriented within ourselves; in theological terminology, this is known as the noetic effect of sin, that sin affects even the way we think. We all have a rather predictable tendency to deceive ourselves and others, and we often attempt to deceive our Creator. Perhaps the most powerful literary rendering of this capacity and tendency for self-deceit is C.S. Lewis's (1956) brilliant novel *Till We Have Faces,* in which the main character, who had spent her whole life justifying her actions, realizes her unreadiness to confront her Judge and asks rhetorically, "How can they meet us face to face till we have faces?" (p.294). In other words, how can we meet God face to face when we spend so much of our lives deceiving ourselves about who and what we really are and hiding our true faces from ourselves and God? Our alienation from God and disorientation within ourselves are regarded as the twin facets of the Fall.

The divine wrath that we are under is not only an expression of God's justice and dignity; it is an expression of his love. Where such vast capacity for fellowship exists, the capacity for hurt is enormous, not unlike that of a broken marital covenant. "What we were made to do and what we were best at doing are now our sharpest and clearest failures" (Hubbard, 1979, p.79).

The Nature of Sin

Sin as state and act. Sin is dealt with in very complex ways in the Scriptures, and getting a clear handle on this slippery concept is difficult. Christians often think of sin as isolated acts that violate moral standards. We think this or that act was a sin. Yet in Scripture sin refers not just to acts but to a state of being. Individual sins testify that we have a "sin nature," which predisposes us to those individual acts of violation against God's law. (Mark 7:20-23 states that individual acts proceed out of a heart of corruption.) As Bloesch (1984) states, "Sin is not just a conscious transgression of the law but a debilitating ongoing state of enmity with God" (p.1012).

Yet sin is even more than a disposition in our natures; it is something palpable beyond ourselves; it is "a power that holds us in bondage" (Morris, 1986, p.57). Among the New Testament writers, Paul especially seems at times to reify sin as a transpersonal "force" acting against God and his purposes (Rom 6–7). Because we are now fallen, we are only able to choose according to our fallen natures—our choices consistently align us against God. As a result of the Fall we have lost our human freedom, the freedom to do God's will. We have lots of choices, but in our own strength they all drive via different roads away from God. So sin is at once acts of transgression, a nature or disposition, and a force in opposition to God.

Rebellion or anxiety? What is the nature of our sinfulness? Why do we commit sins and have a sinful nature? The classic orthodox answer to this question has been to highlight our human rebelliousness against God. Bloesch (1984) states that

> in Reformed theology, the core of sin is unbelief.... Hardness of heart, which is closely related to unbelief, ... means refusing to repent and believe the promises of God (Psalm 95:8; He-

> brews 3:8, 15; 4:7). It connotes ... stubborn unwillingness to open ourselves to the love of God (2 Chronicles 36:13; Ephesians 4:18). (p.1012)

In this formulation sin is a culpable rejection by humans of their rightful submission to God's sovereignty. It is a willful abuse of the freedom God imparted to us.

Another major current understanding of the nature of sin might be characterized as "neo-orthodox." Originating with Niebuhr and Tillich, this view suggests that sin originates in the "union between man's dependence as a creature and his free spiritual life" (Gilkey, 1985, p.231). Confronted with the awesome responsibility of managing the tension between our human finiteness and contingency (dependence on God for our very existence), on the one hand, and our capacity for freedom and transcendence, on the other, we experience anxiety of an existential nature. We don't want to be dominated by our temporal existence, but neither do we want the responsibility of choice. The righteous response to this dilemma is to balance the tension and choose to live in humble submission to the Creator as a dependent being with responsible choice. But the sinful response is to evade the human responsibility of managing this tension by either denying our freedom and living life dominated by the cares of this world (plunging oneself into sensuality with the cry "I can't help myself," for example), or denying our dependence on God and trying to become gods unto ourselves (thus rebelling against God's laws and saying, "No one is going to legislate my life for me!"). Both of these imbalanced responses are regarded as sin, as both shrink from responsibly living out life in the way God created it to be.

There are actually many other understandings of sin (see Bloesch, 1984). Liberation theology, for example, rightly recognizing that sin can and often does become institutionalized, emphasizes the exploitative, oppressive, greedy nature of corporate sin. And many of these views are not mutually exclusive; it is not hard, for instance, to see the Reformed and neo-orthodox views as complementary truths, and orthodox Christians can sadly concur that sin is often institutionalized, while also insisting that there is an inescapable individual aspect of sin.

A Christian understanding of sin that is truly biblical must maintain a balance between seeing sin as a violation of law and as a violation of relationship, of sin as individual and sin as corporate, of sin as driven by rebellion and sin as driven by anxiety, of sin as something we are in bondage to and are yet responsible for.

Moral evil, natural evil, finitude and the satanic. Ethicists commonly make the distinction between moral and natural evil. Moral evil is the result of moral choice—such as intentional theft, for instance. Some things, though, are bad but are not the result of a culpable choice. The accidental injury of a young child who falls down a set of stairs is such a natural evil, as are most instances of disease, decay and death. They may be no one's fault, but they are bad nevertheless, a part of life's reality in a fallen world.

Theologically, the origin of both moral and natural evil is humanity's fall from grace. In Adam and Eve's original choice to turn from God's command and partake of the forbidden fruit (Gen 3:6) lies the beginning of human moral evil. As our first parents chose, now so we choose. Natural evil's origin may be seen in God's judgment on Adam and Eve. They who were given responsibility to care for the garden have the judgment on them extended to the garden that now will produce thorns and thistles (Gen 3:18). Natural evil, therefore, is now understood as nature, the created order, working against human flourishing. Important to note in this discussion is that the temptation to both Adam and Eve, who were created good, arose not from their own natures but from the serpent, or Satan, who was already in the garden. (Genesis 3:1, Revelation 12:9 and Revelation 20:2 identify Satan with the "ancient serpent" of Genesis.)

We can also distinguish moral and natural evil from our finitude, our limitedness as human beings. Our human limitations exist because we are not gods, and thus finitude existed in creation prior to either moral or natural evil. There is much that is beyond our possible reach physically, mentally, emotionally and spiritually. Adam could not run a two-minute mile, will immediate emotional changes, know the future or in any way exceed the capacities God had given him. Humans must confront their finitude and achieve some reconciliation with their limitations. Limitations are not necessarily flaws or sins; they are simply the limits of the raw material from which we are to forge who we are and who we are to become. Thus finitude is part of our God-ordained creatureliness that we might learn to depend and rely on the One in whose image we have been made.

These distinctions become important when sorting out our understanding of human problems. Some human difficulties are due exclusively to human moral evil—sometimes our own, sometimes that of others, but most often both. If we deceive ourselves and engage in immoral behavior, we will bear the consequences.

But many human problems are essentially natural evils rather than moral evils. Chemical brain imbalances appear to be predisposing factors in such disorders as schizophrenia, and are probable factors in other serious disorders. Alternatively, we may experience problems because of our finitude without that problem being a sin. The college student struggling with the difficulty of making decisions about careers is confronting the reality of her finitude—no one knows the answers to all the questions one could ask about careers and the future, and it is not sin not to know these answers and to struggle with the decision.

We must also mention another significant instance of moral evil, that of the active opposition against God's purposes and goodness by the "forces of wickedness" and darkness (Eph 6:12 NASB). Satanic and demonic evil are real. The personal evil of the supernatural forces in rebellion against God must be taken seriously by all Christian mental health workers. Shuster (1987) has argued that there is a demonic element to all evil, and that Scripture suggests that these personal forces of evil have infiltrated all aspects of human life. This further complicates our understanding of moral evil, natural evil and finitude when we grapple with how forces of darkness corrupt our experience and contribute to the evil we are exposed to and commit. Usually, all these elements—the moral evil of ourselves and those about us and of the demonic world, natural evil and human finitude—are involved in the problems of the person who comes for psychotherapy.

We can see the complexity of the human condition as we recognize how all of these aspects of our human experience come together for all of us. A child faces life in the context of human finiteness with a limited capacity to deal with trauma. Perhaps that child is exposed to such unfortunate events (natural evil) as the loss of a mother to cancer. The child's surviving parent, out of his own weakness and fallenness, sinks into alcoholism and begins physically abusing his son in frustration and grief. The demonic forces seek to use these events to pull this child away from any openness to a loving Father God. As that child grows into a young man, he may continue to experience natural evil (a girlfriend killed in a car accident) and moral evil perpetrated against him (the father's abuse turns into chronic emotional abusiveness). In his finiteness he has only so much capacity to strive to overcome all he has experienced but now begins to contribute his own moral evil as he abuses substances to cope and responds abusively to women. And again, supernatural forces for evil seek to use all of this to turn this young man from seeking healing from God.

Johnson (1987) suggested the designation of "moral fault" to describe instances where both moral evil and "weakness" (his term for what we are calling finitude) are involved. We prefer a three-component designation as developed earlier, but his concept of moral fault is a good one, which suggests that often, perhaps almost always, problems involve all these components of moral evil, natural evil, finitude and the satanic.

Sin and Human Freedom

The state of human freedom after the Fall is a topic of mind-boggling complexity. Humanity is now burdened with an impaired capacity for freedom to please and follow God, in that sin now infuses our very being and clouds our every choice. The desperate cries of Paul in Romans 7 are repeated by all Christians who find their desire to follow God in righteousness frustrated by a continual bondage of the will to sin. We can all testify to our impotence to obey God perfectly and to follow him wholeheartedly. And yet God holds us responsible for our disobedience. In short, we have the dual experience of choice *and* bondage, culpability *and* an incapacity to do otherwise. This experience matches the scriptural puzzle of our seeming inability not to sin coupled with our undeniable culpability for sinning.

We can offer no easy resolutions to this matter (see McDonald, 1982, pp.57-67, 92-100). According to Scripture, God's general revelation in nature (Rom 1:20) and the human conscience (Rom 2:15) hold us accountable to God. Yet though this revelation in the created world is indeed part of God's self-disclosure to humanity, it is clear that only by means of God's special revelation, his specific disclosure in Jesus Christ, are humans able to submit to God by his Word, grace and Holy Spirit.

Historically, theological discussion of the matter of free will has usually centered on a specific, crucial choice: the person's choice to become a Christian. Both Calvinists and Arminians hold to a view of theological compatibilism—that God's exhaustive foreknowledge is compatible somehow with humans' exercising responsibility before God. Even so, Calvinists tend to stress the "God" side of the equation, asserting that the act of coming to Christ is wholly the work of God through his grace. They further assert that to believe that any element of being born again is attributable to the person's choice diminishes God's sovereignty, making faith a "work" and thus Christianity a religion of works rather than grace. Arminians, on the other hand, tend to stress the "human responsibility" side, asserting that there is an element of choice or human freedom in becoming a believer. They argue that to assert otherwise is to make humans into moral robots, God into the grand puppet master, and Christianity a deterministic religion. They do not, however, deny our bondage to sin or the central importance of God's work in freeing us from that bondage.

For our purposes here we are not so concerned with the decision of becoming a Christian as we are with the capacity for human freedom in the give-and-take of everyday life. Suffice it to say that in everyday life humans, on a moment-to-moment basis, may not be free to choose the perfect good. Most often this appears beyond our grasp. But the inaccessibility of that choice does not render nonexistent other choices that we can make. For example, we may not be able to choose to be perfectly honest, but we have real choices day by day of particular instances where we can veer either in the direction of being honest or deceitful.

God in his sovereignty may shape human choices to ensure the triumph of his grace and of his redemptive plan for humanity, but human choice is nonetheless real. For example, one of our children may be destined by

God to some work of critical importance to God's purposes on earth, and as such God may be guiding our actions toward them, drawing that child toward him, either through our good example and discipline as parents or through the poverty and pathos of our hypocrisy. In either case, we parents still make choices of how to deal with them and are accountable to God for those actions. There are, from eternity's perspective, no small decisions and no unimportant persons.

Human Motivations After the Fall

Earlier we addressed human motivations implied in the creation narrative. There are also implications for our understanding of human motivation to be drawn from the saga of humanity's Fall, both in terms of new motivations we experience and in the distortions of our most basic creation-grounded motivations.

In terms of new motivations, rebellion against God, the desire to be gods ourselves, now becomes an operative motive in all that we do. Whether we admit it or not, we are all rebels. In addition, to the extent that sin is rooted in the ontological anxiety of grappling with our freedom in light of our limitations, the desire to run away from this burdensome responsibility now operates as an ever-present motivation as well. The story of the Fall makes it clear that Adam and Eve tried to cover up their sin by first avoiding God and then attempting to shift blame and abrogate personal responsibility. This awareness of divine judgment and the desire to avoid that righteous judgment now color all that we do. We are motivated to escape culpability for who we are and what we do.

The Fall also contaminates our most basic good motivations. The good motive for meaningful work and to serve good purposes can become twisted into a drive to dominate others, to be number one, to control or even to rebel against the notion that we have purpose in life and to choose to drift meaninglessly. The good motive of relatedness can be twisted into sensualism and an idolatry of sexuality, into pathetic dependence on another, into a loss of identity in the other, or in a retreat from engagement from others. We no longer experience the pristine original motivations of Adam and Eve before the Fall. Scripture's account of humanity's Fall may additionally offer some insight into spiritual warfare: whenever we find ourselves questioning or disbelieving God's Word ("Did God really say?" [Gen 3:1]) or God's goodness ("God knows that when you eat of it, your eyes will be opened, and you will be like God, knowing good and evil" [Gen 3:5]), we need to be wary of these age-old temptations.

All of this immeasurably complicates our understanding of human motivation. Humans experience compound and conflicting motivations as part of their essential unredeemed natures (and even once redeemed as well). For example, as we approach dating and marriage, we may desire another with the good motive of seeking intimacy and the bad motive of desiring someone to exercise power over. In summary, the constellation of our motivations is vastly complicated by our rebellion against God. Our motivations are seldom pure and never simple.

HUMANITY IN ITS REDEEMED STATE: POSSE NON PECCARE

Using covenant terminology (after Anderson, 1987), we might say that in the midst of the devastation of the Fall, the marriage between humanity and God had been shattered, but from one side only. Grace for reconciliation is needed. God has offered restoration in the life, death and resurrection of Jesus Christ, the pivotal events in all of history and the only source for our hope and salvation. Receiving this grace may lead to significant transformations in the lives of ordinary people through believing and acting on the truths of the faith.

Life Between the Beginning and the End

It is commonly noted that the experience of the Hebrews in being redeemed from Egypt by the Lord (Exodus through Deuteronomy) is a powerful model of our own redemption process. While the Israelites were oppressed, God raised up for them a savior, Moses (a type of Christ). God through Moses freed them from their bondage and servitude to an alien master, and initially they exuberantly celebrated their freedom. But release from captivity was not immediately followed by entering the Promised Land. Rather, the Israelites had to wander in the wilderness for many years before being ushered into the "land of milk and honey." Christians similarly live between the day of emancipation and the day of final deliverance. A battle has been won but the war is not over. Brunner (1939, p.114 and throughout) calls this "life in contradiction"—life suspended between our fallen and redeemed natures.

With the coming of Jesus the King, the kingdom of God has been inaugurated. Thus, we now live between the "already" of the kingdom of God that is present and the "not yet" of the kingdom of God that is to come. We must navigate the struggles and tensions of this "in-between" life by depending on God and others who share this journey. We do this by becoming part of a covenant people, by becoming deeply involved with a local body of believers. Only in the context of a healing community can we learn to cultivate and express the fruits of the Spirit, which along with a deep concern and compassion for others should epitomize mature, committed Christians.

The Goal of the Redeemed Life

Paul's central prayer for the Philippians expresses well the central goal of life in Jesus Christ:

> I consider everything a loss compared to the surpassing greatness of knowing Christ Jesus my Lord, for whose sake I have lost all things. I consider them rubbish, that I may gain Christ and be found in him, not having a righteousness of my own that comes from the law, but that which is through faith in Christ—the righteousness that comes from God and is by faith. I want to know Christ and the power of his resurrection and the fellowship of sharing in his sufferings, becoming like him in his death, and so, somehow, to attain

> to the resurrection from the dead. (Phil 3:8-11)

According to the apostle Paul, the goal of the Christian life is to know Christ, which entails having a righteousness based on faith, being conformed to (or in some way identifying with) Christ's sufferings and death, and finally attaining eternal fellowship with Christ through the resurrection of the dead.

On our contemporary scene, much has been written about emotional wholeness and Christian holiness. Some authors seem to regard the two as essentially identical. Surely growth in Christ means to become more like Jesus, and the more we are like him, the more holy and whole we must be.

Yet wholeness and holiness are actually very different. We live in a fallen world. It is easy for our conceptions of wholeness to become contaminated with sub-Christian notions of well-being, especially those that emphasize easy accommodation with the world. All too often in psychology the goals for clients are to become well adjusted and do one's best at a purely human level, rather than radical realignment of one's life to the claims of Christ.

Curiously, one recent secular acknowledgment of this tension was contained in a prominent report from the American Psychological Association (2009). That report acknowledged that conflict and tension may exist between psychological and religious perspectives on personhood, stating that "Some religions give priority to *telic congruence ...* [while in contrast, certain models of] psychology give priority to *organismic congruence"* (p.18). The term *telic congruence* means that some religions (they clearly had Christianity in mind) formulate the purpose of life to include, against many of our instincts, seeking to reject how we find ourselves to be and striving to become (to develop congruence) with some other goal (Greek *telos)* such as seeking to become like Christ. They contrast this with *organismic congruence,* a psychological valuing of embracing (congruence) what we are already (what is organismic). The APA could not be more on target that this is a fundamental tension—are we okay just as we are, or do we need to be saved from what we are and conformed to something transcendent?

In contrast to such idealized goals as minimizing conflict, total emotional awareness and expression, maximizing life satisfaction and pleasure, and living up to our innate potential, note that Paul prescribes the goals of becoming conformed to Christ's suffering, death and resurrection. Such a calling certainly includes a number of personal experiences that are far from secular psychology's ideals for well-adjusted human living. In short, we are called to a way of life that is often at odds with the ways of the world, a way of life where suffering and pain are an inevitable part of our lot in life, where being holy, which literally means being set apart to God's purposes and manifesting his righteous character, can be difficult and even despised by the world. The Christian life is a way of life in which, as Paul stated, believers know both how to be abased and how to abound, having learned in all circumstances the secret of facing plenty and hunger, abundance and want: "I can do all things through Christ who strengthens me" (Phil 4:12-13 NKJV).

McLemore (1982) cautions that it is quite possible for an individual to be a paragon of mental health, as it is traditionally defined in psychology, yet be living without faith in God through Christ. The peaceful practitioner of Zen Buddhism, unruffled by life's demands as he retreats into an inner world, might be supremely healthy by the definition of some. On the other hand, a "saint" in the local church may be living a life of emotional pain and interpersonal estrangement as she faithfully follows God's calling, thus living a life of holiness that is far from the current psychological understanding of wholeness.

Thus, while there may be much that overlaps between *wholeness* and *holiness* (especially as both are embodied in the concept of Christ-likeness), and the two concepts may not be contradictory in any fundamental way, we must be exceedingly careful when we discuss the two terms. The chief danger is that the pursuit of wholeness is so easily and widely approved of in the Western world that it would be easy for Christians to pursue "growth" as defined by some therapy approach while deluding themselves into thinking that they are thus pursuing holiness as well.

Christian clinicians need to think carefully, critically and courageously about the goals that they are advocating in the context of counseling and psychotherapy, to think in the light of what it means for a believer to be "salt and light" in the world and to be "bearing the marks of Christ." It is imperative that these goals include considerations of Christian faith and experience.

Another unfortunate contemporary development is that of substituting the language of the soul with that of the self. The loss of belief in Scripture as God's Word and concern over Platonic construals of the soul has resulted in a shift within much of the psychological literature of referring to one's "self" rather than one's "soul." Yet these words are far from being synonyms. As Boyd (2001, p.114) notes, to speak of a self is to limit one's perspective to the earthly; to speak of the soul is to acknowledge that there is a life beyond this one and One to whom we must one day give an account.

HUMANITY IN ITS GLORIFIED STATE: NON POSSE PECCARE

Perhaps it is appropriate to end this overview where Augustine did, looking to humanity in its glorified state, no longer able to sin but demonstrating complete freedom to please God in all things. As the Westminster Shorter Catechism notes, one day we will achieve our chief end of fully and without sinful impediment glorifying God and enjoying him forever.

As we struggle with various trials, temptations and earthly suffering, we need to remember that the effects of the Fall are temporary; that one day Christ will wipe away every tear from our eyes (Rev 7:17); that the earthly part of our sojourn is the *short* part of our journey; that one day we will cease to walk by faith and will know our Maker fully by sight, no longer seeing in a mirror dimly, but face to face; no longer knowing in part, but knowing fully even as we have been fully known (1 Cor 13:12); that our earthly labor is not in vain but, in Christ, is full of meaning (1 Cor 15:58). Thus we receive John's encouragement: "Dear friends, now we are children of God, and what we will be has not yet been made known. But we know that when he appears, we shall be like him, for we shall see him as he is" (1 Jn 3:2).

This sure hope is what allows us to persevere in the face of our own suffering and that of others.

CONCLUSION

It is essential for Christian pastors, academicians, clinicians and researchers to take Christian worldviews and control beliefs seriously. As McDonald (1986, p.138) has noted, there is no purely psychological theory of personality that can give an effective account of all the ethical and religious concerns of the human individual. What we have covered here does not constitute a personality theory, but it does form a vision of personhood that should undergird a personality theory acceptable to Christians.

No such theory exists today. Christian psychologists must therefore tentatively work within incomplete personality systems while striving for development of a full-bodied Christian view. As Brunner (1939, p.62) has argued, there can be no Christian psychology if by that we mean a theory of elemental sensory processes or memory. But when we move to the level of a comprehensive understanding of the *person,* then there will be a distinctively Christian approach to psychology.

Does the faith have implications for how we intervene with persons? Does it specify modes of counseling with troubled people? From surveying the writings of Christian counselors, one sometimes gets the idea that God specifies one and only one way of dealing with all problems and difficulties. As we already argued in chapter one, the problem is that each of the Christian counselors specifies a different set of techniques, claiming that his or her system is the one endorsed by Scripture. One emphasizes exhortation to behavior change, another a change to biblical thinking, another healing prayer, another supernatural intervention and yet another the casting out of demons.

Our position on this matter is that we have much to learn from various forms of pastoral intervention recommended and utilized in the Scriptures. In 1 Thessalonians 5:14, the apostle Paul says, "And we urge you, brothers, warn those who are idle, encourage the timid, help the weak, be patient with everyone." Paul's admonition shows that different types of human problems call for different types of responses from counselors. Many other types of interpersonal helping responses are specified in the Bible, including loving, forgiving, providing material charity, teaching, comforting, grieving with, rebuking, excommunicating and so forth. Clearly what is needed is a flexible repertoire of approaches, grounded in coherent theory and deeply respectful of the complexity and profundity of human struggles.

Almost any form of counseling interaction in the Bible can find its counterpart in the practice of secular psychotherapy. It is interesting, though, that each major school of psychotherapy tends to build its identity around a rather limited number of styles of therapist-client interactions so that cognitive therapists are teachers, person-centered therapists are accepting, psychoanalytic therapists are distant and interpretive, and so forth. No counseling model we know of embodies the diversity of interaction styles that seem to be recommended in Scripture. So, as the Christian therapist moves beyond a secular theory, one needed area of growth is an expanded vision of technique that incorporates the eclecticism found in Scripture.

FOR FURTHER READING

Berkouwer, G. (1962). *Man: The image of God* (D. Jellema, Trans.). Grand Rapids, MI: Eerdmans. (Originally published n.d.).

An excellent Reformed study of theological anthropology, emphasizing the image of God.

Blocher, H. (1997). *Original sin: Illuminating the riddle.* Grand Rapids, MI: Eerdmans.

A penetrating and remarkably interdisciplinary reflection on the nature of sin.

Clebsch, W., & Jaekle, C. (1975). *Pastoral care in historical perspective.* New York, NY: Jason Aronson.

One of the best studies of the history of the pastoral care tradition, including "exhibits" of original writings in pastoral care from throughout history.

Cooper, J.W. (2000). *Body, soul, and life everlasting: Biblical anthropology and the monism–dualism debate.* Grand Rapids, MI: Eerdmans.

An insightful critique of monism from an evangelical perspective.

Hoekema, A.A. (1986). *Created in God's image.* Grand Rapids, MI: Eerdmans.

A solid overview of all facets of theological anthropology from a Reformed perspective.

Lewis, C.S. (1946). *The great divorce.* New York, NY: Macmillan.

A moving and thought-provoking depiction of physical existence after the resurrection.

McDonald, H. (1982). *The Christian view of man.* Westchester, IL: Crossway.

An excellent overview of Christian anthropology.

McMinn, M.R., & Phillips, T.R. (Eds.). (2001). *Care for the soul.* Downers Grove, IL: InterVarsity Press.

A collection of essays from the 2001 Theology Conference at Wheaton College, this compilation offers thoughtful insights about the integration of theology and psychology from a number of perspectives.

REFERENCES

Adams, J. (1979). *More than redemption: A theology of Christian counseling.* Phillipsburg, NJ: Presbyterian & Reformed.

APA Task Force on Appropriate Therapeutic Responses to Sexual Orientation. (2009). Report of the Task Force on Appropriate Therapeutic Responses to Sexual Orientation. Washington, DC: American Psychological Association. Retrieved from www.apa.org/pi/lgbt/resources/therapeutic-response.pdf.

Anderson, R. (1987). *For those who counsel.* Unpublished manuscript, Fuller Theological Seminary, Pasadena, CA.

Augustine (Intro. by Thomas Hibbs). (1961). *Enchiridion on faith, hope, and love.* Washington, DC: Regnery Publishing.

Beck, J.R., & Demarest, B. (2005). *The human person in theology and psychology: A biblical anthropology for the twenty-first century.* Grand Rapids, MI: Kregel.

Berkouwer, G. (1962). *Man: The image of God* (D. Jellema, Trans.). Grand Rapids, MI: Eerdmans. (Originally published n.d.).

Bloesch, D. (1984). Sin. In W. Elwell (Ed.), *Evangelical dictionary of theology* (pp.1012-1016). Grand Rapids, MI: Baker.

Boyd, J.H. (2001). In defense of the word *soul.* In M.R. McMinn & T.R. Phillips (Eds.), *Care for the soul* (pp.102-117). Downers Grove, IL: InterVarsity Press.

Brunner, E. (1939). *Man in revolt* (O. Wyon, Trans.). Philadelphia, PA: Westminster Press. (Originally published 1937).

Clebsch, W., & Jaekle, C. (1975). *Pastoral care in historical perspective.* New York, NY: Jason Aronson.

Cooper, J.W. (2000). *Body, soul, and life everlasting: Biblical anthropology and the monism–dualism debate.* Grand Rapids, MI: Eerdmans.

Engel, G.L. (1977). The need for a new medical model: A challenge for biomedicine. *Science, 196* (4286), 129-136.

Evans, C. (1977). *Preserving the person: A look at the human sciences.* Grand Rapids, MI: Baker.

Evans, C. (1990). *Søren Kierkegaard's Christian psychology.* Grand Rapids, MI: Zondervan.

Foster, R. (1985). *Money, sex, and power: The challenge of the disciplined life.* San Francisco: Harper & Row.

Gilkey, L. (1985). *Maker of heaven and earth.* Lanham, MD: University Press of America. (Originally published 1959).

Green, J. (1998). Bodies—that is, human lives: A re-examination of human nature in the Bible. In W.S. Brown, N. Murphy & H.N. Malony (Eds.), *Whatever happened to the soul? Scientific and theological portraits of human nature* (pp.149–174). Minneapolis, MN: Fortress.

Greidanus, S. (1982). The use of the Bible in Christian scholarship. *Christian Scholar's Review, 11,* 138-147.

Gunton, C.E. (2002). *The Christian faith: An introduction to Christian doctrine.* Malden, MA: Blackwell.

Hoekema, A.A. (1986). *Created in God's image.* Grand Rapids, MI: Eerdmans.

Hubbard, D. (1979). *What we evangelicals believe.* Pasadena, CA: Fuller Theological Seminary.

Jewett, P. (1975). *Man as man and female.* Grand Rapids, MI: Eerdmans.

Johnson, E. (1987). Sin, weakness, and psychopathology. *Journal of Psychology and Theology, 15,* 218-226.

Jones, S., & Hostler, H. (2005). The role of sexuality in personhood: An integrative exploration. In W.R. Miller & H.D. Delaney (Eds.), *Human nature, motivation, and change: Judeo-Christian perspectives on psychology* (pp.115-132). Washington, DC: American Psychological Association.

Lewis, C.S. (1956). *Till we have faces.* New York, NY: Harcourt Brace Jovanovich.

Lewis, C.S. (1963). *Letters to Malcolm: Chiefly on prayer.* New York, NY: Harcourt Brace Jovanovich.

McDonald, H.D. (1982). *The Christian view of man.* Westchester, IL: Crossway.

McDonald, H.D. (1986). Biblical teaching on personality. In S. Jones (Ed.), *Psychology and the Christian faith: An introductory reader* (pp.118-140). Grand Rapids, MI: Baker.

McLemore, C. (1982). *The scandal of psychotherapy.* Wheaton, IL: Tyndale.

Morris, L. (1986). *New Testament theology.* Grand Rapids, MI: Zondervan.

Oden, T. (1984). *Care of souls in the classic tradition.* Philadelphia, PA: Fortress.

Plantinga, C. (1988). Images of God. In M. Noll & D. Wells (Eds.), *Christian faith and practice in the modern world* (pp.51-67). Grand Rapids, MI: Eerdmans.

Shuster, M. (1987). *Power, pathology, and paradox: The dynamics of good and evil.* Grand Rapids, MI: Zondervan.

Storkey, E. (2007). Evangelical theology and gender. In T.R. Larson & D.J. Treier (Eds.), *The Cambridge companion to evangelical theology* (pp.161-176). Cambridge: Cambridge University Press.

Straub, R.O. (2006). *Health psychology: A biopsychosocial approach* (2nd ed.). New York, NY: Worth.

Webber, R. (1986). *The church in the world.* Grand Rapids, MI: Zondervan.

Wolterstorff, N. (1984). *Reason within the bounds of religion* (2nd ed.). Grand Rapids, MI: Eerdmans.

Wolterstorff, N. (1987). *Lament for a son.* Grand Rapids, MI: Eerdmans.

3

CLASSICAL PSYCHOANALYSIS

Stanton L. Jones, Robert Watson and Richard E. Butman

***

Although psychoanalysis is the grandparent of all psychotherapeutic methods, it tends to be unpopular in many conservative Christian circles. The specific concerns focus around three troubling themes in classical Freudian psychoanalysis: (1) the emphasis on sexual and aggressive drives as the motivational bases for behavior, (2) the deterministic and naturalistic assumptions of the model, and (3) the direct attacks on religion Freud made in his later writings.

Despite these reservations, many Christian mental health professionals have a profound respect for this tradition (see, for example, Sorenson, 2004; Crabb, 1988; McLemore, 1984; Narramore, 1984; Peck, 1983). Certainly the reservations are legitimate, but to dismiss psychoanalysis as irrelevant to the real problems of life is to fail to see its potential significance for the church and the society (Browning & Cooper, 2004).

Classical psychoanalysis has reemerged in contemporary conversations between neuroscience and psychoanalysts. While there is no clear consensus, a number of key neuroscientists suggest that the basic contours of Freud's view of the mind may serve as a theoretical framework or template that can organize the empirical findings (Kandel et al., 2005). In fact, recent Nobel laureate in physiology and medicine Eric R. Kandel (1999) said that in light of the findings of contemporary cognitive neuroscience, psychoanalysis is "still the most coherent and intellectually satisfying view of the mind" (p.505). The direct impact of psychoanalysis as a system of thought can be seen in nearly all academic disciplines, including history, literature and philosophy. The more indirect influence on the larger public consciousness can hardly be overestimated (Jones & Wilson, 1987). Thus, Freudian thought continues to be relevant at a cultural level, and its broad impact profound (and despite the legitimate Christian objections we will raise here, we seriously doubt that all the influence has been negative).

Given the brevity of our treatment, we cannot trace the development of psychoanalytic thought over time. Freud's thinking evolved over his productive years; the most striking example of this is his gradual move away from a harshly biological approach to his subject matter, and his widening of his understanding of motivation to include not just the sexual drive but the aggressive/death drive as well (Mitchell & Black, 1995). For the sake of economy, we will present Freud's system as if it were a static whole, though we recognize that this fails to capture the evolution of classical psychoanalytic ideas. We will appraise contemporary derivatives of the classical Freudian analytic tradition (called psychodynamic theories) in chapter four.

DESCRIPTIVE SURVEY

Classic psychoanalysis assumes that all human behavior is determined by the impact of early childhood experiences on the management of psychic energy. In order to make sense of a person's current behavioral patterns, it is necessary to understand the behavior's roots in largely unconscious conflicts and motives. The forces that "move" us are irrational and strong, and are related to aggressive or sexual drives that arise from biological instincts. Consequently, the goal of psychoanalysis is to make the unconscious conscious: to bring into conscious awareness disavowed desires, feelings, fantasies, fears, memories and wishes whose expression has been thwarted. Often, this involves exploration of memories of critical life events in the formative childhood years thought to be related to the psychopathological symptoms and problems in living that emerge throughout the remainder of the lifespan. Only through greater self-knowledge and self-regulation can mature adults increase their capacity to love and work effectively.

This theory is best understood when we grasp the historical-cultural milieu or context of psychoanalysis. We will highlight three aspects of Freud's historical-cultural context: (1) the Enlightenment worldview of the late nineteenth century, (2) the Darwinian assumptions underlying Freud's anthropology, and (3) his Victorian-era Austrian cultural milieu.

The early modern era, beginning in the early 1600s, brought to an end the medieval era in Europe. For our purposes, this transition marked dramatic shifts in cultural (including theological) views of personhood. Cushman (1995) observed,

> What was once a spiritual being who contained a soul and was embedded within a community that was in turn held in the hand of God, had become an early modern individual who contained a mind which was dependent upon the domination of reason

> and will over the wild emotions of the body. (p.93)

The modern, Enlightenment view of persons construed the individual's mind as ruled by reason, but construed the emotions (and the body) as wild and primitive; it also entailed a dramatic shift toward an individualistic view of the self. Order, domination and control emerged as key values in the post-medieval European world that supported its burgeoning market economies, republics and politics. The individual mind and its capacity to bring order, rationality and control over itself (including the body and its passions) preoccupied much intellectual discourse. The use of science and technology to bring a rational sense of order and control over the natural world, human institutions and people groups also became hallmarks of the modern era. Freud was not just an uncomplicated Enlightenment figure, however; the Romantic movement that competed with rationalistic Enlightenment thinking is also reflected in and took inspiration from Freud, who never saw rationality alone as the route to understanding or achieving human wholeness. The emotional realities of the human psyche were irrefutable and inevitable contributors, even determinants, of human experience. Freud never manifested the bland optimism that reason was the answer to all problems, which characterized other Enlightenment figures. Further, with his relentless search *behind* our current conscious experience for hidden explanations in our unconscious, Freud helped set the stage for the development of postmodernism, particularly in terms of the way in which his "hermeneutic of suspicion" (i.e., an instinct that the surface explanation for human experience is rarely the fundamental one) became one of the pillars of postmodern epistemology (Westphal, 1998). Thus, it is probably less accurate to call Freud an Enlightenment thinker, and better to identify him as an exemplar of modernity.

Freud formed his psychoanalytic theory and treatment approach against this historical-cultural backdrop, informed by his work as a research neurologist and clinical psychiatrist. At the center of his theory building, Freud viewed mind as a kind of internal, psychological battleground for the three *modern* forces of the human condition: instincts, rationality and culture (Cushman, 1995). The connection between Freud's model of mind and his context seem clear on this point: his awareness, particularly as an Austrian Jew, of the long history of war, bloodshed, repression and strife in Europe influenced his view of the interior struggles of the individual. For Freud, as a quintessential modern man, "Life is a constant contest, a struggle to determine which aspect of the mind would dominate and which suffer from the consequences of submission" (Cushman, 1995, p.115). This was, of course, represented theoretically in his structural theory of mind as a battleground between three intrapsychic "agencies" (more on this later).

It is also against this historical-cultural background that Freud's focus on sexuality as central to personality, development and psychopathology developed. The Enlightenment (and Romantic) view of persons suggested that beneath rational civilization and individual mind lays the primitive, pleasure-oriented bestial aspects. Consistent with the cultural perspective of his day, Freud linked pleasure-seeking, primitive instincts and a Romantic view of animals with human sexuality. "Thus, Freud established sexuality as a realm of unfettered pleasure, free from the tyranny of the object and social necessities, a 'nature preserve,' like a zoo in the middle of an urban setting" (Mitchell, 1988, p.121). For Freud the inevitable conflict in the mind between agencies of rationality, culture and instinct best explains human behavior, development, psychopathology and personality.

The second of the cultural-historical factors influencing the classical psychoanalysts were the Darwinian assumptions underlying Freud's anthropology. Darwin's evolutionary perspective exerted profound influence over the thinking of Freud's late-nineteenth-century European scientific milieu. Consistent with Darwin's emphasis on evolutionary development from primitive (or lower) to advanced (or higher) organisms, Freud considered mental development to follow a similar trajectory. We develop as our "bestial," primitive core is brought under control by our rationality and cultural constraints. Freud made use of the Darwinian shift from the Platonic-Judeo-Christian portrayal of humankind as fallen from harmony with and designed by a divine Creator to humankind evolving from below. "Man was not a fallen angel, a chip off the divine block gone astray, but a more or less refined beast. This reversal provided a fresh and exciting perspective on human nature and experience, and Freud was very much a beneficiary" (Mitchell, 1988, p.73). This perspective, of course, put classical psychoanalysis on a direct collision course with theistic worldviews of his day (and ours).

The third contextual aspect influencing classical psychoanalysis is the highly repressive and obsessively proper Victorian-era Austrian cultural milieu in which Freud worked and lived. Being an astute clinician and an ethnic outsider, he saw through the superficial propriety and popular piety of the day. His patients' stories reflected darker aspects of everyday human experience: lust, envy, possessiveness, ambivalence, hatred and self-deception—things no one addressed directly in proper conversation. In fact, his clinical work eventually brought him to a conceptual (and personal) crisis: his patients' stories of childhood sexuality, including abuse and seduction, led him to suspect that children from good Viennese families had actually been seduced sexually by parents and parent figures. Ultimately, Freud resolved this crisis in his thinking and practice (in part) by assuming that these stories were, by and large, fantasies generated by his patients when they were *children.* He thus construed these fantasies as not only fearful, nightmarish sexually traumatic fantasies, but also as wish-fulfilling, pleasure-seeking fantasies—that is, as what they as children wanted to experience with their parent(s) emotionally and sexually. What was, of course, lost in this theoretical resolution of the problem was the distinct likelihood that Freud was actually hearing about *real* traumatic memories of sexual abuse—a prospect the magnitude of which he may have been unable to face.

As a result Freud brought into the open what polite Victorian society tried to avoid. And he argued that this very avoidance of what is most primitive, instinctual and uncivilized about us is at the core of psychological problems and symptoms. Cushman (1995) writes,

> [Freud] thought the unthinkable, and uttered the unspeakable; no one was safe from his gaze, not mothers, not children. Paul Ricoeur has called psychoanalysis a "hermeneutics of suspicion," and for good reason. Freud saw psychopathology as a product of urges, conflicts, and self-deceptions common to all persons, regardless of social class, race, religion, or gender. According to Freud's theory, if peoples' inherent physiological drives are not repressed by the "internalized" norms of society, acts of violence or sexual perversity would destroy society. But repression, in turn, causes its own problems, which are manifested through various psychological symptoms: what is repressed "returns" in creative but ultimately self-destructive or dangerous behavior. (pp.110-111)

Ironically, while Freud clearly valued the role that culture played in civilizing our base, animal instincts, he also pioneered a worldview and method that helped to bring to an end the Victorian view of persons as rational, pious and civilized at the core.

Philosophical Assumptions and Model of Personality

Philosophically speaking, psychoanalysis reflects the influence of classical empiricism as well as the Enlightenment tradition (cf. Rychlak, 1973). Freud adopted a materialistic or naturalistic worldview as the backdrop for his model. Ultimately, Freud believed that his psychology would be understood in terms of brain physiology. For example, Freud (1914) once opined, "We must recollect that all of our provisional ideas in psychology will presumably one day be based on an organic substructure" (p.78). Classical psychoanalysis makes at least five core assumptions about persons (Brenner, 1973; Arlow, 1984): (1) topographical, (2) genetic, (3) dynamic, (4) structural and (5) economic.

The *topographical assumption* asserts that there are three levels of consciousness: (1) the conscious experiences we are aware of (e.g., thoughts you have as you read this page), (2) the preconscious experiences that we can voluntarily recall but are not currently cognizant of (e.g., the memory of your best experience in the fifth grade), and (3) the unconscious experiences that are the primary determinant of psychic life but are not directly accessible to conscious examination (e.g., unresolved conflicts from your childhood). All behavior is assumed to have largely unconscious determinants. Although we may be aware of our conscious motives for writing this book (e.g., contributing to the work of the church), at a somewhat deeper and perhaps more powerful level, we may be unconsciously looking for approval from parents or significant others.

The *genetic assumption* essentially asserts that current behavior and experience, but most notably troubling repetitive behavior, is over-determined by past events. All the influences that we believe to be shaping us in the present (e.g., conflict with a supervisor at work or love for our spouse) have their real power through the unresolved issues of our past (e.g., conflict with a parental figure that was strictly authoritarian or overly permissive). In other words, the experiences that trouble us largely derive their meaning from activating unresolved difficulties from the formative years of childhood. Consequently, psychoanalysis has a strong historical as well as deterministic bias (cf. Ford & Urban, 1963).

The *dynamic assumption* contends that all behavior is ultimately dependent on the interaction of two fundamental human drives. The *libidinal drive* is largely erotic or sexual in nature. Broadly defined, the libido focuses on far more than genital sexual release and pleasure—it includes the desire or urge to create, to develop or maintain intimacy, to love self or others, to form ideals and values, and more (Munroe, 1955). The other major drive is primarily oriented around the twin themes of aggression and death. Both drives have creative or destructive potential (Prochaska, 1979). Libido and the death instinct also are the impetus for attachment and separation behavior. Both drives can be understood as deterministic at the intrapsychic, interpersonal or societal levels. These "life instincts" and "death instincts" are at the core of the Freudian view of human nature and of what drives human behavior.

The *structural assumption* asserts that the psychic apparatus can best be understood in terms of three separate but interdependent psychological entities known as the *id, ego* and *superego.* The id is the repository for our most primitive sexual and aggressive drives and urges. Id processes are assumed to be present at birth and to be largely unconscious, illogical, demanding and relentlessly driving toward personal gratification (this is called the pleasure principle). The ego is reality based and develops as an individual interacts with the external world. The ego is largely conscious and serves a vital role in mediating the primitive urges of the id with the constraints or opportunities of reality. Finally, the superego places restrictive demands on both the id and the ego. It is generally understood as a split-off from the ego and as the repository of the moralistic standards one has absorbed from significant others, most often parents and society. Often seen as a primitive kind of conscience, the superego is assumed to be only partially conscious.

Finally, the *economic assumption* asserts that human personality can best be understood as a closed or quasi-hydraulic system. In other words, a certain amount of energy is introduced into the psychic system in the form of the basic drives. Exactly how instinctual energy (bodily, primitive instincts) became psychic energy (i.e., that powers the structures of the personality) was never explained by Freud. He, like all thinkers of his time, was limited by the mind-body dualism introduced by Descartes. Since this energy must be released, ways must be found to disperse it in a direct or transformed manner. This is *economic* in the sense that energy is neither gained nor lost; the bank account always balances. The goal of psychoanalytic treatment is to develop the capacity for the release of id energy in socially acceptable and appropriate ways. In contrast, psychopathology is understood as the consequence of a compromise negotiated by the ego between the demands of the superego to comply with the internalized rules of others and of the id to allow for partial gratification of unacceptable wishes (e.g., a psychosomatic symptom that elicits attention and also expresses aggression). At more severe levels, psychopathology may also be understood as gratifying release of id energy with little regard to the constraints of reality or external social norms (e.g., psychotic regression).

For Freud consciousness was only a small part of the total psyche. Although it cannot be studied directly, Freudians believe the existence of the unconscious can be inferred from direct observation of behavior or through conscious experiences such as dreams, slips of the tongue or material derived from free association. Freud hypothesized that all the stored experiences, memories and repressed material of a lifetime can be found in the unconscious. Since unconscious material influences all behavior, the deeper contents of the mind must be explored at some level to achieve any significant measure of health and wholeness. Awareness and insight of this material alone isn't curative—it must be worked through, ideally in the context of a psychotherapeutic relationship.

In the absence of such working through, however, means must be found to deal with the anxiety that develops out of the conflict between the id, ego and superego over the control of the available psychic energy. Ideally, the ego can control the anxiety through direct and rational means, but more often than not the largely unconscious and often primitive ego defense mechanisms must be utilized. These defense mechanisms transform the threatening anxiety into some alternate form the person can deal with and thus help one cope with threatening unconscious conflicts. The more primitive defense mechanisms often result in marginal coping. Most abnormal psychology, personality or psychotherapy textbooks contain summaries of the most important defense mechanisms. The main lesson to be learned about defense mechanisms is that overt behavior rarely means what it seems to, because in transforming the anxiety caused by unconscious conflicts, the true reasons for our behavior become largely inaccessible.

The classic Freudian understanding of the development of personality asserts the existence of a series of psychosexual stages. According to this perspective, the personal and social development that occurs in these critical stages of infancy, childhood and adolescence lays the foundation on which further maturation can be built. Both healthy and unhealthy personality development reflect the manner in which the relevant tasks were accomplished. Each stage is distinguished by the focal area of the body where the gratification of libidinal impulses is concentrated.

The *oral stage* (first year of life) is foundational to later personality development. The caregiver's focus is on feeding and nurturing the infant, and gratification for the baby centers on the mouth; sucking and chewing are primary. Failure to get one's needs met potentially leads to greediness or an unhealthy preoccupation with possessions in later life.

The *anal stage* (ages one to three) centers around the child's experience of parental demands, discipline and expectations, especially as they relate to toilet training. Psychic gratification centers on retention and expulsion of feces and urine. Unresolved issues at this stage potentially lead to unhealthy attitudes about the body or bodily functions. Extremes of orderliness or messiness are also assumed to be related to unresolved issues in this period.

In the *phallic stage* (ages three to six) the focus for gratification moves away from the mouth and anus to the genitals. It is during this stage that the child learns much about sex-role identity and develops an interest in sexual matters. Parental attitudes in particular are communicated verbally or nonverbally, and negative experiences can affect feelings about sexuality throughout the remainder of the life span.

The phallic stage is assumed to be the period in which Oedipal (for boys) or Electra (for girls) conflicts emerge, in which the child develops threatening, erotically charged feelings for the parent of the opposite sex. Freud developed his notions of what happens at this stage for boys to a much greater extent than for girls, so we will focus on those. (The Oedipal crisis was named after the famous Oedipus myth of Greek mythology, in which Oedipus was destined to murder his father and marry his mother.)

The boy, Freud proposed, comes to experience vague libidinal longings for union with his mother. These are rarely experienced consciously. These feelings are often exhibited by intense attachments to mother, jealousy for her attention and so forth. Realizing that the father is a competitor for the love of the mother, the boy first experiences an angry competitiveness with the father, followed by a fearful realization that he cannot, as a child, hope to compete for the attention of the mother (assuming the basic health of the parental relationship). The healthiest resolution to this terrible dilemma is for the boy to identify with the father and actually absorb parts of the father's personality, so that at least the boy can have some sense of special attachment to the mother on a vicarious level by being like the father. Part of what is absorbed becomes the foundation for the superego.

In the *latency stage* (ages six to twelve), increased socialization with other children typically replaces the inwardness of the phallic period. Coupled with new interests in others, the child develops academic, athletic, interpersonal or recreational competencies. These social themes are predominant throughout the prepubescence period.

In adolescence the child moves into the *genital stage* (ages twelve to eighteen) where again sexual impulses become predominant. Interest in the opposite sex develops, often with some sexual experimentation. Ideally, libidinal energies are redirected in socially appropriate activities (e.g., dating friendships). The genital stage is assumed to continue throughout the remainder of life as one searches for a healthy balance between love, work and play.[4]

Even the most ardent critic of psychoanalysis would agree that the approach is comprehensive and that its model of personality has heuristic value (Ryckman, 1985). Unfortunately,

---

4 Somewhat parallel but complementary understandings of these stages can be found in the work of Erikson (1982) or other major developmental theorists (cf. Berger, 1988).

the theory all too often lacks precision and testability, and runs the risk of leading to "nothing-but," or reductionistic interpretations of behavior (e.g., everything becomes the result of aggressive or sexual drives). Still, as Silverman (1976) has observed, aspects of psychosexual theory can be clinically demonstrated. For example, persons with primitive defenses against aggressive and sexual impulses do seem to exhibit greater rates of neurotic psychopathology, an observation consistent with Freudian theory.

Model of Health

In the psychoanalytic tradition, healthy individuals have enough conscious awareness of their wish-fulfilling aims to have self-control and self-awareness (as Freud [1933] said, "Where id was, there shall ego be. It is a work of culture—not unlike the draining of the Zuider Zee" [p.80]). Both wish fulfilling and painful and traumatic memories have largely been worked through and are no longer denied or distorted. To a meaningful and significant degree, aspects of the unconscious have been made conscious. Important dimensions of the personality structure have been reconstructed as neurotic processes have been undone, thereby facilitating greater movement toward maturity.

The healthy person has good ego strength. Destructive impulses exert less pressure on the individual so that he or she is increasingly able to make responsible decisions about how to deal with the tasks of everyday living. The clash between the biological urges and the demands of social reality is still there, but effective compromises, choices and commitments have been made. Self-knowledge about these and other tensions are of supreme importance in this tradition, so much so that it is often viewed as a necessary, if not sufficient, condition for growth toward an autonomous and productive life (Korchin, 1976, pp.326-332).

Maturation, then, is seen as a lifelong process of increasing the capacity to understand and regulate one's self. Obviously, this will require a high level of self-awareness and intelligence, a fair degree of willingness for painfully honest self-assessment, and a strong motivation for change and growth in one's life. Perfection is impossible to reach.

Model of Abnormality

According to this tradition, everyone is pathological, to a greater or lesser degree, due to the inevitable conflicts and fixations that develop in our formative years. The specific symptoms that develop reflect both the psychosexual stage in which the conflicts and fixations first developed and the particular manner in which immature or primitive ego defense mechanisms are utilized to deal with the resulting anxiety. In other words, psychoanalysis assumes that problems in living are universal, since nobody proceeds through the developmental stages without difficulty. At the intrapsychic level, all symptoms "work," in that they help us cope with the demands of everyday living, even though the symptoms may be self-defeating and perhaps even self-destructive.

The model is thoroughly intrapsychic in its assessment of the etiology and maintenance of emotional difficulties. The more intense the conflicts and fixations are, the more severe the psychopathology. Given sufficient environmental or internal stress, the defenses can be overwhelmed and symptoms emerge. These internal threats are typically avoided rather than dealt with directly, and the person is highly motivated to keep unacceptable impulses or childish, primitive anxieties out of direct consciousness at whatever cost. When the avoidance strategy is coupled with often well-meaning attention from family and friends that help continue the unhealthy way of dealing with the conflict, the cycle of avoidance can become a deeply ingrained pattern (what has come to be designated "the neurotic nucleus").

In short, stress stirs up unacceptable wishes and makes the person anxious (i.e., creates internal conflict); the anxiety is avoided at all costs (which can be highly reinforcing); and a vicious cycle becomes established. A more direct strategy of resolving the core conflict itself is not adopted because the deeper unconscious "primary process" is nonlogical (irrational) and atemporal (makes no differentiation with respect to time) (cf. Prochaska, 1979, pp.34-35).

According to the model, conflict is not incidental to being human. Rather, conflict is intrinsic to human nature and forms the core of our being. At the minimum the positing of two distinct fundamental drives creates the potential for confusion and tension in human motivation. Freud thus differed from later humanistic theorists who consistently see motivational confusion and tension as the result of external interference with the uncomplicated motivations of persons; for Freud, confusion and tension was often intrinsic. But more consistently, the instincts of the id conflict with the repressive dictates of the superego, such that the two seem to do battle, like two powerful horses, with the ego astride them both, trying to get them to cooperate. Consequently, conflict is as much a part of normalcy as it is of pathology.

Anxiety is at the core of all psychopathology, operating largely at the unconscious level.

Generally speaking, the person has no awareness of the deeper significance of immediate precipitating events and how they affect the underlying impulses or unresolved conflicts and fixations. As the largely unconscious anxiety intrudes on consciousness, the person tends to experience feelings ranging from a mild sense of dread to feelings of panic. Anxiety at any level serves a signal function: it signifies (painfully) the presence of a threat—from the inside or the outside. Depending on where these conflicts and fixations first developed psychosexually, and the specific ego defense mechanisms utilized to bind the anxiety, the full spectrum of psychopathology takes shape. Obviously, certain responses to immediate precipitating events are healthier than others. But at some level all symptoms are gratifying, even to highly functioning individuals. This inevitable tendency to deny and distort reality is apparently generic to the human condition (cf. Munroe, 1955, for an especially insightful treatment of these themes).

Model of Psychotherapy

For Freud the ultimate goal of psychoanalysis is the complete analysis of all aspects of personality and the resolution of virtually all intrapsychic conflicts (which is the highest and most difficult goal of any system of psychotherapy). In order to accomplish this goal psychoanalysts argue that it is necessary to relive memories of certain painful childhood experiences and work them through. This process is called abreaction or catharsis, but a patient, careful therapeutic focus on the patient's avoidance of these memories via defense mechanisms, precedes it. In making the unconscious conscious, the ego is strengthened, thereby facilitating a greater capacity for managing the demands of the instinctual urges within the constraints of reality. The resulting self-awareness and insight is more than merely intellectual—it is deeply felt and experienced after an agonizingly difficult and often painful process of change, and thoroughly integrated by the patient.

Classical psychoanalysis usually involves multiple appointments every week for at least two or three years, and often more. Obviously, this can be an expensive and demanding commitment. In actual practice, analysts work in diverse and varied ways, depending on their personal styles and the needs of their clients. Despite these differences, concerned analysts early recognized the need to reduce the length of the standard treatment, without sacrificing the technique's unique properties (Korchin, 1976, p.325).

But it is precisely because of the typical length, expense and intensity of the treatment that psychoanalysis is so widely disparaged in both lay and professional circles. Specifically, it is asserted that psychoanalysis is an elitist therapy, geared toward the rich and self-indulgent who find that talking about themselves to a highly trained analyst a great deal promotes their own sense of well-being. In their defense, classical Freudian psychoanalysts assert that promoting lasting and significant change is of necessity a difficult and time-consuming process. Not only do clients need to unlearn self-defeating coping strategies, but they must also develop new and more effective ones. Further, change is resisted because these same patterns have historically worked for the client, in that they bind anxiety, provide some degree of instinctual gratification, and often lead to attention from others. As Korchin (1976) has summarized it, "the process of character reorganization... is about on par with learning a new language to replace one's mother tongue, particularly if the student is ambivalent in his motivation, fighting the new experience while seeking it" (p.325).

Classical Freudian psychoanalysts usually agree that they should remain *relatively* neutral and personally anonymous to their clients. This way of relating to patients is thought to help by bringing out into the open and into the therapeutic relationship the very psychological conflicts that are related to their psychopathological symptoms. So, for example, if their symptoms are about feeling anxious at work in relation to a critical supervisor, the neutral stance of the analyst may evoke similar feelings of anxiety toward another authority figure (i.e., the analyst) that can be worked through in the therapeutic relationship. They assert that more directive and supportive approaches have lesser value for many patients, in that they tend to promote dependency rather than autonomy. Further, psychoanalysts assert that these therapies run the risk of becoming anti-developmental, in that they tend to lessen the necessity of the "legitimate suffering" that will occur when the client works at self-exploration. Only deep self-awareness and understanding can lead to the kind of insight needed to promote lasting change (see Meissner, 1985). On the other hand, contemporary Freudian psychoanalysts (e.g., Gabbard, 1994) also understand that some patients—typically with more severe psychopathology—cannot tolerate nondirective, highly emotionally stimulating interventions typical of the classical approach. For these patients, directive and supportive interventions are targeted at supporting and scaffolding healthier defenses, coping strategies and overall ego functioning (Gabbard, 1994).

The most basic method of psychoanalysis is free association. Clients are asked to minimize conscious control and tell everything that comes to their minds, with the expectation that more and more significant material bearing allusions to unconscious conflicts will emerge. This basic rule of psychoanalysis is exceedingly difficult to follow even with the best of intentions. Most of us are loathe to speak directly and truthfully, even in the best of situations. This is especially pronounced in the context of a clinical relationship, where difficult and often painful material must be explored and worked through. Resistance to free association often builds in direct proportion to the psychic significance of the unconscious material emerging. Indeed, classical psychoanalysis asserts that the forces that are striving toward recovery are usually met with equally strong opposing ones. And it is the analysis of these blocks or disruptions in free association (i.e., resistances to the process of analysis owing to defense mechanisms) that often give the analyst clues as to the nature of psychic conflicts and fixations. If they can be brought to awareness and effectively dealt with, increased insight can result.

Another major theme in this tradition is the analysis of the transference relationship that occurs between the therapist and the client. Strong, personal feelings of both a positive and a negative nature usually develop between client and therapist that go beyond the actual or real clinical relationship. Specifically, both client and therapist bring to the current relationship issues that are brought forward (transferred) from earlier relationships with significant others. Assuming that the analyst has dealt with his or her own countertransference issues (basic conflicts that might be transformed into feelings, expectations and attitudes toward the client), the focus can be on bringing the client's hidden and repressed conflicts or feelings from the past, which are transferred into feelings about the therapist, into the present where they can be examined, understood and resolved. The neutrality of the therapist encourages the development of transference, as the more unknown the therapist, the easier it is for the client to project his or her internal material on that therapist. Thus client reactions toward the therapist are vitally important. Indeed, they can develop to the point where a transference neurosis will emerge, which then becomes the major focus of therapy. A potential transition between illness and health also becomes possible if the deeper meaning of the neurotic origins of the expressed feelings can be explored and worked through in the context of the client's current difficulties and needs.

Interpreting the client's resistances and defensive maneuvers is another fundamental strategy utilized in psychoanalysis. Good interpretations are appropriate in timing, tact and sensitivity. Specifically, they must be given at the level at which the client can hear, understand, appreciate and incorporate them. They not only make sense intellectually, they *feel* true at a deep emotional level. If the interpretations are premature or inappropriate, they only lead to greater resistance. If they are well-suited, they can contribute to greater understanding and perhaps relief. Ideally, good interpretations help the client to make sense of current thoughts, feelings and behavior in light of his or her past.

Psychoanalysts assert that dream analysis is especially helpful in uncovering important unconscious material. During dreams, normal conscious controls are relaxed, perhaps even more deeply than they are in free association. Through inquiry, inference and eventually interpretation, the meanings of both current and longstanding conflicts or difficulties can be explored and worked through. Although Freud once described dreams as "the royal road to the unconscious," they are "hardly a freeway with unlimited visibility, nor do hidden meanings roll forth with simple clarity" (Korchin, 1976, p.328). As with free association, resistance and transference, working through the material is hard work that takes time and an extremely high degree of commitment on the part of the psychoanalyst and patient.

In summary, psychoanalysis consists of a variety of methods to make unconscious conflicts conscious so that they can be worked through in the context of the psychotherapeutic relationship. In particular, the "then and there" conflicts and fixations of the formative years of childhood and early adolescence are explored as they relate to "here and now" concerns. These must be "reconstructed, discussed, interpreted, and analyzed" (Corey, 1986, p.38) with a view toward the strengthening of the reality-oriented ego—one's best hope of lasting change. Since the therapeutic goals are so high and difficult to obtain, and the self-defeating patterns so deeply established with the client, it is inevitable that most treatment be intensive and long-term.

Few clinicians alive today can deny that they have felt the impact of Freudian theory and technique. Hardly any well-developed approach to people-helping lacks a conception of an unconscious, an appreciation of the role of early childhood development, or an understanding of the relevance of such clinical concepts as transference and countertransference, resistance or the ego defense mechanisms. The model stresses biological and instinctual factors to the neglect of other psychosocial, interpersonal or sociocultural factors, but it does speak broadly and deeply to certain dimensions of the human experience. On the other hand, as Alston (1967) has noted (p.516), psychoanalytic concepts need to be more explicitly stated and anchored in objective criteria if they are going to be the basis for further interdisciplinary dialogue. The works of Hackett (1986), Oakland (1977) and Walters (1973) are good initial examples of such interdisciplinary work.

Contemporary psychotherapists are indebted to the legacy of classical psychoanalysis. While many aspects of Freud's theory—most especially his drive theory—appear to have limited value, many other pieces of classical psychoanalytic theory and technique have held up well over the course of time. Empirical research and vast clinical experience would seem to support ongoing interest in and utility of six clinical concepts grounded in psychoanalysis, namely, the dynamic unconscious, psychological ambivalence, defense mechanisms and resistance, the compulsion to repeat, the centrality of the therapeutic relationship and mourning of illusion.

Dynamic unconscious. That a significant portion of our consciousness is beneath our own awareness is unquestionable from the standpoint of classical psychoanalysis and of contemporary cognitive neuroscience. The remaining questions about the unconscious mental processes revolve around questions of what the content is. For example, neuroscientists working at the interface of psychoanalysis and cognitive neuroscience suggest that Freud's dichotomy of unconscious instinctual life into sexuality and aggression is not comprehensive enough. At present, at least four basic instinctual "circuits" seem to underpin our instincts (Solms, 2004). They are a "pleasure" system (which motivates us toward the pursuit of pleasure), the "anger-rage" system (which is related to aggression associated with fight or flight when threatened), the "fear-anxiety" system (which helps alarm us into action in the face of potential threat), and the "panic" system (which is related to instincts associated with social bonding and attachment). That these systems operate much of the time out of our awareness is fairly obvious—particularly in terms of their motivational aims. Knowing that most of human consciousness is not directly accessible is useful to any clinician. Having a basic map of the terrain of the unconscious is particularly helpful when attempting to understand human behavior.

Ambivalence. Classical psychoanalysis provided us with a basic framework for understanding and working clinically with a fundamental reality of human beings; namely, that we live between what we *wish* for and what we *fear* will happen if we get what we wish for. Freud and the classical psychoanalysts recognized that wishes and fears are linked: you cannot have one without the other surfacing nearby. If a patient feels anxiety about an upcoming family event—a reunion, perhaps—the therapist can safely assume that there are corresponding wishes that are tethered to the fears. For example, the individual anxiously anticipating the event may wish (perhaps unconsciously) that this time she might feel welcomed and secure in her mother's presence. On the other hand, getting what we wish for often triggers unexpected fear or anxiety. For example, the pleasure of a wished-for promotion at work is often followed by feelings of dread regarding whether she can now perform up to a new set of standards and expectations.

Defense mechanisms and resistance. Another enduring contribution from classical psychoanalysis involves methods of psychological self-protection and self-preservation. When examined outside of a relational context (e.g., the psychotherapy relationship), these methods are called defense mechanisms. When explored within a relational context, these are called types of resistance. Defense mechanisms have been cataloged and stratified over many years. Many contemporary approaches cluster individual defense mechanisms from most primitive and least adaptive to most mature and most sophisticated psychologically (see the *Adaptive Functioning Scale* of the American Psychiatric Association, 2000).

Repetition compulsion. One of Freud's most poignant and useful clinical observations is summed up in the following from his 1914/1963 article: "the patient remembers nothing of what is forgotten or repressed, but that he expresses it in action. He reproduces it not in his memory but in his behavior; he repeats it, without of course knowing that he is repeating it" (p.160). Freud goes on to provide, as an example, the story of the patient who does not remember being defiant and critical of his parents' authority in his childhood, but behaves precisely in that way toward the therapist. This very human propensity to express in action that which is too painful to remember is an essential clinical phenomenon for psychotherapists of all theoretical orientations to understand. It is this dynamic that drives transference phenomena.

Patients that have histories of psychological trauma—particularly *chronic* trauma over many years—are most vulnerable to the compulsion to repeat. In this attempt at self-protection (to not remember) coupled with a wish to "revisit the scene of the crime" to try to have a different outcome in the present, many people unconsciously orchestrate present-day scenarios to reenact their painful historical experiences. This can take the form of trying to please authority figures in the present that are withholding approval, choosing a romantic partner or mate who behaves like an abusive or neglectful figure from childhood, or (unconsciously) choosing a vocation that holds out the promise that the practitioner can finally help people in the present in ways that they could not help their own families in the remote past—a common motivation for people who become psychotherapists!

Centrality of the therapeutic relationship. Classical psychoanalysis was the first psychotherapeutic system to insist that what happens within the therapeutic relationship figures centrally in the outcome of the treatment. The assumption is that patients deliver into the relationship with the therapist the very patterns of thinking, feeling and behaving that caused them to seek treatment. And this aspect of the repetition compulsion (and of the patient's resistance to becoming aware of what is being repeated) is highly significant grist for the mill of what happens in psychotherapy sessions and what ultimately leads to making progress and experiencing healing.

In recent years empirical support for the link between the quality of the therapeutic relationship and the outcome of treatment has been mounting. In fact, the psychotherapy outcome research literature suggests that 30 percent of the variance in courses of psychotherapy with positive results is accounted for by the quality of the therapeutic relationship and other factors common to all therapies. This percentage of the variance is second only to the 40 percent of the variance attributed to "patient qualities and extratherapeutic change" (Lambert & Barley, 2001). While contemporary psychotherapy outcome research does not prescribe a classical psychoanalytic model for the therapeutic relationship, it certainly argues for the potency of the relationship between therapist and patient. And the psychoanalytic tradition clearly is the most thoughtful and comprehensive in its reflection on making use of the therapeutic relationship on behalf of the patient's healing.

The perceived effectiveness of Freud's psychoanalysis was enhanced by the clinical insightfulness he demonstrated in his writings, but according to Storr (1989, pp.100ff.), while Freud mentioned 133 cases in his writings, he only provided extensive reports on six cases. Of these six, he only saw two for over six months, and only one for a full course of psychoanalysis. This last, full case, the famous "Wolf Man," was "not quite the advertisement for psychoanalysis which Freud might have hoped for" (pp.106-107). Apparently while Freud reported his analysis to be a complete success, a follow-up study suggested that the Wolf Man's analysis with Freud was only somewhat helpful, allowing him to live a life of moderate maladjustment. Thus, while Freud encouraged a helpful understanding of the therapeutic relationship as central, it is by no means clear that his own clinical work demonstrated a high success rate.

Mourning of illusion. Perhaps Freud's most useful and enduring contribution to contemporary psychotherapists was his elucidation of the relationship between the process of mourning of illusion and growth. In fact, it can be argued that mourning and growth are two sides of the same coin (Shabad, 2001). Freud's clinical work with depressed patients helped him to recognize that the failure to disengage the wishes and desires bound up in one's relationship with, for example, a lost parent sets the stage for a kind of thwarted mourning. In normal mourning the wishes and desires—the emotional attachment to the lost parent—are transferred from the actual person to the memories of that person. In pathological mourning the grieving person is vulnerable to clinical depression if she *psychologically* keeps the lost parent alive in her mind in order to meet psychological needs that she believes she cannot meet apart from the lost parent, like feeling confident or loved. Using a psychological sleight of hand, human beings who cannot let go of the other keep the other alive by identifying with them—in essence, allowing their own self to be *eclipsed* by an internalized version of the other. This attempt to hold onto the relationship leads to one of the characteristic symptoms of thwarted mourning—the self-loathing and anger-turned-inward that many depressed people manifest (Freud, 1915/1957). Listening clinically to this type of self-loathing pretty quickly leads to the conclusion that the very things the depressed person is angry about themselves are actually attributes of the lost other. So, for example, the son who cannot come to terms with the death of his mother finds himself berating himself for being mean-spirited and critical of others' mistakes—a quality clearly more related to his mother's personality and behavior than to his own.

So what does this have to do with mourning of illusion *and* growth? Freud recognized that to grow—to become less conflicted, more integrated, more free to choose—requires that we negotiate well the "necessary losses" (Viorst, 1986) that life presents. And the process of negotiation involves willingness on our part to face reality courageously, to endure the necessary dis-illusionment, and to re-member aspects of our hopes and dreams that have been thwarted by the reality of the loss. This last aspect, re-membering or re-collecting, is the least intuitive piece of the mourning process (Shabad, 2001). It involves intentionally thinking about (and feeling about) how we would have wanted/hoped life to have been if the inevitable loss had not occurred. So, for example, it is essential to the healing of the broken heart of the young woman who prematurely loses her father to cancer that she think about how she would have wanted her graduations, wedding and birth of children in the future to have been with her father present—all the while knowing that he will not be a part of those events. This is a type of re-membering—of joining back to her own heart and soul those pieces that have been torn apart by the loss of her father. It is a costly thing for the mourner, for she comes face to face with the very thoughts that evoke the deepest feelings of grief.

For a person with a Christian worldview it is not difficult to sense something paschal about this psychological formulation: it alludes to the deepest pattern and rhythm of reality—that *death precedes new life.* In this case, facing "death" in the form of what was and will be lost in terms of hopes and dreams is a necessary step toward discovering new life. And this type of psychospiritual pilgrimage takes both faith and hope. This integrative theme will be developed further in the next section.

CHRISTIAN CRITIQUE

As might be evident from the previous section, Freudian thought has come under fire from many sectors. As Hurding (1985) notes, Freud receives criticism "from the academic psychologists for being unscientific, from humanistic and theistic psychologists for being too reductionistic, and from the behaviourists for not being reductionistic enough" (p.70). Still, a balanced and fair assessment would recognize that we owe much to Freud in assisting us in our efforts to make sense of the often bewildering complexity of our psychospiritual natures.

Philosophical Assumptions

Freud is perhaps best known in religious circles for his attacks on religion. Classical psychoanalysis is essentially an agnostic or atheistic system, since Freud treated religion as a wish-fulfilling illusion. Genuine religious motivation and the spiritual life are ignored or treated negatively in psychoanalysis (Vitz, 1987, p.66). Exemplified in works like *The Future of an Illusion, Civilization and Its Discontents,* and *Moses and Monotheism,* the essence of Freud's argument is that the religious believer in adolescence or adulthood comes face to face with a cold, ambiguous and threatening universe in which annihilation, isolation or meaninglessness are seen as likely options, and death is the inevitable outcome. This creates overwhelming anxiety. In a primitive, self-protecting gesture, we create a comforting illusion with which to shield ourselves. The illusion we embrace stems from real or distorted memories of our childhood years, when as weak and vulnerable persons we felt nurtured and protected by what we perceived to be omnipotent, omniscient and loving parents, and, specifically, an idealized father.

In a desperate attempt to maintain that sense of security and well-being, and to meet our adult needs and wants, we embrace some form of religion, creating an imaginary deity, a divine father figure. Freud specifically argued that religion fulfilled three needs: "[The gods people believe in] must exorcise the terrors of nature, they must reconcile men to the cruelty of Fate, and ... they must compensate them for the sufferings which a civilized life in common has imposed upon them" (quoted in Storr, 1989, p.89). Indeed, the illusions we create for ourselves can also serve as a symbolic means to meet unfulfilled childhood longings as well. From the psychoanalytic perspective religion is seen as a kind of universal neurosis that civilization substitutes for a more authentic personal reality based on scientific (objective) knowledge.

In light of Vitz's (1988) treatment of the deeper motives for Freud's rejection of religion, it seems reasonable to assert that important events in his own life contributed to his antipathy toward matters of faith. In fact, Freud's profound ambivalence about Christianity in particular appears to be as much a function of projection of his own conflicted wishes and fears about God and religion as it is the logical outcome of his theorizing. Vitz suggests, for instance, that the traumatic early loss of a nanny who may have been a devout Catholic believer could have complicated Freud's feeling about religion. Vitz also documents Freud's possible dabbling in matters of the occult. There is apparently more to Freud's contention that religion lacked integrity than his "adulation of the scientific method of the day" (Hurding, 1985, p.73). His attitudes about Christianity reflected his complex hostility and attraction to a faith that meant something to him at a deeply personal level, at the level of Freud's unconscious.

The analysis by Vitz and Gartner (1984a, 1984b) of Freud's understanding of religion also reveals some interesting weaknesses in the theory. They argue that if one presumes God is an illusion, then the "projection of a father figure" understanding of religion makes sense. But if one starts with a presupposition that God exists, psychoanalysis does equally well in explaining atheism!

How would the denial of a real God happen psychologically if classical psychoanalysis is true? If God is a heavenly "father," then disbelief in God must clearly be attributable to the Oedipal period of development. During this period the child feels infantile rage at the same-sex parent who competes with the child for the love of the opposite-sex parent. If the child does not adequately resolve that unconscious rage at the parent during the genital stage, the unconscious rage might be played out as atheism in adulthood; after all, what better way to get back at (or murder) a father figure than to simply not believe in him! Since one can only go so far in rejecting the earthly parent, a deeper rage, an even more primitive aggressive impulse, can be vented on God by denying his very existence.

This theme was developed in Ernest Becker's (1973) classic text *The Denial of Death.* Becker suggested that, from the point of view of the Christian philosopher Søren Kierkegaard, the real problem identified in Freud's Oedipal formulation was that the child wishes to be the father of himself—to be *causa sui,* self-caused. This hostile denial of fatherhood and contingency, Becker argues, is at the center of Oedipal rage:

> In Kierkegaard's understanding of man, the *causa-sui* project is the Oedipus complex, and in order to be a man one has to abandon it completely. From this point of view Freud still had not analyzed away his Oedipus complex, no matter how much he and the early psychoanalysts prided themselves that they had. He could not yield emotionally to superordinate power or conceptually to the transcendental dimension. (p.257)

For Becker (1973), it is pride that holds back the Oedipal child and the atheist alike from yielding intellectually or relationally to contingency (the father, the concrete embodiment that I did not create myself) and to the transcendent (the Father).

While interesting in itself, we can also see in this brief sketch that one frequently noted problem of the theory of psychoanalysis is its very adaptability. Psychoanalysis can literally explain anything, as in this case it both explains religion and atheism! This is quite a conundrum, in that a true and comprehensive theory would have to explain all facets of human experience, but a theory that is so flexible that it is impossible to come up with any human facts that refute the theory ceases to be a theory and achieves the status of a worldview or dogma.

This case study of Freud's view of religion also highlights the epistemological problems latent in the theory. Because the theory is deemed to explain everything, and because all human experiencing (including rational reflection on truth) is viewed as shaped and determined by irrational, unconscious forces, it follows that we are ultimately locked in a closed system where everything that humans think or believe can be rendered as a function of early childhood factors. If atheism can be explained in as facile and convincing a fashion as religion, then there is no ultimate hope of ever knowing anything truly. We can all point at each other and say, "Well you believe 'X' because of your unresolved issues with your mother and father." Such an all-encompassing psychologizing of our capacity to know is repugnant to Christians, who believe that we are capable of knowing truly, at least at some level. Positively, it is an asset of psychoanalysis that it deeply understands our profound capacities for self-deception (which we will develop later).

Further, psychoanalysis tends to be thoroughly mechanistic and naturalistic in terms of its core hypotheses, in that it assumes that all mental events are ultimately biological and instinctual in origin. This inevitably leads to reductionistic explanations about religious matters and indeed about all that we regard as distinctively human. Freud is consistent in asserting that biological and physical laws determine every important aspect of human existence. And naturalism was not just a working hypothesis for him: "Freud was dogmatic about it" (Browning & Cooper, 2004, p.37).

Such a philosophical and scientific commitment allows no room for anything supernatural, for the kind of general or special revelation so central to the Christian faith, nor for a more constructive perspective about our spiritual urgings for deeper meaning and significance in life. Freud's system is a closed system of cause and effect with no room for a transcendent reality. It is at this point that there is no possible reconciliation with the fundamental assertions of the Christian tradition and the dictates of Freudian psychoanalysis. We concur with Hurding (1985), who states:

> The Christian believes in a creator God who brought all that exists into being and who sustains the universe by his power and love; he also declares a redeemer God who has intervened in history in countless ways but supremely in the incarnation, life, death and resurrection of His Son, and in the sending of the Holy Spirit. This is a God who calls man, both individually and corporately, to choose good rather than evil, life rather than death, the Lord's way rather than the Enemy's. This blend of divine determinism ... and man's freedom to choose ... is at the heart of biblical revelation and is a far cry from Freud's naturalistic world view. (pp.74-75)[5]

---

5 Other helpful treatments from a variety of perspectives on the philosophical tensions between psychoanalysis and Christian theology can be found in Browning and Cooper (2004), Burnham (1985), Irwin (1975), Kristol (1970), Robinson (1985), Wallace (1983) and Wood (1980).

Model of Personality

Narramore (1985) argues that the personality concepts in psychoanalysis should stand or fall on whether or not they enable us to make sense of the complexity of human nature in light of biblical revelation and human experience. As with nearly every major theory we will discuss in this book, we contend that it would be a mistake to reject hypothetical constructs because their exact equivalent cannot be found directly in the Scriptures.

Our perspectives on some of the Freudian notions of psychosexual development have changed since our initial exposure to these concepts as undergraduates. Initially, we were quite skeptical, but our experiences since with our own children and clients have taught us that, broadly understood, these developmental themes have some contemporary relevance. As we listen to the struggles of our clients and students, certain themes often emerge, including powerful "feelings towards parents of the opposite sex, ... guilt over sexual feelings and actions, fears related to sexual intimacy and loving, fears of abandonment, struggles in the area of defining one's own sexual identity, anger and rage in not getting what one wanted as a child, and love/hate conflicts" (Corey, 1986, p.39). Psychoanalysis speaks directly and deeply to the roots of these concerns. One does not need to accept all the tenets of orthodox psychoanalysis to appreciate the potential contribution of these emphases for our awareness and understanding of our client's difficulties. In fact, most contemporary psychoanalytic perspectives reject the notion of hard-and-fast stages of development in favor of viewing the developmental issues identified in the stage theories from a life-cycle perspective. In other words, the anal wish to be neat, orderly and tidy is understood less as a developmental outcome related to mastery of bodily functions and more as an aspect of the lifelong developmental task of self-regulation and control that spans all phases of one's life.

Psychoanalytic thought is certainly a unifying perspective that stresses the developmental, historical and unconscious dimensions of the human experience. Although we find the approach to be overly deterministic, we share Korchin's (1976, p.332) assessment that many of the central tenets of Freud's intrapsychic theory are perhaps less biological and universal than originally posited, and more overtly interpersonal or sociocultural. This is certainly the direction that psychoanalytic "revisionists" (who added onto Freud's ideas) and "heretics" (who rejected the core of Freud's ideas in favor of their own) took psychoanalysis after Freud's death.

Browning and Cooper (2004) summarize several scholars who suggest that Freud himself was actually quite torn on this point, writing sometimes in a mechanistic, deterministic, individualistic vein, but at other times in an "intersubjective or ... dialogical one" (p.39). Several psychoanalytic writers have pointed out that part of the reason why classical psychoanalysis seems so conflicted about this is because the first psychoanalyst never underwent psychoanalysis with another person. Freud was his *own* analyst, and thus didn't experience first-hand the intersubjective, dialogical nature of the therapeutic relationship. It is largely from an emphasis on the nonmechanistic aspects of Freud that the broad popularity of the contemporary psychodynamic theories has grown. There is certainly more possibility for Christian appreciation of psychoanalytic thought when theorists move away from the mechanistic, reductionistic aspects of psychoanalysis; we shall find this to be precisely the case in chapter four.

Freud made his understanding of personality the backdrop for understanding all of existence. By doing so, he presented Christians with an unsatisfactory scheme for understanding the foundations for life. As Browning and Cooper

(2004) say, "By taking the position that the psychobiological realm is the only relevant context for human action he has indeed elevated eros [libido drive] and death [aggression drive] to metaphors of ultimacy, that is, to metaphors which represent the only effective and relevant ultimate context of experience" (pp.43-44).

Are eros/libido and death/aggression the ultimate motivational contexts for life? These id-drives could be described as aberrant and distorted reflections of the relational and dominion motivations we gleaned from Genesis 1–2 (see chap.2). Biblically, we are seen to be positively motivated to procreate, to create and to love, and certainly the biblical attention paid to the distorted and evil sexual motivations we experience also suggests some centrality to sexual motivation in life. Further, the Scriptures assert very clearly that sinful humanity is bent on death and self-destruction. Aggression is sometimes understood as an aspect of control, making it possible that Freud's "darker drive" is a depraved version of our dominion drive.

We also note (with Van Leeuwen, 1985, 1990) that Freud's description of humans as having two intrinsically opposed core motivations places conflict as central and endemic to being human. Unlike the humanistic theories which say that humans are basically good but "messed up" by external influences, psychoanalysis says that to be human is to be torn by conflict. This darker reading of the human plight is much closer to biblical reality than Romantic humanism. Christianity does not paint the conflict in the same way, but suggests that our conflict is most fundamentally between longing for God and being in rebellion against him. A Christian point of view is not completely incompatible, however, with the psychoanalytic view of motivation.

We appreciate Freud's stress on the reality of dynamic unconscious mental processes. Certainly there is a reality beyond, or perhaps, beneath that which we are immediately aware, perhaps most directly evident in the content of our dreams. In the clinical context both free association and other psychoanalytic techniques strongly suggest that there is a level of thinking, perceiving and feeling beyond direct consciousness. These assertions are not inconsistent with the scriptural understanding of persons.

We share the widespread appreciation for the psychoanalytic understanding of the defense mechanisms, especially as they are developed in clinical treatments (e.g., Meissner, 1985). The Scriptures speak directly to our tendencies to be deceitful to self and others and to avoid facing painful realities (cf. Jer 17:9). As

Narramore (1985) says, psychoanalysis's "understanding of the role of the defense mechanisms... goes beyond scriptural descriptions of how we avoid facing painful reality but is consistent with that scripturally described process" (p.900).

Psychoanalysis can contribute much to our awareness of both the unhealthy and healthy ways that conflict and sin can be dealt with in the context of our religious communities. Indeed, the language of the ego defense mechanisms has so widely and thoroughly permeated contemporary Western culture that it is difficult to imagine how we could discuss our avoidant tendencies without such terminology. Psychoanalysis asserts that we can learn more adaptive and goal-oriented means of managing anxiety. The limitation, however, of the psychoanalytic approach is that there are serious constraints on that potential due to our sinful nature (i.e., we are in need of divine intervention; we can't heal ourselves).

Psychoanalysis essentially contends that all behavior is purposeful and motivated. This assertion is not inconsistent with scriptural teachings about the nature of human beings. Nor is the assumption about the crucial importance of early childhood experience. Indeed, the Scriptures assert that the parenting relationship, like the marital relationship, ought to reflect the divine-human encounter (cf. Narramore, 1979; Prov 22:6), with all the inherent risks and responsibilities. The psychoanalytic assertion of the importance of familial, early life experiences alone does not, however, constitute a substantial contact point with Christianity, as any reasonable understanding of human life would emphasize these primary relationships as formative.

Model of Health

It should be evident from the earlier section on Freudian notions of health that the model stresses individualism over and against interdependence. We find this to be a matter of deep concern, since our understanding of the Christian tradition emphasizes a deep awareness of our utter dependence on God and the absolute necessity of developing meaningful and significant relationships with others, both within the body of Christ and in the broader community and society we live in. Our concern is that the insight and self-awareness so deeply valued in the psychoanalytic tradition won't necessarily translate into appropriate other-directed behaviors. Rather, it will remain largely self-directed or self-serving.

Psychoanalysis is actually so oriented to understanding the person as a self-contained psychological system that even for the healthy person, "relationships with other human beings are of value only in so far as they facilitate instinctual gratification" (Storr, 1989, p.91). Browning and Cooper (2004) noted that a literal interpretation of the Freudian paradigm would inevitably make us skeptical about whether there is such a thing as authentic and legitimate altruistic service toward others that is free of self-serving gain. How could Freudian thought, for example, account for the sacrificial service of Mother Teresa in the slums of Calcutta?

A clearly articulated, stable ethical system is lacking in psychoanalysis (Browning & Cooper, 2004, pp.48ff.), though like all systems, it actually contains an implicit system in its view of health. The best description of its implicit ethic might be that of a "cautious but fair reciprocity" (p.49). It is a reciprocity system because Freud recognized that if each person ultimately cares only about his or her own gratification, then we must each trade gratifications to keep everyone satisfied. It is cautious because Freud believed that libidinal energies are ultimately for our own satisfaction. We cautiously give to others so we can get what we want.

But the stance of "cautious reciprocity" stands in stark contrast to the kind of costly discipleship and risk-taking inherent in Christian morality and in a Christian conscience. Authentic love for the other *(agape)* is not based on reciprocity but on our common family membership, on Christ's example and on the Spirit's enablement. Granted, many of our efforts to be loving or distinctively and decidedly Christian in our compassion are less than noble or pure. But the assumption in psychoanalysis is that there is no normative basis for responsible ethical decision-making and action. In particular, psychoanalysis is profoundly skeptical about whether there can be any *genuine* commitment to an absolute like the love of God or the love of one's neighbor that is not ultimately a derivative of the sexual instinct. Its commitments to a Darwinian worldview lead it to view love in survival-of-the-fittest evolutionary terms. Psychoanalysis is brutally honest about our propensity toward extrinsic motivation, but asserts that intrinsic motivation, especially in a religious context, is largely a wish-fulfilling illusion.

Another concern about the Freudian notion of wellness is its extreme emphasis on subjectivity. Self-awareness tends to become a major goal of the maturation process. Our fear is whether a preoccupation with the "inner reality" of one's psychic life will replace any appropriate concern about the "outer reality" of God or the relational obligations to the local church and community. Our worst fear is that the view of persons that classical psychoanalysis prescribes may breed an unhealthy narcissism and self-absorption that removes one from engaging with the world of everyday living. But in practical application this seems an exaggerated concern: Classical psychoanalysis's vision of adult maturity—the capacity to love and work meaningfully and purposefully—seems to be appropriately other-directed and pro-social. Ultimately, though, human beings are motivated at the deepest levels to maximize pleasure and to minimize pain. As such, even the most altruistic behaviors are understood to be self-serving in that they bring pleasure or the avoidance of pain to the individual.

No doubt there is a need for greater self-awareness and understanding in our Christian communities, but this should not develop into an escape from active involvement in the local church or with the lives of suffering persons. Obviously, a healthy balance between escape and engagement is essential. The need to "know thyself" must not replace the command to "love God and others."

What is desperately needed in our Christian communities today are persons who can balance a desire and willingness to know self with an equally strong passion to know God. This accords marvelously with John Calvin's discussion in the first chapter of his *Institutes of the Christian Religion* (1559/1981):

> Our wisdom, in so far as it ought to be deemed true and solid wisdom, consists almost entirely of two parts: the knowledge of God and of ourselves. But as these are connected together by many ties, it is not easy to determine which of the two precedes, and gives birth to the other. For, in the first place, no man can survey himself without forthwith turning his thoughts toward God in whom he lives and moves.... On the other hand, it is evident that man never attains to a true self-knowledge until he has previously contemplated the face of God, and come down after such contemplation to look into himself. (1.1.1-2)

A final fear relates to our concern about the ultimate direction of the maturation process in psychoanalysis. As Christians we must continually remind ourselves that our ultimate salvation comes from without, not from within. There is the distinct danger in psychoanalysis of a kind of gnosticism where self-knowledge is seen as a means to self-salvation (Vitz, 1987, p.73). From the standpoint of the Christian contemplative tradition, self-knowledge produces humility, not salvation. Specifically, the cultivation and expression of the Christian virtues (Roberts, 1982, 1984) should be seen as the apex of sanctification for the committed believer, not self-awareness and insight. The search for psychological wholeness ought not replace our desire to know God or pursue authentic holiness, but be seen as *one* means of pursuing God and holiness.

A wonderfully helpful example of how concerned and committed Christian theoreticians can correct some of these inadequacies can be found in two articles by Vitz and Gartner (1984a, 1984b). At the core of the Freudian critique of Christianity is the assertion that unresolved Oedipal issues are foundational in the formation of one's superego (e.g., the son tries to take over the role of the father). In contrast, a more theologically informed understanding of the sacrificial love of the Son for the Father and how the obedient death of the Son brings ultimate redemption can illustrate how the life of Jesus becomes a needed corrective for the unresolved issues of the "unredeemed self" caught in unresolved Oedipal tensions. In short, Jesus serves as a kind of anti-Oedipus who finds life by obediently doing his Father's will rather than trying to destroy the Father. Part of the good news of the gospel, then, is the potential power that comes when the perpetual fear and hatred of the Father due to the Oedipal crisis can be replaced by a thorough transformation of the mind through conversion and

Christian commitment. The "unredeemed self" studied by Freud can be changed into a "redeemed self" in Christ through the mystery of belief in the incarnation, crucifixion and resurrection of Jesus.

Model of Abnormality

The psychoanalytic approach speaks deeply and meaningfully to the origins and functions of symptoms. It seems foolish to disregard the impact of critical life events in the formative years or to neglect the role of the ego defense mechanisms in the etiology and maintenance of problems in living. On the other hand, it does not necessarily follow that one must dwell exclusively on these matters in order to help clients make sense of the roots of their difficulties.

Psychoanalysis contends that the root of much of our psychopathology can be found in aberrant psychosexual development. In particular, aggressive or sexual impulses are major determinants of our neurotic tendencies. This is not consistent with the thrust of Scripture, where our own drive to be autonomous and godlike (i.e., pride) is seen as a more basic source of maladjustment and sin (Narramore, 1985, p.900). Sexual or aggressive impulses are sometimes troublesome but have become so because of our rebellion against God.

The Freudian tradition is prone to reductionistic interpretations of the etiology and maintenance of symptoms. This is inconsistent with the thrust of contemporary thought in the human sciences, where etiology is more accurately seen as a function of multiple factors for almost all disorders. Despite its strong emphasis on the biological and instinctual bases for behaviors, Freudian thought has very little to say about more recent advances in biological psychiatry and medicine (e.g., neurotransmitters, chemical imbalances, genetic predispositions and so on). In its defense, psychoanalysis was originally focused on the concerns of reasonably high-functioning neurotics in a particular cultural and historical context. Even so, the theory that emerged from that work has been asserted to have near universal applicability, and the scope of psychoanalytic practice has been considerably broadened since its inception, and thus fundamental revision to incorporate a broader range of concepts is indicated.

Traditional psychoanalysis needs a much broader base of social motivations and dynamics to be closer to a more biblical understanding of persons. The more one views psychoanalysis as not just a tool in the therapist's armamentarium but as a worldview as well, the more difficult it seems to reconcile psychoanalysis and legitimate religious concerns (Wallace, 1983). Indeed, the developments in psychoanalytic thinking and practice of the past sixty years have begun to bridge somewhat the gap between the limited viewpoint of the classical perspective and biblical understandings of persons.

Model of Psychotherapy

Responsible eclectic therapists find psychodynamic concepts like resistance, transference and countertransference, repetition compulsion, mourning of illusion, and the ego defense mechanisms to be extremely useful in exploring current difficulties in a client's life. Further, awareness of the psychoanalytic distinctives probably helps these same clinicians to have a greater depth of awareness and understanding in their efforts to assist their clients. Broadly understood, Freudian thought can be a powerful model for understanding behavior.

Psychoanalysis, when practiced in its strict classical form, is widely perceived as impractical for the majority of mental health settings in this country or abroad. The great time commitment and expense that is involved and the limited availability of highly trained psychoanalysts make this an inefficient approach. Few potential clients have the necessary financial and personal resources (e.g., introspective and verbal skills) and fewer still are willing to make the kind of commitment of those resources that would be necessary for a successful analysis. The lofty goal of personality reconstruction is probably inappropriate and unrealistic for the vast majority of suffering persons.

But there might be ways to transcend certain of these limitations. Klein (1970), for example, suggests that society should underwrite part of the cost of psychoanalysis for truly needy clients as well as a limited number of future psychotherapists. He suggests that this would contribute much to the continued development of the mental health movement and to the direct well-being of the persons involved. The Institute for Psychoanalysis in Chicago (Desruisseaux, 1983) has been exemplary in offering low-cost psychoanalytic training and treatment to human-service providers (e.g., teachers, child care workers, etc.). By investing in the lives of those persons in the trenches, they are making a long-term contribution to the mental and emotional well-being of the lives their clients will touch. Gabbard (1994) also argues for a place for classical psychoanalytic practice within the current health care system. He advocates for shorter-term treatment, more circumscribed goals for treatment, and interventions along a spectrum from emotionally stimulating (e.g., interpretation) to supportive (e.g., prescriptive strategies like giving therapeutic homework).

We respect the emphasis of this tradition on the training and supervision of future therapists. No major system of psychotherapy takes the personal development of the clinician more seriously than does psychoanalysis. Only after years of personal therapy, specialized coursework and careful supervision of select cases can the psychoanalyst become certified. With the incredible proliferation of people-helpers in our society, the careful and meticulous preparation of the psychoanalyst is certainly to be commended.

Such training, however, is not without its risks. Psychoanalysis is often accused of being an arrogant, exclusive professional guild. But even within that establishment many articulate and vocal critics can be found (e.g., Robert Coles, a committed Christian psychiatrist and Harvard professor). But all too often the professional isolation remains, creating for all practical purposes rather exclusive clubs of the fully initiated "true believers." This has done little to create goodwill with other traditions within the mental health field. The proliferation of managed care in North America over the past twenty years or so served as a bit of an antidote to the arrogance and haughtiness of some of the psychoanalytic community.

We also have a concern that classic psychoanalytic treatment is not necessarily a good model for either clinical or personal relationships. Certainly there is a need for clinicians to listen attentively and respectfully to the stories of their clients. But the risk is that the often cold, distant, anonymous style of the classical Freudian analyst can replace a more balanced and genuinely warm style that we more often associate with authentic Christian love and concern. The anonymous relationship that may be necessary for the formation of a transference neurosis can covertly or even overtly communicate deeper values about relationships in general. As Miller and Jackson (1985) have noted, notions of ideal clinical or personal relationships should be deeply informed by both societal standards and religious belief systems. Psychoanalytic therapy raises tough questions about what it means to care for others and be fully present to them. Specifically, it asserts that there is an essential place for the quiet receptivity of the psychoanalyst (Kovel, 1976). But whether it should be the primary relational modality of the psychoanalyst is a matter of intense debate both within and without psychoanalytic circles. Indeed, the question of the moral dimensions of psychotherapy is a key point of discussion in the psychoanalytic literature and at conferences.

Finally, we sense a certain fatalism and pessimism in intensive and long-term psychoanalytic treatment. Obviously, a tremendous commitment of time, energy and expense is needed to bring about increased self-control and self-regulation through greater insight and self-awareness. Although we agree with Wheelis (1978) that change is all too often painfully slow and agonizingly difficult, the Christian faith commitment raises the possibility of quick, dramatic change in an individual's life (cf. McLemore, 1982). Granted, persons bring their "raw material" into their Christian conversion, but the possibilities for change are certainly greater than classical psychoanalysis would have us believe, although perhaps less dramatic and sudden than many Christians would like to believe. In fact, Freud himself believed that "the end result of analysis was the replacement of neurotic misery by everyday unhappiness" (Breuer & Freud, 1895/1957, p.305).

It is at this point that the classical psychoanalytic perspective alludes to but does not quite provide a more hopeful vision for human suffering. As mentioned earlier, Freud's brilliant work on the relationship between mourning of illusion and growth offers the Christian mental health professional a framework to understand at least one dimension of the most profound theological mystery—that death precedes new life. While most authentic, devout Christians express earnest belief in this most central piece of our doctrine and history, many fail to recognize the reality of this paschal pattern in their own lives. In fact, one could argue that many theologically orthodox churches in North America have swallowed whole the cultural mandate to avoid loss, pain or legitimate suffering whenever possible. This perspective is promoted because, in subtle and not so subtle ways, we are encouraged to believe that we are entitled not to suffer, that we should be able, somehow, to transcend the pain associated with loss, death, grief and mourning. And so, in many churches, we celebrate Easter morning with joy—having thought (or, more importantly, felt) very little about Good Friday.

The necessity of mourning of illusion calls us back to this basic paschal process, because it insists that in order to grow—psychologically or spiritually—we must be open to the process of mourning. This makes sense when we consider that all change—even the most positive change—necessarily entails loss. These losses may be of relationship, of status, of role, of a stage or era of life. They may even involve the way that we understand God—our own personal working theology. At such times Christians need ways to face their loss courageously, directly, and to feel their grief acutely. And this process happens best in relationship—in community with others. We need, like Mary Magdalene outside the empty tomb of Christ (Jn 20:11-17), to be willing to not cling to what or whom we have loved (i.e., Jesus before ascending to the Father) in order to be given something much better (i.e., the Holy Spirit) (Rolheiser, 2001). We can imagine how wrenching and painful and confusing it must have been for her to let go of her own hopes, dreams, desires and wishes embodied in the man who stood before her on the same morning that she discovered his body was missing and two days after she had watched him murdered by the authorities. Her hope that what he told her was the best thing for both of them, and her faith to see beyond her own grief and disillusionment, together are a powerful example for us to follow. To become people capable of mourning opens us to becoming people available to the Holy Spirit, whose aim is to re-form, form, and transform us.

CONCLUSION

Psychoanalysis deserves to be more than a whipping boy for conservative Christians. It is a comprehensive and exhaustive system of personality, psychopathology and psychotherapy that should be carefully considered by committed and thoughtful persons of faith. Our primary concerns have to do with some of the metapsychological assumptions of the Freudian worldview.

In our judgment psychoanalysis as a therapy is probably inappropriate and impractical for all but a very few carefully selected individuals. The model certainly needs to be more clearly articulated so that the central tenets are amenable to more rigorous clinical and empirical investigation. But we still assert that it is highly advisable to think, on occasion, in psychoanalytic terms so as to give greater structure and direction to our efforts to be effective change agents. On the other hand, the committed Christian needs to offer clearly articulated correctives to some of the deficiencies that can be found in this tradition, especially with reference to the overly deterministic and naturalistic assumptions. We fully suspect that classic psychoanalysis will serve as a springboard for discussion, debate and dialogue for decades to come in Christian counseling circles. Perhaps its most enduring legacy will be that it gave birth to the approaches discussed in chapter four.

FOR FURTHER READING

Becker, E. (1973). *The denial of death.* New York, NY: Free Press.

Becker critiques classical Freudian psychoanalysis from the perspective of Christian philosopher Søren Kierkegaard.

Gay, P. (1989). *The Freud reader.* New York, NY: W.W. Norton.

The best of the many edited readers available in print today. Gay is a highly respected Freud scholar.

Mitchell, S.A., & Black, M.J. (1995). *Freud and beyond: A history of modern psychoanalytic thought.* New York, NY: Basic Books.

An excellent overview of the psychoanalytic tradition that puts Freud's ideas in the context of contemporary psychoanalytic thought.

Storr, A. (1989). *Freud.* New York, NY: Oxford.

A readable brief introduction to Freudian thought.

Wallace, E. (1983). Reflections on the relationship between psychoanalysis and Christianity. *Pastoral Psychology, 31,* 215-243.

One of the best of the many introductory articles available that speaks directly to integrative issues.

Westphal, M. (1998). *Suspicion and faith: The religious uses of modern atheism.* New York, NY: Fordham University Press.

A Christian philosopher helps us to see our own spiritual growth potential by taking the insights of Freud, Marx and Nietzsche seriously.

REFERENCES

Alston, W. (1967). Psychoanalytic theories, logical status of. In P. Edwards (Ed.), *The encyclopedia of philosophy* (Vols. 5-6, pp.512-516). New York, NY: Macmillan.

American Psychiatric Association. (2000) *Diagnostic and statistical manual* (4th ed.). Washington, DC: American Psychiatric Association.

Arlow, J. (1984). Psychoanalysis. In R. Corsini (Ed.), *Current psychotherapies* (3rd ed., pp.14-55). Itasca, IL: F.E. Peacock.

Becker, E. (1973). *The denial of death.* New York, NY: Free Press.

Berger, K. (1988). *The developing person through the life span* (2nd ed.). New York, NY: Worth.

Brenner, C. (1973). *An elementary textbook of psychoanalysis.* Garden City, NY: Anchor/Doubleday.

Breuer, J., & Freud, S. (1895/1957). *Studies on hysteria. Complete psychological works, Standard edition, Vol.2.* London: Hogarth Press.

Browning, D.S., & Cooper, T.D. (2004). *Religious thought and the modern psychologies* (2nd ed.). Minneapolis, MN: Fortress.

Burnham, J. (1985). The encounter of Christian theology with deterministic psychology and psychoanalysis. *Bulletin of the Menninger Clinic, 49,* 321-352.

Calvin, J. (1981). *Institutes of the Christian religion* (H. Beveridge, Trans.). Grand Rapids, MI: Eerdmans. (Original work published 1559).

Corey, G. (1986). *Theory and practice of counseling and psychotherapy* (3rd ed.). Monterey, CA: Brooks/Cole.

Crabb, L. (1988). *Inside out.* Colorado Springs, CO: NavPress.

Cushman, P. (1995). *Constructing the self, constructing America: A cultural history of psychotherapy.* New York, NY: Perseus.

Desruisseaux, P. (1983, January 12). Psychoanalysis: Off the couch and into the streets of Chicago, IL. *The Chronicle of Higher Education.*

Erikson, E. (1982). *The life cycle completed: A review.* New York, NY: Norton.

Ford, D., & Urban, H. (1963). *Systems of psychotherapy: A comparative study.* New York: Wiley.

Freud, S. (1933). *New introductory lectures on psychoanalysis* (W.J.H. Sprott, Trans.). New York, NY: Wiley.

Freud, S. (1957). *Mourning and melancholia. Complete Psychological Works, Standard edition, Vol.14.* London: Hogarth Press. (Original work published 1915).

Freud, S. (1957). *On narcissism: an introduction. Complete Psychological Works, Standard edition, Vol.14.* London: Hogarth Press. (Original work published 1914).

Freud, S. (1963). Further recommendations in the technique of psychoanalysis: Recollection, repetition, and working through. In *Therapy and technique.* New York, NY: Macmillan. (Original work published 1914).

Gabbard, G.O. (1994). *Psychodynamic psychiatry in clinical practice: The DSM-IV edition.* Washington, DC: American Psychiatric Press.

Hackett, C. (1986). Psychoanalysis and theology: Two dialectics. *Journal of Religion and Health, 25,* 29-45.

Hurding, R. (1985). *Roots and shoots.* London: Hodder & Stoughton.

Irwin, J. (1975). Reinhold Niebuhr critique of Freudian psychoanalysis. *Journal of Religion and Health, 14,* 242-254.

Jones, J., & Wilson, W. (1987). *An incomplete education.* New York, NY: Ballantine.

Kandel, E.R. (1999). Biology and the future of psychoanalysis: A new intellectual framework for psychiatry revisited. *American Journal of Psychiatry, 156,* 505-524.

Kandel, E.R. (2005). *Psychiatry, psychoanalysis, and the new biology of mind.* Washington, D.C.: American Psychiatric Association.

Klein, G. (1970, August). *Is psychoanalysis relevant?* Paper presented at the annual convention of the American Psychological Association, Miami, FL.

Korchin, S. (1976). *Modern clinical psychology.* New York, NY: Basic Books.

Kovel, J. (1976). *A complete guide to therapy.* New York, NY: Pantheon.

Kristol, I. (1970). God and the psychoanalysts. In A.H. Cohen (Ed.), *Arguments and doctrines.* New York, NY: Harper & Row.

Lambert, M.J., & Barley, D.E. (2001). Research summary on the therapeutic relationship and psychotherapy outcome. *Psychotherapy: Theory/research/practice/training, 38,* 357-361.

McLemore, C. (1982). *The scandal of psychotherapy.* Wheaton, IL: Tyndale House.

McLemore, C. (1984). *Honest Christianity.* Philadelphia, PA: Westminster Press.

Meissner, W. (1985). Theories of personality and psychopathology: Classical psychoanalysis. In H.I. Kaplan & B.J. Sadock (Eds.), *Comprehensive textbook of psychiatry* (Vol.4, pp.337-418). Baltimore, MD: Williams & Wilkins.

Miller, W., & Jackson, K. (1985). *Practical psychology for pastors.* Englewood Cliffs, NJ: Prentice-Hall.

Mitchell, S.A. (1988). *Relational concepts in psychoanalysis: An integration.* Cambridge, MA: Harvard University Press.

Mitchell, S.A., & Black, M.J. (1995). *Freud and beyond: A history of modern psychoanalytic thought.* New York, NY: Basic Books.

Munroe, R. (1955). *Schools of psychoanalytic thought.* New York, NY: Holt, Rinehart & Winston.

Narramore, S. (1979). *Parenting with love and limits.* Grand Rapids, MI: Zondervan.

Narramore, S. (1984). *No condemnation.* Grand Rapids, MI: Zondervan.

Narramore, S. (1985). Psychoanalytic psychotherapy. In D.G. Benner (Ed.), *Baker encyclopedia of psychology* (pp.896-900). Grand Rapids, MI: Baker.

Oakland, J. (1977). The introjected and the intrinsic in psychology and Christianity. *Journal of Psychology and Theology, 5,* 91-94.

Peck, S. (1983). *People of the lie.* New York, NY: Simon & Schuster.

Prochaska, J. (1979). *Systems of psychotherapy: A transtheoretical analysis.* Homewood, IL: Dorsey Press.

Roberts, R. (1982). *Spirituality and human emotion.* Grand Rapids, MI: Eerdmans.

Roberts, R. (1984). *The strengths of a Christian.* Philadelphia, PA: Westminster Press.

Robinson, L. (1985). The illusion of no future: Psychoanalysis and religion. *Journal of the American Academy of Psychoanalysis, 13,* 211-228.

Rolheiser, R. (2001). *The holy longing: The search for a Christian spirituality.* New York, NY: Doubleday.

Rychlak, J. (1973). *Introduction to personality and psychotherapy.* Boston, MA: Houghton Mifflin.

Ryckman, R. (1985). *Theories of personality* (3rd ed.). Monterey, CA: Brooks/Cole.

Shabad, P. (2001). *Despair and the return of hope.* Northvale, NJ: Jason Aronson.

Silverman, L. (1976). Psychoanalytic theory: The reports of my death are greatly exaggerated. *American Psychologist, 31,* 621-637.

Storr, A. (1989). *Freud.* New York, NY: Oxford.

Solms, M. (2004). Freud returns. *Scientific American Magazine, 290* (5), 82-89.

Sorenson, R.L. (2004). *Minding spirituality.* New York, NY: Routledge.

Van Leeuwen, M. (1985). *The person in psychology: A contemporary Christian appraisal.* Grand Rapids, MI: Eerdmans.

Van Leeuwen, M. (1990). *Gender and grace: Love, work and parenting in a changing world.* Downers Grove, IL: InterVarsity Press.

Viorst, J. (1986). *Necessary losses.* New York, NY: Fawcett Gold Medal.

Vitz, P. (1987). Secular personality theories: A critical analysis. In T.J. Burke (Ed.), *Man and mind: A Christian theory of personality* (pp.65-94). Hillsdale, MI: Hillsdale College Press.

Vitz, P. (1988). *Sigmund Freud's Christian unconscious.* New York, NY: Guilford.

Vitz, P., & Gartner, J. (1984a). Christianity and psychoanalysis, Part I: Jesus as the anti-Oedipus. *Journal of Psychology and Theology, 12,* 4-14.

Vitz, P., & Gartner, J. (1984b). Christianity and psychoanalysis, Part II: Jesus as the transformer of the superego. *Journal of Psychology and Theology, 12,* 82-90.

Wallace, E. (1983). Reflections on the relationship between psychoanalysis and Christianity. *Pastoral Psychology, 31,* 215-243.

Walters, O. (1973). Psychodynamics in Tillich's theology. *Journal of Religion and Health, 12,* 342-353.

Westphal, M. (1998). *Suspicion and faith: The religious uses of modern atheism.* New York, NY: Fordham University Press.

Wheelis, A. (1978). *How people change.* New York, NY: Harper & Row.

Wood, B. (1980). The religion of psychoanalysis. *The American Journal of Psychoanalysis, 40,* 13-26.

4
CONTEMPORARY PSYCHODYNAMIC PSYCHOTHERAPIES

Michael W. Mangis, Stanton L. Jones and Richard E. Butman

***

The contemporary psychodynamic psychotherapies are those schools of thought influenced by Freud and classic psychoanalysis that have evolved substantially beyond orthodox analytic thought. Christians have not been alone in being dissatisfied with the deterministic and mechanistic assumptions of the Freudian system, which paint a picture of humans as isolated beings irrationally driven by biological, primitive drives welling up within them, their personalities molded by discrete psychic structures interacting mechanically and unconsciously to achieve compromises leading to drive gratification. Christians have also not been alone in seeing the rich possibilities of a system that seeks to understand the profound impact of early relationships on our character, the mysterious way in which we are shaped by unconscious processes, and the pervasive presence of psychological conflict in our lives.

In fact, many argue that Freud himself led the way in attempting to resolve some of the mechanistic and deterministic problems in his own model. The focus of much of Freud's later work was on the ego as presented in *The Ego and the Id* (1923/1961). In his earliest theorizing, when he was working from his seduction theory, Freud emphasized interpersonal environment as the cause of pathology. He quickly moved away from that position to a more "scientific" view where psychological development was seen as an almost entirely internal and self-contained process. The person was seen as controlled by biological instincts and drives, and by the actions and fantasies associated with those drives. The ego had little true efficacy. But in *The Ego and the Id,* Freud began to acknowledge again the role of the environment, of relationships, in the development of the internal workings of the mind.

Some theorists have suggested that Freud intended *The Ego and the Id* to be a major paradigm shift, a new direction in his thinking, but others vehemently disagree. The classical psychoanalytic school (see chap.3) believes Freud was not overhauling his thought but fine-tuning it. They have remained true to the bulk of Freud's work and see psychological development as being entirely controlled by biological drives; the psychic structures of id, ego and superego; and the effects of psychosexual development. For the traditional psychoanalyst the instinctual drive model was and continues to be the only viable focal point for understanding human nature.

DESCRIPTIVE SURVEY

Whether it was his intent or not, Freud's new thinking about the ego did create a dramatic shift in some psychoanalytic circles, resulting in several new models and paradigms. These neo-Freudian, or post-Freudian, theorists share an appreciation for the way traditional psychoanalysis illuminates the complexity of our conflicting motivations and the influence of unconscious processes. Their key differences with classic psychoanalysis have to do with the ways in which these intricate processes are explained. Generally speaking, their formulations are less biological and mechanistic, and more respectful of cognitive and interpersonal processes, precisely because they have shifted from Freud's emphasis on id and drive to an emphasis on ego, self and relationships. As Guntrip (1969) noted,

> Emphasis has moved away from "instinct entities" and their control, on to the vital problem of how we begin to grow an ego, the core of a personal self, in infancy; and how this growth in personal reality is rooted in the baby's environment of personal relations, first with the mother, then the father, family, neighbours, school, and the ever-widening world around. (p.326)

Post-Freudian psychodynamic thinking has usually been divided into three camps (Pine, 1988): ego psychology, object-relations theories and self psychology.

Ego psychology, usually dubbed the "American school," stresses the development of personality across the life span. It does not deny that certain conflicts reflect id impulses striving for immediate gratification, but it does assert that the ego strivings for adaptability, competency and mastery are at least as important. The model is mostly an adaptation of Freud's original thought with a heightened emphasis on ego and relationships. Beyond the tensions surrounding sex and aggression, issues of identity, intimacy and integrity become especially striking and salient in this tradition. Erik Erikson, Anna Freud, Heinz Hartmann, Rudolf Lowenstein and David Rapaport are among the major theoreticians in this tradition (cf. Korchin, 1976; Prochaska, 1984).

Object-relations theorists similarly emphasize the outward focus of the ego, reject Freud's narrow range of hypothesized instincts and deemphasize or ignore his main psychic structures. Collectively called the "British school," these theorists concentrate on those first few years of life, where they believe the foundation of the personality is laid. Experiences and relationships in these early years, they assert, leave impressions on the personality that profoundly affect the individual throughout the life span. The main determinant of personality is presumed to be the internalized images that we each carry within us of the primary relational figures in our past ("objects" such as mother and father). Personality is then understood primarily in terms of the relationships among and characteristics of these internalized "objects." These internal images or objects then are the primary psychic structures, replacing id, ego and superego. The interrelations of the objects create our psychological drives, rather than them welling up from the id (Edkins, 1985). The drives themselves are deemed relational rather than crudely sexual and aggressive. Well-known theorists in this tradition include W.R.D. Fairbairn and Otto Kernberg.

Self psychology, established by Heinz Kohut and his followers, also emphasizes the experiences of the early years in the development of a sense of identity after a process of differentiation and integration (to be explained shortly). If early relationships are healthy and nurturing, a stable or "true" self will develop that is capable of mature relationships. If the early environment is characterized by deprivation, however, the resulting "false" self remains limited in its relationship capacity (i.e., the individual cannot value both autonomy and community). A more mature identity is one that is open to input from others without a competing fear of being overwhelmed. Whereas the object-relations school focuses on psychological relations between internalized objects, self psychology goes the further step of positing a strong entity of self that is not a separate psychic structure but rather "might be said [to be] the sum of all these [intrapsychic] entities plus an unnamed integrating function" (Johnson, 1985, p.1052). Such a cohesive and higher-order entity is quite a departure from Freud's original thought.

Greenberg and Mitchell (1983) point out that the three traditions share a common view of the primacy of cognitive and interpersonal processes as the building blocks of personality. The ego psychologists accommodate classic psychoanalysis by building on it. They modify the classical id-drive model by emphasizing early, formative relationships. A more radical alternative strategy, adopted by the object-relations theorists, requires complete replacement of the drive concept with a strong interpersonal model. Greenberg and Mitchell suggest that a third category, one of model mixing, describes the self psychology of Heinz Kohut and his followers; they have adopted drive-model concepts and mixed them with the relational model.

Our focus in this chapter will be on the commonalities of the psychodynamic models. Because each of the three models, and indeed different theorists within the three traditions, can be radically different from one another, we will stay at a general level in our presentation. Because of the popularity of object-relations theory, we will discuss it more than the other models. In recent years the contemporary psychodynamic models have coalesced somewhat into an eclectic whole. Authors cite theorists from any of the traditions, and practitioners seldom cite one theorist as their primary anchor.

As should be evident from chapter three, many of the fundamental tenets of classic psychoanalysis are simply irreconcilable with an orthodox Christian worldview. It is our judgment, however, that these contemporary variations on Freudian thought deserve a closer inspection because of their rich integrative potential. These contemporary psychodynamic movements have generally inherited the distrust of organized religion because of their roots in traditional psychoanalysis. But there seems to be considerably less overt hostility toward religion in general in the writings of these contemporary theorists than was true of Freud himself.

Hoffman has noted that British object-relations theory, in fact, is particularly grounded in biblical perspectives of the nature of the person. She notes that Fairbairn and Winnicott were especially influenced by their religious upbringing and affiliation. Fairbairn's immersion in the Calvinism of the Scottish Presbyterian Church and Winnicott's involvement in the Wesleyan church greatly influenced their views of the nature of a self and the inherent draw of humans toward relationship, particularly with God. Hoffman (2004) notes that "the study of 'persons in relationship' that emerged not only in object relations, but in the greater British academic culture, was undoubtedly influenced by the prevailing Judeo-Christian narrative, a narrative that made it particularly probable that the personal would make its entry into psychoanalysis by way of that culture" (p.801).

Psychodynamic psychotherapy has become enormously influential in recent decades. In the judgment of many academicians and clinicians, these approaches have been fertile ground for broad-ranging discussions about personality, psychopathology and psychotherapy. It is not surprising, then, that growing numbers of Christian mental health professionals have found these ever-evolving formulations to be useful in relating their Christian faith and practice with their professional lives. We suspect that the majority of Christian psychologists today would describe themselves as psychodynamic or at least "psychodynamically informed."

Philosophical Assumptions

Few if any of the psychodynamic theorists have made the kinds of broad dogmatic assertions that Freud did, and this makes it difficult to explicate any fundamental philosophical presuppositions in these models. Since all are revisions of Freudian thought, all are likely to share the naturalistic or materialistic assumptions of psychoanalysis. Yet all of the models have rejected the mechanistic metapsychology of Freud and have thus opened up the possibility for a more satisfactory resolution of the determinism/causality issue than was possible with Freud. Nevertheless, none of the models, to our knowledge, have explicitly embraced a limited human freedom stance compatible with Christian belief. We will develop in the later critique how this might, in fact, be attainable.

Workman (1988) convincingly argues that these models share what might be called a "subjective epistemology" that is congruent with contemporary thinking in philosophical epistemology. The core of this view is that knowable reality is a "function of the inner world of experience as perceived" by the person (p.3). External reality is ultimately unknowable except through the intermediary of psychological experience.

In fact, several approaches to Christian counseling have their roots in this tradition, though this is sometimes not acknowledged. The work of Lake (1966, 1986), called "clinical theology," is fundamentally a derivative from contemporary psychodynamic thought, specifically of the object-relations variety. The "healing of memories" phenomenon (e.g., Linn & Linn, 1978; Seamands, 1985) is best understood as a lay derivative of a psychodynamic understanding of persons, though it proposes a directly supernatural methodology for healing. Hurding (1985) has developed a thoughtful critique of the clinical theology and healing-of-memories approaches. Larry Crabb's widely read book *Inside Out* takes a psychodynamically influenced perspective on the individual's relationship with God (Crabb, 1998).

Model of Personality

Object representations, or introjects, are intrapsychic structures that are significantly affected by interpersonal relations. More specifically, introjects are the mental representations of the self and others (the objects). As mentioned previously, the central tenet of psychoanalysis and of psychodynamic theories in general is that each individual has an internal world that is affected by the past and which, in turn, affects one's functioning in the present, external world. According to object-relations theories the past affects us through internalized memories and images of events and relationships. We are usually not conscious of these imprints, but they influence our daily lives in profound and significant ways.

When we interact with a person we are relating not just to the real person that stands before us but to an internal representation or idea that we have of who that person is. It is seldom possible for that internalized representation of the person to be wholly based on the raw reality of who the person before us is. Rather, our perception is colored by past images of events and people. In a sense, we relate to real people through our internal representations of past relations. For example, a person may look like someone we once knew, or someone may be in a position of authority and therefore stir up memories of our parents; a person's mannerisms or tone of voice may set off other cues, and so forth. In short, we transfer parts of past images of people onto others. If these past images are strong enough, and if our ability to sort out the distortions from the reality is weak enough, we may act and feel in quite unrealistic ways toward this person. We may feel resentful toward others when they have done nothing to anger us. We may feel dependent on them for no apparent reason. Our feelings may vary dramatically toward them in any given encounter or across time.

In addition to these internal representations of others, we have internal representations of ourselves. In our earliest interactions with the important people in our environment we form ideas of who we are. A common example is the "gleam in the mother's eye." When an infant gazes up into his mother's eyes, her expression provides the child with a mirror image of himself. These mirror images form the earliest perceptions of self. If we are treated with adequate nurturing and protection, we will develop a whole and integrated sense of self. This representation will include a realistic awareness of both good and bad qualities coexisting. In an environment where the needs are not adequately met, however, this integrated sense of self cannot develop. Instead, an incomplete or inaccurate sense of who we are is formed.

The development of the mature or integrated self is thought to take place in several stages through the first few years of life. To adequately complete a stage, parents need to meet the needs of the child in a loving and consistent fashion. In their study of young children, Mahler (1968) and her associates (Mahler, Pine & Bergman, 1975) utilized object-relations theory to provide a model of the psychological birth of the child, which is considered to take place over the two years following the biological birth. They suggest that the self develops in three primary stages. From physical birth (or perhaps even within the womb) until approximately two months, the normal infant exists in the autism stage, characterized by what is called "absolute primary narcissism." During this phase infants are aware only of physical sensations they experience as globally pleasant or unpleasant. Children are not able to distinguish between self and external world; they have no sense of identity whatsoever.

In the symbiotic stage, from about two to six months, the infant experiences a sense of oneness or symbiosis with the primary caregiver. The child is presumed to be only aware of the functions that the parent serves in meeting the needs of the infant. Thus, the infant views the parent as something of an "object." The parent's task in this stage is to be readily available and attentive to the needs of the infant. If the parent is "good enough" at meeting these needs, to use Winnicott's well-known phrase, the infant develops the capacity to trust the world and also to look within for some capacity for comfort and meeting of needs.

From six months to two years the child is engaged in the process of separation and individuation, which has several stages. The child first begins to focus externally, rather than on her own bodily sensations. As she begins to move about and explore her world, and is able to affect her world (by grabbing things, etc.), her sense of separateness or differentness from the external world is heightened. This usually results in ambivalence as the child is conflicted between feelings of independence and wonder, on the one hand, and fear, on the other, which results from the loss of the ever-present sense of the parent's reassuring presence. These feelings feed the infant's sense of the parent as good and loving but also bad and frustrating.

Similarly, the child begins in this stage to realize that she, herself, can also be good and bad. For normal development to occur, the parent must walk the fine line of both encouraging independence while continuing to serve as a source of protection and nurturance. Overemphasis on either extreme can result in personality disturbances. If this phase is successfully navigated, the child achieves the optimal resolution of being able to internalize mental representations of parent and self that are stable, realistic (recognizing good and bad in self and parent) and comforting (because the parent's love and protection are with the child even when separated from the parent). The child feels loved and lovable, and has a sense of her capacity for independence and interdependence.

Since we carry around internal images of ourselves and others, relationships are necessarily complicated. Not only are two real people interacting, but one's internal image of oneself is relating to the internal image of the other person, and the same is happening in the other person as well. In a reasonably mature individual, the internal objects, or representations of self and others, have been allowed to develop adequately and come close to external reality. In a person who has been subjected to inadequate or nonexistent parenting there is little ability to discriminate between the reality and the distorted internal objects; this person seems to be responding to an "inner agenda" rather than true interpersonal reality. This function of discriminating between the internal images and the external reality belongs to the ego, and this emphasis on the relation between the internal images and the external reality is the primary differencebetweencontemporarypsychoanalysis and its classical ancestry. (This interest in relationships is also what led to the establishment of an object-relations school of family therapy, as discussed in chapter 9.)

Model of Health

As just described, the infant begins the process of maturation essentially unaware of the existence of others. As the child develops, a process of learning to separate and individuate from others takes place. The child learns to differentiate self from other, and can carry on a healthy, interdependent relationship with another person. Such a relationship is characterized by a valuing of other persons for more than their usefulness in meeting needs and desires. Maturity is, then, "the realization of our full potentialities as persons in personal relationships" (Guntrip, 1969, p.324).

One of the most refreshing aspects of contemporary psychodynamic psychology is its definition of health. This is somewhat ironic since it, like its psychoanalytic counterpart, is essentially a psychology of sickness. This focus on the abnormal is obvious in light of the way the previous discussion of personality theory turned quickly to a discussion of disruptions of development. Psychodynamic theory has been constructed through the clinical experiences of the theorists who practice therapy. Such a system is necessarily skewed toward finding pathology. Nevertheless, by extrapolating from the theories of pathology and by observing the health that is there, as well as the health that develops, a model of maturity can be developed.

The mature adult, according to the relational model, sees self and others in a constant way that deviates only minimally from reality. The adult is, as a result, capable of enjoyable and interdependent relationships. Such individuals have learned to value others for qualities beyond their usefulness (unlike the narcissistic person). They can also view self and others as having an integration of both good and bad qualities without having to either reject or idealize others on the basis of passing moods or pressing needs (unlike the person with a borderline personality disorder).

Since the mature individual perceives the world and other people accurately, there is no need for exaggerated psychological defenses. Defenses are built initially against the real hazards of the world—pain inflicted, accidentally or intentionally, by people or events of our childhood. Later, however, we continue to project the threats of pain onto the world or people in the world when, in reality, those threats do not exist. The mature individual trusts others but remains aware that at times of potential pain the self may need to be defended.

The mature individual is able to build new, creative relationships with other healthy individuals. Immaturity is marked by seeking out unhealthy individuals with whom to engage in pathological relational patterns that repeat old, unresolved interactions. Like its classical counterpart, contemporary psychoanalysis sees the mature individual as freed from the prison of unconsciously and unnecessarily reliving the past.

Model of Abnormality

Given an adequate environment where the parent nurtures the child and meets his needs, the process of maturation is thought to unfold naturally. But for many the necessary nurture is not provided and the resulting immature personality, deprived of such a relationship, remains stuck in the early phase of viewing others for their usefulness in meeting internal needs. The object-relations literature primarily focuses on categorizing and treating the disorders of the personality that can result when the needs of the developing self are not adequately met.

A fragmented internal sense of self most frequently occurs when the primary parent is not healthy enough to provide adequately for the psychological needs of the child. Such a parent never had those needs adequately met for him- or herself. The parent will provide either little or no love, inappropriately intimate attention, love in an unpredictable way or love only when the child acts as the parent wants him or her to act. In such an environment the child's internal sense of self can become distorted in many ways. One common example is an inability to "own" or experience as part of us those aspects that our parents found unacceptable, as when a parent rejects a child when she is needy. This may result in a fragmented psychology wherein the "bad" parts are split off from the acceptable parts, and the person's sense of a coherent identity is damaged.

Freud essentially divided psychopathology into two categories, neurosis and psychosis. Psychosis, the inability of the ego to interact with the reality of the external world, was seen as largely untreatable through traditional psychoanalysis. Neurosis, however, reflected unresolved conflicts from the Oedipal period of development. The individual generally remained cognizant of reality and had established the capacity to develop a transference relationship that was seen as essential for a successful course of psychoanalysis.

Other analysts, working with populations more diverse than those visiting Freud in Victorian Vienna, found that many nonpsychotic patients were untreatable using the techniques of classic psychoanalysis. These patients were not capable of sustaining a consistent sense of self or of others and were, therefore, unable to invest in the necessarily intense analytic relationship. The consistent variable in the personality of such patients was the focus on pre-Oedipal disturbances in their relationships, disturbances rooted in problems before the age of four. The existence of such patients suggested a realm of abnormality between neurosis and psychosis.

Initially, these patients were seen as walking a fine line between neurosis and psychosis, what some called a "borderline" state. In time, psychodynamically oriented clinicians began to view this state as an entirely separate cluster of syndromes, the "personality disorders," with features unlike either the neurotic or psychotic constellation of symptoms.

Disruptions in the early development of object relations are usually considered to lead to the formation of either narcissistic or borderline disorders. What any two theorists mean by either of these terms, however, can vary widely. Stone (1986), for example, identified six different uses for the term *borderline* in describing personality dysfunction. While theorists may disagree as to the number, differentiation and organization of personality disorders, they consistently assert that disruptions in early relationships leave the personality in an immature or incomplete state, largely incapable of forming healthy and mature adult relationships. By definition, an individual with a personality disorder has remained stuck in pre-Oedipal development and is thus always looking for ways to satisfy unmet needs. A neurotic individual, by comparison, has a reasonably well-developed personality but is still unable to effectively manage anxiety in his or her life.

There is disagreement as to whether the infant is born with a complete and unblemished ego or a fragmented ego in need of further development. Relational model theorists agree, however, that the adequate development of the personality depends on the care and nurture provided by the primary parental figure(s). The parent who adequately meets the child's needs, or to use Winnicott's (1965) term, the "good enough parent," provides the child with the necessary raw materials for the development of a consistent and healthy sense of self and the world. As mentioned earlier, the parent whose needs were not adequately met in her or his own childhood probably cannot adequately meet those needs for the child. Instead the child will be provided with conditional love and an inconsistent or negative sense of worth.

The relational model's emphasis on the effects of the behavior and motivations of the parent on the personality of the child has been criticized by feminists and others as "mother-bashing," particularly since the mother is typically the primary caregiver (cf. Van Leeuwen, 1990, pp.125-143). Indeed, the responsibility for the adequacy of the child's personality is placed disproportionately on the shoulders of the parents. The child is not able to have much volitional control over the development or reparation of his or her personality until late adolescence at the earliest. This certainly places an awesome responsibility on the primary caregiver(s).

Model of Psychotherapy

One of the strengths of the psychodynamic model is the direct link between theory and therapy. The theory is derived from the clinical work of the theorists with their clients. Because we are fundamentally relational beings, healing can only come through relationships. The core assumption is that healthy relationships have therapeutic potential.

In the classical approach to psychoanalysis the patient-analyst relationship is defined by transference and its interpretation. The analyst is an anonymous and blank canvas on which the patient recreates the vicissitudes of his or her past. Any feelings or personal involvement on the part of the analyst are seen as countertransference, the therapist's own unresolved neurotic conflicts. Thus, it is fair to say that the classic analytic relationship is not a real relationship at all.

Greenberg and Mitchell (1983) argue that the relational psychodynamic models see therapy quite differently from the classical model. Therapy is a relationship. The analyst and the patient participate in a dynamic interaction. Transference is an important part, but the therapist cannot be a blank canvas. Who she is as a person will necessarily influence the transference. Countertransference (the reaction of the therapist to the client) also plays an important part. Rather than being seen as the immaturity or "unfinished business" of the therapist, it is understood to be an essential tool and empathetic guide to the patient's inner experience of the world. In a sense the transference and countertransference interact as in a dance, a mutual event. In all likelihood therapy may be the first authentic or consistent intimacy that many patients have encountered. The impersonal and artificial methods of classical analysis had to be discarded because in this model the only hope for real change for the client is through a real relationship, and not through technique:

> The task of the analyst is not to remain outside of a process which is unfolding from within the mind of the patient, because this is theoretically impossible in the terms of the model's basic premises, but to engage the patient, to intervene, to participate in, and to transform pathogenic patterns of relationship. (Greenberg & Mitchell, 1983, p.390)

Object-relations theories do not prescribe techniques or exercises for therapy. On the contrary, the spontaneity and mutual exploration of the relationship constitute the healing process. The therapist does not keep the theory always in mind. It becomes second nature, "the invisible backdrop, the unseen framework, within which the analyst hears the patient's story" (Greenberg & Mitchell, 1983, p.15).

Contemporary writers on the psychotherapy process have come to refer to four different modes or channels of listening to the therapeutic relationship. Some have labeled these modes the one-person, one-and-a-half-person, two-person and three-person approaches. The first, or one-person model, describes the classical Freudian approach. The goal of the therapist's personal analysis was complete objectivity. The analyst was believed to be free of countertransference that would distort his or her capacity for providing accurate interpretations of the patient's unconscious defenses. The only person in the room, so to speak, is the one person of the patient. The analyst is more of a reflective object with personal perspectives removed.

Such a confidence in objectivity as Freud's could only have thrived in the modernist ethos of his time. Ricoeur (1970) noted that Freud's very method of observing the depth of the human capacity for self-deception helped demolish all confidence in the capacity of the analyst, or anyone else, for true objectivity. While the contemporary psychodynamic therapist might glean insights from Freud's classical theory, few will hold out any confidence for the analyst's capacities of neutrality, abstinence and anonymity that Freud believed in. Further, since the advent of object-relations theory, few would suggest that such detachment is even desirable.

The one-and-a-half-person mode has been the dominant mode of thinking about therapy for several decades. In this perspective the therapist is half of a person in the equation. Therapeutic relational boundaries and the rules of the therapeutic frame keep the therapist from being fully present. This model proposes the therapist as an empathic tool. By providing empathy, insight and corrective emotional experiences, the therapist brings about change in the patient. But the therapist in never fully present, because the therapeutic relationship is always about the needs of the client.

The two-person mode involves both the therapist and the patient fully in the relationship. But perhaps the circle of those present must be expanded further. Altman (1995) and others have pointed out that psychoanalysis has largely been developed and practiced in a very homogeneous world of privileged Europeans and Americans. Such homogeneity makes it possible to ignore the presence of a "third" person, the intersubjective experience uniquely created by the two people in the room. The idea of this third presence is a strong theme in contemporary relational theorists. The bringing together of two people and their intersubjective worlds is thought to create something entirely unique while also vaguely familiar to both of them. This three-person model of thinking about development and therapy (generally, now referred to as relational psychoanalytic psychotherapy) has become, if not a theory of its own, at least a strong and growingly cohesive tradition. For an excellent overview of theorists and seminal ideas of this tradition, see Mitchell (1999).

For both the two- and three-person models, therapy is thought to provide a context where the vital internal representations of primary figures, which form the core of personality, will begin to emerge. Therapy will focus on past and present experiences to encourage this uncovering. What makes therapy different from other relationships (where internalized representations are just as operative) is that the trained therapist can recognize distortions based on maladaptive inner images and can maintain the relationship in such a way as to allow the client to begin to change these images and come to have a more accurate understanding of self and the interpersonal environment.

The countertransference, or responsive and reactive state of the therapist, is her or his primary tool. Therapy hinges on it (Racker, 1957; Winnicott, 1956). The subtle confrontations or interpretations of the patient's experience of the world are chosen and worded through the matrix of the therapist's experience of the world. In the one-and-one-half-person model, the therapist seeks to limit the distortion of her own perspective by relying on empathic listening and by making the patient's transference the focus of discussion. In the three-person model the therapist actually selectively discloses her experience of the relationship with the patient, even acknowledging mistakes and countertransference reactions to the patient.

A healthy therapist will judge the maturity of the patient's behavior with reasonable effectiveness and accuracy. She can momentarily step outside herself to monitor the countertransference and separate much of what is her internal interpretation of reality from that of the patient. An immature therapist, however, can model a distorted sense of maturity and influence the client to develop according to the therapist's faulty perspective. Little possibility exists, in this theoretical framework, for the therapist leading the patient to a greater level of maturity than the therapist has personally attained.

Unlike the classical model of psychoanalysis that required longer-term therapy with multiple sessions per week, contemporary dynamic therapists are likely to work within more realistic constraints. The Vanderbilt Psychotherapy Study of Strupp and his colleagues, in fact, has demonstrated that the helpful effects of psychodynamic therapy can be experienced in a time-limited context of twenty-six sessions (Strupp & Binder, 1985). Using Strupp's time-limited method the therapist anticipates that each patient suffers from a cyclical maladaptive pattern that interferes with all of his significant relationships. The therapist monitors her relationship with the patient, watching for the emergence of this pattern.

Unlike the classical model that demanded the therapist's objectivity, the emerging relational model assumes that the therapist will, at times, lose all objectivity and become lost in the patient's cyclical relational pattern, enacting past relational failures. This comfort with intersubjectivity is built on the object-relations theorists' trust in the relational process over the therapist's ability to provide constructive interpretation of the patient's unconscious conflicts. The therapist is trusted to help the patient see the cycle they have both fallen into and to disclose her feelings about that experience. This type of immediacy is quite unlike the classical Freudian model of abstinence and anonymity. By breaking free from the morass of the cyclical maladaptive pattern, the patient is thought to receive both a new experience and a new insight that will help him to bring change into other relationships in his life. While capacity for insight is important, some patients are thought to benefit from the experience of healthy immediacy without simultaneous insight into the source of their problems.

CHRISTIAN CRITIQUE

Philosophical Assumptions

In reacting against the scientism and mechanism of classical drive theory, contemporary psychodynamic psychology has adopted a theoretical understanding of human nature based primarily on the analysis of human relationships. Object-relations theorists look first and foremost at the primary attachments made between children and the caregivers in the early developmental years. Other biological, psychosocial and sociocultural variables are deemed as less formative on later personality development and functioning. These influences are not seen as irrelevant, only less uniquely and fundamentally "human." Who we are and who we tend to become, they argue, can best be understood in the interpersonal context.

In basing the foundation of its psychology on the relational rather than biological components of personality, psychodynamic theory has essentially taken a step back into the phenomenological and philosophical realms in which psychology as a discipline began. In embracing such an emphasis and in moving away from a mechanistic model, psychodynamic theorists have removed many major obstacles for Christians who appreciate their model. In particular, as Hoffman (2004) has noted, Fairbairn and Winnicott—two of the primary theorists to form the contemporary psychodynamic movement—were thoroughly immersed in Protestant worldviews and developed theories consistent with those roots. Because of that influence, object-relations theories lend themselves to questions of human nature, values and subjective experience. Not surprisingly, contemporary psychodynamic theories have become a realm for creative discussion among theologians and Christian mental health professionals.

Object-relations theorists claim that humans have an inherent capacity and need for relationships. Guntrip (1969), for example, suggested "the universe has begotten us with an absolute need to be able to relate in fully personal terms to an environment that we feel relates beneficently to us" (p.328). Such a statement is reminiscent of the discussion in chapter two about the relational nature of humankind and how some say this is the central feature of what it means to be created in the image of God.

Vanderploeg (1981a, 1981b), White (1984), Greenlee (1986) and others have noted how this common ground—an emphasis on the centrality of relationships—provides a foundation for the integration of the relational model and Christian thought. Hoffman (2011), in fact, notably demonstrates the long-unrecognized influence of the "Christian narrative on the theories, clinical practices and history of psychoanalysis" (p.2).

Further, the notion that we internalize our relationships, that they become part of us, corresponds with Christian belief in marital union (Eph 5), family relatedness in the body of Christ (1 Cor 12) and even the notion of God residing in our very being when we become his child. Surely theirs is a purely psychological understanding of relatedness, but it is at least a step in the right direction.

Since the relational model addresses itself to that which is fundamental to human nature, the place of sin and particularly of original sin plays a prominent role in a Christian critique of its theories. Henderson (1975, 1977) points to a parallel between the object-relations view of the infant's earliest stage of primary narcissism, or egocentrism, with the Judeo-Christian view of original sin as selfishness, a sense of omnipotence or of viewing self as the center of the universe. He suggests, however, "the approach of dynamic psychology, in contrast to that of theology, is to assist the individual ego to search for, discover and know its inherent quantum of badness in the view that a badness which is well-known and familiar is thereby rendered impotent" (1975, p.114). Christianity, however, goes further by offering forgiveness for and victory over sin, rather than merely rendering it psychologically impotent. Again, though, this is a step in the right direction, and there are almost certainly helpful aspects of this psychodynamic understanding of how we come to overcome our own "badness."

One result of the classic psychoanalytic approach has been a gradual erosion of a concept of sin. What theology had ascribed to sin, Freud ascribed to symptoms of illness, especially to psychological defenses. A person is not "bad" but "ill." Henderson (1977) resists this tendency with the accurate rationale that such a view tends to steer us away from "individual human accountability for the human situation" (p.427). He suggested "psychotherapists should bring a concept of sin back into their work and emphasize personal moral culpability and accountability as vital to mental health" (p.432). This is consistent with the view of psychodynamically oriented clinicians such as Peck (1983) and Menninger

(1973), and is a move all Christians can applaud.

The importance of individual moral culpability notwithstanding, a psychodynamic perspective may have something to teach us about sin. To search for a psychological factor in some forms of sin does not require a corresponding diminution of personal accountability. Since early deprivation can leave the personality in an immature and vulnerable state, it seems feasible that some means of protecting the self could reflect our sinfulness (cf. Mangis, 2008). This would not equate sin with defense, but some sins could serve a defensive function. Sexual sins, for example, might, in some cases, be motivated by early unmet needs for intimacy. A propensity toward gossip might be motivated by an inner need to feel superior to others. This controversial area of human accountability may provide fertile ground for dialogue between theologians and psychodynamically oriented clinicians. Specifically, greater awareness and understanding of the nature of sinful behavior may aid in more effective (albeit limited) interventions that address it. Obviously, human beings in and of themselves are powerless to ameliorate either the ultimate causes or effects of sin. But they can serve an important and vital role as being agents of reconciliation and renewal in human relationships.

Discussions concerning moral accountability inevitably raise philosophical questions as to the existence of free will. On first glance, contemporary psychodynamic thought, in abandoning or altering the emphasis on biological instincts and drives, appears to have rejected the accompanying assumptions of determinism. In an apparent rejection of determinism, Guntrip (1969) states that

> we have non-dynamic behaviour theories describing human beings as just repertoires of behaviour patterns to be treated by techniques of reconditioning.... Over and against this is the dynamic psychology of the psychoanalytic and psychotherapeutic schools, standing for man's basic freedom and right not to be manipulated, but to be supported till he can find his own proper mature selfhood. (pp.330-331)

While proponents of the relational model may seem to have wholly accepted the concept of free will, it is more likely that most have, in Evans's (1984, 1989) terms, rejected a "hard" determinism, which acknowledges the incompatibility of psychological causation and human freedom, for a "soft" determinism, which simply redefines freedom to make it seemingly compatible with psychological determinism. In both cases, internal forces exert powerful influences on our thoughts, feelings and behaviors.

But the relational models are much more amenable to a "libertarian" perspective on personal responsibility than is classic analysis. Evans (1984) has, in fact, argued forcefully that contemporary psychodynamic theory really has no need to retain the deterministic assumption of psychoanalysis. Eliminating that assumption would eradicate a stumbling block for Christian utilization of this approach. He argues that these approaches are quite compatible with a type of "limited freedom." We exist in the context of our personal histories. We are certainly influenced in powerful and significant ways by past relationships. We do not have to assume, however, that this history forces us to behave in a predetermined way, but rather provides probabilities of how we will act. Within certain boundaries, we have freedom and are, therefore, still accountable for our actions.

Models of Personality and Abnormality

While the emphasis of object-relations theorists is on the parents' impact on the child's personality, they do stress that no parent can be perfect, only "good enough." Kohut even emphasizes the importance of occasional failures by the parents so as to aid the internalization of the child's sense of responsibility for the maintenance of her or his own self-image.

It is difficult to criticize the relational model for its emphasis on the importance of the relationship between parent and child for personality development. If the *imago Dei* (the image of God) is at some level a need for relatedness, it follows that our healthy development would depend largely on adequately meeting that need, and that our earliest and most profound relationships would leave powerful impressions on us. Greenlee (1986) has pointed out that the dynamic of persons deprived of adequate caring in childhood in turn depriving their own children might be seen as a way in which the sins of the fathers are passed on to the succeeding generations (Ex 34:7). Certainly the notion of intergenerational sin and psychopathology deserves more serious attention in our religious circles in light of the alarmingly high rates of childhood trauma (e.g., physical and sexual abuse).

The view of *imago Dei* as "need for relatedness" certainly is not restricted to relations with other humans such as parents. According to a Christian creational perspective, the need itself arises from the fact that humankind was created for relationship with God and others. It is not surprising, then, that being created for a relationship with God and being born into a world where we find only broken and fallible images of God, we should have difficulty finding adequate resources for the building of a mature self capable of healthy relationships. It is also not surprising that we should have just as much difficulty developing a healthy relationship with God as with other human beings. Though created for this relationship, we are nevertheless on this earth separated from God, and thus there will always be a hunger for a greater sense of connectedness with him.

This latter difficulty of relating to God has been a prominent area of discourse between object-relations theorists and Christian theologians. The center of this discussion has been how individuals image or conceptualize God. This area of research developed out of the common and puzzling observation that people have radically different core views of God even within the same religious groups (e.g., God as Daddy, Judge, Distant Originating Cause, Buddy, Cosmic Vending Machine, etc.). Ana-Maria Rizzuto (1974, 1979, 1996) is probably best known for her work in this area. She draws on the object-relations concept of internal representations, developed in early childhood, which later influence our interactions with other people and our world. She suggests that in infancy the child, dependent on the parents for the provision of even the most elemental needs, creates an idealized representation of the parent (primarily mother) as God. While later development will lead to separate representations for the parents, this original God-image remains.

This concept is not new to psychodynamic thought. As discussed in chapter three, Freud saw the child's view of the parents as the origin of belief in God. He employed play on words of the Genesis account of God making humankind in his own image and suggested that, instead, humankind makes God in its own image. Freud saw God as an individual and corporate myth arising out of early relations with our own human fathers.

The healthy adult must, therefore, abandon the infantile belief in a supreme being and resign her- or himself to the relative and impersonal nature of the universe. The object-relations perspective of our image of God is decidedly more tolerant than that of Freud. Rizzuto sees one's image of God as a dynamic and creative part of the self that can grow and change, particularly as our perceptions of our parents, the original models for the God image, grow and change. Guntrip (1969) argued that "'religious experience' is the same kind of 'stuff' as human 'personal relations experience'" (p.328), and that a relationship with God is the "personal heart of reality" (p.331). Such a relationship, he suggests, can contribute to the maturation and integration of the developing personality. Rizzuto (1974) did not take her interpretation this far but did suggest that

> such a systematic grasp of the sources and the adaptive or maladaptive potential of internalized God-images within the larger theory of object relations would be, I submit, a useful tool, not just in the hand of the clinician, but also in the hands of the minister, rabbi and priest in their pastoral work as well as in the religious education of children. (p.98)

But there is still potential here for views that are destructive of true faith as conceived in orthodox Christianity. Guntrip (1969), for example, regards God as an "indefinable term" (p.331). Similarly, religion as a relationship with God is

> an overall way of experiencing life, of experiencing ourselves and our relationships together; an experience of growing personal integration or self-realization through communion with all that is around us, and finally our way of relating to the universe, the total reality which has, after all, evolved us with the intelligence and motivation to

> explore this problem: all that is meant by "experience of God." (p.326)

An internal relationship with a healthier image of God or the universe will remain, however, a unidirectional relationship. It is relating to an image (even illusion) within. When we form an internal image or representation of our parent, on the other hand, it originates out of an attempt to relate to the real person of the parent. No matter how distorted that internal image of the parent is, the potential always exists for further interactions with the parent and further maturing of the self to lead to a more accurate and reality-based internal image. Such a relationship is bidirectional. We can test aspects of our internal image against the real person, and the real person can take action to attempt to alter our internal image of her or him.

A secular object-relations theory cannot conceive of an internal relationship with an internal image of God as bidirectional. In fact, any belief in a real supernatural world in which the real God exists would be interpreted as "out-of-date dogmas or inadequate symbolisms of worship" (Guntrip, 1969, p.329), a projection of our own subjective beliefs onto an impersonal external world. If this view were true, then Christianity would subsist purely of personal or collective autobiography, representations and images of God as recorded by our ancestors, together with our individual inner images of God formed in the context of relationships with significant others. Obviously this runs the risk of developing into a theology of personal subjective experience only.

Such a perspective by a secular object-relations theorist could allow for our image of God and our religion to be healthy, important, even artistic and poetic, but could not see it as a real relationship with a real person. The temptation, of course, is to believe that the discovery of the source and the distortion of our image of God is the end, to conclude that "we have discovered God and he is us." It is tempting to see an "almost" relationship with our internal image of God as the same thing as a relationship with God, to confuse sentimentality about vague religious impulses with a true relationship. It seems plausible, after all, that our images of God could be distorted by our experiences with fallen people, especially parents, in a fallen world. The slope can be quite slippery from that point, however. Having "psychologized" our experience of God, it may then seem logical to conclude that what Christians often interpret as their experience of God is actually the work of the unconscious, and so, perhaps, we should worship the "God image" in all of us. To counter this, more accurate and "objective" concepts of the Creator God must be shaped in the context of Christian worship, education, fellowship and service. We need the input of these external sources for corrective feedback against our subjective and projective tendencies.

The seductiveness of these arguments does not invalidate the possible helpfulness of the object-relations theories. Knowledge of early development may truly inform us about distortions in our images of God; this knowledge could serve to lead us to a truer and more intimate relationship with God and others, just as understanding how our spouse is in reality quite different from our internalized image of "Mommy" or "Daddy" can aid the maturation of our marriages. It can take on an important role in therapy, especially when we know that in Christ we have a current, two-way relationship with a living, objective God both through the Word in us and the written Word, "living and active, sharper than any double-edged sword" (Heb 4:12 ESV).

The relational model of contemporary psychodynamic psychology may also provide helpful insights into how our image of God can grow and become healthier as our capacity for relationships goes through its necessary healing and maturing process (cf. Hoffman, 2011).

We would note in closing that this notion of the God image being profoundly shaped by parental images has been subjected to careful empirical assessment. Spilka, Hood and Gorsuch (1985, p.81) summarize the results of this research by stating that the complexity and the subtlety of the hypothesis, and the difficult and challenging measurement issues involved, make this a very complicated question indeed. The existing data provide some modest support for the projective hypothesis, suggesting mild similarity in concepts of God and concepts of the same-sex or most-liked parent.

Theory of Health

According to psychodynamic theory, the mature individual values relationships and can maintain a commitment to them, even when the other person is not present. Such maturity requires a valuing of self since our perceptions of others are highly dependent on our internal representation of self. This notion is certainly in accord with the commandment to "love your neighbor as yourself" (Mt 22:39). It is significant, in light of the object-relations view of God, that this is the second greatest commandment. Jesus said that it was like the greatest commandment to "love the Lord your God with all your heart and with all your soul and with all your mind" (Mt 22:37). Our greatest commandment, to love God, places love of self and other second, an impossibility if self and other are real while God is only an internal representation. Perhaps the primary point should be, though, that love is central to what God wants in us when we are fully human, and it is to their credit that these models put the kind of interpersonal bonding that might be called love at the very center of their model of normalcy.

The psychodynamic system, like all psychotherapy systems, contains an implicit ethical system embedded in its understanding of normalcy. Altruism and mutual dependence are valued within the contexts of close (especially family) relationships, but self-sacrifice, giving to the point of allowing pain to be inflicted on the self, would not be highly valued. The hidden ethical vision of this tradition "is that one has a moral obligation to do that which deep down one wants to do. Or to say it differently, it is morally justifiable to do what one is inclined to do because what one is inclined to do is also moral" (Browning & Cooper, 2004, p.225).

Because of our relational natures we are inclined to care for those close to us because they care for us and nurture us. This view directly parallels that of classic psychoanalysis. Thus a self-sacrificial act would generally be thought of as a self-induced punishment for irrational guilt or the result of an inaccurate view that others are more worthy of love than oneself. While this is probably often true (e.g., the self-styled Christian "doormat"), this model has little place for the reality of Christ's unilateral sacrifice and our commandment to model ourselves after his example (cf. Smedes, 1988). Since contemporary psychodynamic psychology is agnostic regarding the existence of reality or truth outside of this temporal world, it cannot allow for choices or values that call for the sacrifice of the needs of the self. It cannot envision a relationship with a real God that could empower one to make a truly self-sacrificial act.

In calling for the importance of equal and trusting relationships, and in highly prizing interrelatedness, however, it fares decidedly better than some theoretical systems which seem to actively embrace narcissism alone (Browning & Cooper, 2004, chap.8). Its ethic is still partial and incomplete, but it is an important improvement.

Model of Psychotherapy

Benner (1983), Workman (1988) and others have suggested provocative parallels between the process of psychodynamic psychotherapy and God's work of salvation and sanctification. Salvation and sanctification, it is argued, might be loosely understood as the process by which in intimate relationship with God we grow by the process of God himself, through Christ, taking upon himself our "badness." Through Christ's death, "he is open to receive all our sin, able to contain anything we can project onto him. In this relationship, we are offered the opportunity to become whole persons" (Workman, 1988, p.21). These authors suggest this is an analog to the psychotherapy relationship wherein the therapist acts as a human mediator who accepts, on behalf of God, the "bad introjects," the "psychic split-offs," that the client must be rid of to become whole.

This conception does parallel our call to be "Christ's ambassadors" (2 Cor 5:20-21), reconciling sinners with God. These authors do not wish to stretch these analogies too far, and we would agree with this caution. The analogies are fascinating, but the dangers of rendering God's work into a purely psychological framework and of elevating the redemptive work of the therapist to a grandiose level are great. The analogies may be helpful, but surely Christ's work is of an entirely different order than anything we can accomplish at a human level.

The psychodynamic methods of therapy may also be criticized for their seeming lack of appreciation for methods for change other than having a curative relationship. The pastoral instruction of the New Testament gives a great deal of attention to removing the characterological barriers to good relationships. We are to lay aside jealousy, envy, malice and so forth. But there is also ample biblical attention paid to other functions such as correcting our thinking, disciplined prayer and seeking restoration of shattered relationships. In the psychodynamic camp such interventions are often regarded as trivial or necessarily ineffectual. Further, these models are subtly humanistic in assuming that all will be well if the client has one really good relationship. The person will, as it were, be able to function autonomously through the direction of the ego once the bad internalized objects are straightened out. What is missing is an understanding of health that includes a long-term relationship with a living God and an appreciation for anchoring self in commitments to the church and God's revelation of himself in the Bible.

From a Christian perspective the faith of the therapist is important, though not the only factor, in determining effectiveness in psychotherapy. The worldview of a Christian is, presumably, substantially different from that of a non-Christian therapist. A non-Christian therapist with a healthy capacity for relationships may do far more good toward the healing of the personality than an immature Christian therapist, and a mature Christian therapist could possibly lead a patient away from true Christlikeness. On the whole, however, the greatest capacity for healing must certainly come from a Christian therapist directed by the Holy Spirit. As people, and in a profound and sobering way as therapists, we are imagers of God. The more that the therapist can be an accurate imager of God and therefore direct the individual to a greater capacity for relationship with God, the more healing will take place. A Christian object-relations therapist would, therefore, realize and help to facilitate the importance of a relationship between the patient and God in which God actively participates.

While the intimate connection between theory and therapy may be considered the strength of contemporary psychodynamic models, those who aspire to a more objective science of psychology will view it as a fatal weakness. Because all knowledge of internal dynamics comes from the therapy process in which the therapist is intimately involved, all conclusions are subject to the interpretations and distortions of the therapist. This might help explain the substantial disagreements between psychodynamic theorists from different schools and different eras. It is impossible to separate the conclusions of the theorist from his or her own individual dynamics.

To the question, Have the premises of contemporary psychoanalytic psychotherapy been adequately researched? the answer has, until recent years, depended on one's theoretical orientation. In a meta-analysis of psychodynamic psychotherapy outcome research, Shedler (2010) notes considerable empirical evidence for the efficacy of psychodynamic psychotherapy. Psychodynamic therapy was found to be as effective as other therapeutic modalities. And he noted that the effectiveness of other therapies is likely rooted, at least in part, in their similarities to the foundational principles of psychodynamic psychotherapy. Further, Shedler found that the effects of psychodynamic therapy were longer lasting than with other approaches, with patients continuing to find improvement after therapy had ended.

The fact that psychoanalytic theory grows out of the personal interactions of theorists with their patients provides an urgent call for Christian psychodynamically oriented therapists. One of the strongest voices in this area was Randall Lehman Sorenson. The thoughtful integration of contemporary psychoanalytic theory with Christian faith was dealt a terrible blow by his untimely death. Respected within both the secular and the Christian psychoanalytic communities, he mentored many practitioners and researchers in the relational psychodynamic tradition. We rely now on his writings and on the wisdom gained from those who were mentored by him (c.f. Sorenson, 1994a, 1994b, 1997, 2004).

CONCLUSION

The psychodynamic psychotherapies are among the broadest, most comprehensive systems in use today. In moving beyond Freud's narrow commitment to a biologically rooted, "scientific" theory, contemporary psychodynamic theorists have developed a system that does not present many of the problems to the committed Christian psychotherapist that classical analysis does.

These models are relational in nature, balance a cautious optimism with a deep appreciation of our capacity for self-deception and have a substantial (though secondary in emphasis) understanding of our rational capacities as humans. The values imbedded in the model are broadly compatible with Christian values, though of course there is not a perfect match.

The observant reader will note that our criticisms of this model were not devastating. Rather, they took the form of cautions. We think it fitting that this is one of the models that many Christian therapists are embracing;

it holds much promise as a possible foundation for future elaboration of a thoroughly Christian understanding of human personality.

FOR FURTHER READING

Altman, N. (1995). *The analyst in the inner city.* Hillsdale, NJ: Analytic Press.

Altman challenges the Eurocentric and socioeconomic assumptions of psychodynamic therapies.

Berzoff, J., Flanagan, L.M., & Hertz, P. (1996). *Inside out and outside in: Psychodynamic clinical theory and practice in contemporary multicultural contexts.* Northvale, NJ: Jason Aronson.

This introductory textbook covers the major psychodynamic theories and therapies and examines them from a multicultural perspective.

Browning, D.S., & Cooper, T.D. (2004). *Religious thought and the modern psychologies* (2nd ed.). Minneapolis, MN: Fortress.

Browning's sympathetic analysis of the potential contributions of Kohut and Erikson to a Christian understanding of persons in his chapter eight is a model of scholarly thoroughness, though in the mainline denominational rather than evangelical tradition.

Hoffman, M. (2004). From enemy combatant to strange bedfellow: The role of religious narratives in the work of W.R.D. Fairbairn and D.W. Winnicott. *Psychoanalytic Dialogues, 14* (6), 769-804.

This article explores the faith-based roots of two of the most significant object-relations theorists.

Lake, F. (1986). *Clinical theology.* (Edited and abridged by M. Yeomans). New York, NY: Crossroad.

A readable abridged introduction to the fascinating thought of a dedicated Christian expounding a thoroughly psychodynamic view of the counseling process.

Levenson, H. (1995). *Time-limited dynamic psychotherapy: A guide to clinical practice.* New York, NY: Basic Books.

This application of Strupp's research on time-limited psychotherapy is extremely practical and readable.

Mitchell, S.A. (Ed.). (1999). *Relational psychoanalysis: The emergence of a tradition* (Vol.14). Hillsdale, NJ: Analytic Press.

Until his untimely death Mitchell was the foremost relational theorist in the contemporary psychodynamic scene. In this volume he gathered some of the seminal works of relational psychoanalysis.

Stark, M. (1999). *Modes of therapeutic action: Enhancement of knowledge, provision of experience, and engagement in relationship.* Northvale, NJ: Jason Aronson.

This readable and practical book utilizes the three modes of listening discussed in this chapter and translates them into very practical advice for psychotherapists.

REFERENCES

Altman, N. (1995). *The analyst in the inner city.* Hillsdale, NJ: Analytic Press.

Benner, D. (1983). The incarnation as a metaphor for psychotherapy. *Journal of Psychology and Theology, 11,* 287-294.

Browning, D.S., & Cooper, T.D. (2004). *Religious thought and the modern psychologies* (2nd ed.). Minneapolis, MN: Fortress.

Crabb, L.J. (1998). *Inside out.* Colorado Springs, CO: NavPress.

Edkins, W. (1985). Object relations theory. In D. Benner (Ed.), *Baker encyclopedia of psychology* (pp.769-771). Grand Rapids, MI: Baker.

Evans, C.S. (1984). Must psychoanalysis embrace determinism? Or can a psychologist be a libertarian? *Psychoanalysis and Contemporary Thought, 7,* 339-365.

Evans, C. (1989). *Wisdom and humanness in psychology.* Grand Rapids, MI: Baker.

Freud, S. (1961). The ego and the id. In J. Strachey (Ed. and Trans.), *The standard edition of the complete psychological works of Sigmund Freud* (Vol.19, pp.3-66). London:

Hogarth Press. (Original work published 1923).

Greenberg, J., & Mitchell, S. (1983). *Object-relations in psychoanalytic theory.* Cambridge, MA: Harvard University Press.

Greenlee, L., Jr. (1986). Kohut's self psychology and theory of narcissism: Some implications regarding the fall and restoration of humanity. *Journal of Psychology and Theology, 14,* 110-116.

Guntrip, H. (1969). Religion in relation to personal integration. *British Journal of Medical Psychology, 42,* 323-333.

Henderson, J. (1975). Object relations and the doctrine of original sin. *International Review of Psychoanalysis, 2,* 107-120.

Henderson, J. (1977). Object relations and the psychotherapy of sin. *Canadian Psychiatric Association Journal, 22,* 427-433.

Henry, W.P., Strupp, H.H., Schacht, T.E., & Gaston, L. (1994). Psychodynamic approaches. In A.E. Bergin & S.L. Garfield (Eds.), *Handbook of psychotherapy and behavior change* (4th ed., pp.467-508). New York, NY: John Wiley.

Hoffman, M. (2004). From enemy combatant to strange bedfellow: The role of religious narratives in the work of W.R.D. Fairbairn and D.W. Winnicott. *Psychoanalytic Dialogues, 14* (6), 769-804.

Hoffman, M. (2011). *Toward mutual recognition: Relational psychoanalysis and the Christian narrative.* New York, NY: Routledge.

Hurding, R. (1985). *Roots and shoots.* London: Hodder & Stoughton.

Johnson, R. (1985). Self psychology. In D. Benner (Ed.), *Baker encyclopedia of psychology* (pp.1051-1053). Grand Rapids, MI: Baker.

Korchin, S. (1976). *Modern clinical psychology.* New York, NY: Basic Books.

Lake, F. (1966). *Clinical theology.* London: Darton, Longman & Todd.

Lake, F. (1986). *Clinical theology.* (Edited and abridged by M. Yeomans). New York, NY: Crossroad.

Linn, M., & Linn, D. (1978). *Healing life's hurts: Healing memories through five stages of forgiveness.* New York, NY: Paulist Press.

Luborsky, L., Barber, J., & Crits-Christoph, P. (1992). Testing psychoanalytic propositions about personality change in psychotherapy. In J.W. Barron, M.N. Eagle & D.L. Wolitzky (Eds.), *Interface of psychoanalysis and psychology* (pp.572-585). Washington, DC: American Psychological Association.

Mahler, M. (1968). *On human symbiosis and the vicissitudes of individuation.* New York, NY: International Universities Press.

Mahler, M., Pine, F., & Bergman, A. (1975). *The psychological birth of the human infant.* New York, NY: Basic.

Mangis, M. (2008). *Signature sins: Taming our wayward hearts.* Downers Grove, IL: InterVarsity Press.

Menninger, K. (1973). *Whatever became of sin?* New York, NY: Hawthorne Books.

Mitchell, S.A. (Ed.). (1999). *Relational psychoanalysis: The emergence of a tradition* (Vol.14). Hillsdale, NJ: Analytic Press.

Peck, S. (1983). *People of the lie.* New York, NY: Simon & Schuster.

Pine, F. (1988). The four psychologies of psychoanalysis and their place in clinical work. *Journal of the American Psychoanalytic Association, 36,* 571-596.

Prochaska, J. (1984). *Systems of psychotherapy* (2nd ed.). Chicago, IL: Dorsey.

Racker, H. (1957). The meanings and uses of countertransference. *Psychoanalytic Quarterly, 26,* 303-357.

Ricoeur, P. (1970). *Freud and philosophy: An essay on interpretation* (D. Savage, Trans.). New Haven, CT: Yale University Press.

Rizzuto, A.-M. (1974). Object relations and the formulation of the image of God. *British Journal of Medical Psychology, 47,* 83-99.

Rizzuto, A.-M. (1979). *The birth of the living God: A psychoanalytic study.* Chicago, IL: University of Chicago Press.

Rizzuto, A.-M. (1996). Psychoanalytic treatment and the religious person. In E.P. Shafranske (Ed.), *Religion and the clinical practice of psychology* (pp.409-431). Washington, DC: American Psychological Association.

Seamands, D.A. (1985). *Healing of memories.* Wheaton, IL: Victor Books.

Shedler, J. (2010). The efficacy of psychodynamic psychotherapy. *American Psychologist, 65* (2), 98-109.

Smedes, L. (1988). *Caring and commitment.* San Francisco: Harper & Row.

Sorenson, R.L. (1994a). Ongoing change in psychoanalytic theory: Implications for analysis of religious experience. *Psychoanalytic Dialogues, 4* (4), 631-660.

Sorenson, R.L. (1994b). Therapists' (and their therapists') God representations in clinical practice. *Journal of Psychology and Theology, 22* (4), 325-344.

Sorenson, R.L. (1997). Transcendence and intersubjectivity: The patient's experience of the analyst's spirituality. In C. Spezzano & G.J. Gargiulo (Eds.), *Soul on the couch: Spirituality, religion, and morality in contemporary psychoanalysis* (Vol.7, pp.163-199). Hillsdale, NJ: Analytic Press.

Sorenson, R.L. (2004). *Minding spirituality.* Hillsdale, NJ: Analytic Press.

Spilka, B., Hood, R., & Gorsuch, R. (1985). *The psychology of religion: An empirical approach.* Englewood Cliffs, NJ: Prentice-Hall.

Stone, M. (1986). Borderline personality disorder. In A. Cooper, A. Frances & M. Sacks (Eds.), *Psychiatry: Vol.1. The personality disorders and neuroses* (pp.203-217). New York, NY: Basic Books.

Strupp, H.H. (1993). The Vanderbilt psychotherapy studies: Synopsis. *Journal of consulting and clinical psychology, 61,* 431-433.

Strupp, H.H., & Binder, J.L. (1985). *Psychotherapy in a new key: A guide to timelimited dynamic psychotherapy.* New York, NY: Basic.

Vanderploeg, R. (1981a). Imago dei, creation as election: Foundations for psychotherapy. *Journal of Psychology and Theology, 9,* 209-215.

Vanderploeg, R. (1981b). Imago dei as foundational to psychotherapy: Integration versus segregation. *Journal of Psychology and Theology, 9,* 299-304.

Van Leeuwen, M. (1990). *Gender and grace.* Downers Grove, IL: InterVarsity Press.

White, S. (1984). Imago dei and object relations theory: Implications for a model of human development. *Journal of Psychology and Theology, 12,* 286-293.

Winnicott, D. (1965). *The maturational process and the facilitating environment.* New York, NY: International Universities Press.

Winnicott, D.W. (1956). On transference. *International Journal of Psycho-Analysis,* 386-388.

Workman, D. (1988, April). *An analysis of object-relations theory.* Paper presented at the Christian Association for Psychological Studies convention, Denver, CO.

5
BEHAVIOR THERAPY

Stanton L. Jones, Kelly Flanagan and Richard E. Butman

***

Traditional behavior therapy (BT) is perhaps the most straightforward and direct of all approaches to human change. It has attempted to define a set of problem behaviors (including thoughts and emotions), determine the conditions that cause the problem behaviors to occur, and then intervene to eliminate or decrease the occurrence of those problem behaviors in the most efficient and effective way possible, all using the tools of "scientific psychology" or the "laws of learning."

The history of BT includes several phases. The first phase in the 1950s and 1960s was purely behavioral in focus. BT gained rapid popularity, undoubtedly due to its ability to demonstrate clear empirical success in accomplishing change with certain tightly defined problems. With the recognition that behavioral principles did not deal adequately with the role of thoughts and feelings in patients' mental health problems or with more complex problems, the second phase, beginning in the 1970s, involved the broadening of its models and techniques to incorporate the growing emphasis on cognitive models.

The third phase is an even more dramatic departure from the early foundations of BT. It is now difficult to define BT apart from its cognitive counterpart, as indicated by the (controversial) change in name of the flagship organization from the Association of the Advancement of Behavior Therapy to the Association of Behavior and Cognitive Therapies. Further, to improve the effectiveness of BT, current approaches often consider the role of factors and the use of methods once considered "soft and unscientific" by the movement's founders, factors such as therapeutic relationships, mindfulness, acceptance, personal values and emotional deepening (Hayes, Follette & Linehan, 2004; Tsai et al., 2009). These "third-wave behavior therapies" differ in focus and technology from traditional behavioral approaches that focused solely on basic behavior or learning principles by incorporating consideration of context and combining BT techniques with utilization of a broadened scope of experiential and indirect change strategies (Hayes, 2004; Kohlenberg & Tsai, 1994).

Two examples of mainstream BT today show how dramatically the field has incorporated nonbehavioral elements in therapy. Parent-child interaction therapy (PCIT; Eyberg, 1988) is a parent-training intervention for disruptive behavior problems in young children. The first stage of PCIT is humanistic in approach, seeking to establish warm, loving relationships between parents and children. Only then is more traditional BT offered in the form of instruction in effective behavior management based on behavioral learning principles. Sheila Eyberg, the developer of PCIT, recognized the importance of developing warm and safe therapeutic and parent-child relationships, and thus the intervention is conducted within play interactions between parent and child (Hembree-Kigin & McNeil, 1995).

Similarly, behavioral marital therapy focused on direct behavior change in couple interactions (e.g., replacing fighting with more effective problem-solving behavior) was recognized as having limited effectiveness. Despite immediate reductions in distress, many couples relapse two to four years later (Baucom, Shoham, Meuser, Daiuto & Stickle, 1998). Thus, a new approach was developed. In integrative behavioral couple therapy (IBCT; Jacobson & Christensen, 1996; Jacobson, Christensen, Prince, Cordova & Eldridge,

2000), traditional behavioral marital treatment techniques (e.g., effective communication training, problem-solving, behavioral exchange strategies) are combined with a focus on "acceptance." Specifically, couples are encouraged throughout the therapy to compromise, accept aspects of their spouse that are unlikely to change, and actively collaborate.

The evolution of BT over the past fifty years highlights not only the shortcoming of traditional BT but also the resiliency of this therapeutic model with its ideological focus on learning principles and its strong support within psychology. In this chapter, BT in its older, purer and more stringently behavioristic form will be the focus, with particular attention paid to its foundational principles and to those contemporary practices still defined by their utilization of more classic behavioral techniques. The more cognitive approaches of cognitive-behavior therapy and third-wave therapies focused on mindfulness and acceptance will be discussed in the next chapter.

DESCRIPTIVE SURVEY

Philosophical Assumptions

Behavior therapy is an outgrowth of *behaviorism,* which in turn is a product of two factors: a view of metaphysics, specifically that of naturalism; and a view of science, first that of inductive empiricism and later that of logical positivism (see Van Leeuwen, 1979, for an expanded discussion). Naturalism assumes that the universe is composed exclusively of matter and energy, and hence there are no such things as supernatural entities such as gods or spirits. The human qualities that distinguish us from the rest of the universe (especially "mind"), and which are commonly assumed to transcend nature, are in this view presumed either not to exist or to be understandable by the same physical laws that explain the rest of existence. Human beings are not viewed as special in the sense of transcending these laws of the universe.

Behaviorism took shape under the influence of a particular view of science, that of logical positivism and its predecessor, inductive empiricism. According to logical positivism, all meaningful assertions must be either analytic (statements that are true by definition, such as 2+2=4) or be *empirically verifiable* or *falsifiable.* Statements such as "God exists" are, in this view, not merely false but rather are meaningless because they are neither analytic nor verifiable by empirical means. In this view, empirical data become the highest court of meaning and hence determine truth. Contemporary philosophers of science have convincingly documented the problems with this view of science and proposed outlines for a better understanding of the process of human knowing (see Evans, 1989; Jones, 1994; and Van Leeuwen, 1982, for Christian analyses: Brown, 1977; and Kuhn, 1996, for a more standard treatment of this issue from the perspective of the philosophy of science; and Berry, 2001, for an intriguing complementary perspective). Further, in postmodern analysis, the validity of truth claims made through empirical study has been called into question, with stark consequences for psychological science (Dueck & Parsons, 2004; Gergen, 2001; Gorsuch, 2002).

If the material universe, understandable only as matter and energy operating according to universal laws, is all that is, then human beings are material beings only and hence explainable by natural laws. Because psychological events were not accessible to empirical study, classic behaviorism eschewed all "mentalism." Philosophical behaviorism was first given clear articulation by John B. Watson. In the 1920s he directly challenged the notion that mind or consciousness ("psyche") was the proper subject matter of psychology because it could not be empirically examined. For Watson the road to progress in psychology was to follow after the natural sciences in dealing only with empirically verifiable constructs (i.e., behavior); thus behavior was understood through its material and causal relationships to other behaviors and environmental events. The specific formulas for understanding behavior were supplied later by the learning theories of Pavlov, Thorndike, Skinner and others.

Behavior therapy has been described, in addition to being an outgrowth of empirical psychology, as also a reaction against "the bizarre, symbolic interpretations of behaviors" offered by psychoanalysis; BT was construed in contrast as a "direct, humble, rational, and empirical" therapeutic approach (Hayes, 2004, p.2). In general, the leaders in the development of BT were critical of what they viewed as unfounded, vague and poorly researched theories and treatments of mental disorders (Wolpe & Rachman, 1960).

Behaviorism's embrace of naturalism gave rise to what has been called reductionism, the principle of breaking down more complex phenomena into simpler, more elemental ones. Thus, human language became understood as "verbal behavior," operating by the same principles as all overt behavior and reflexes. Thought in turn became "subvocal verbal behavior." These complex phenomena were in turn believed to be understandable in terms of the most elemental processes of learning. In this view, what we call "mental events" (such as thoughts and beliefs) and affect (feelings and emotions) may be part of human functioning, but are important only in their direct ties to overt behavior (e.g., dispositions to engage in behavior, initial cues to ensuing behavior). Everything, it was believed, can be reduced to elemental processes, and human behavior can be understood by breaking it down into parts. Without identification and analysis of these elements, complex human behavior cannot be studied, comprehended or effectively altered.

At the most basic level, then, an additional assumption of behaviorism can be termed *environmentalism,* not in the ecological sense but in the sense that behaviors are caused by factors outside of or external to themselves. All human and animal behavior is viewed as caused by environmental events. Thus, the reading of this chapter by graduate students is seen by the strict behaviorist as having been compelled by reinforcement contingencies exerted on them by the environment (i.e., demanding professors who dole out passing grades only in response to completion of educational tasks) and generated by the stimuli of the book lying on their desk.

The word *compel* signals that we must deal with the concept of determinism as well. Generally speaking, behaviorists accept the notion that all behaviors are the inevitable results of the causally relevant conditions that preceded them *(metaphysical determinism)* (Erwin, 1978). Skinner (1976) stated, "A person is not an originating agent; he is a locus, a point at which many genetic and environmental conditions come together in a joint effect" (p.185). If the behaviors of human beings are merely part of the stream of natural material events occurring in a mechanistic cosmos, then it can logically follow that all our actions, including even what we call our decisions and choices, are caused in such a way that, as Wolpe (1978) put it, "We always do what we must do" (p.444).

Although some modern behaviorists view behavior as a result of a system comprising random events (termed *metaphysical probabilism* or *probabilistic determinism),* human choice cannot be an originating source of that variability (Galuska, 2003). In fact, the concept of free will has been labeled "an illusion based on ignorance of the factors determining behavior" (Baum, 1994, p.15). Thus, in this view human free will is ultimately illusory; our actions are the inevitable results of the causal forces impinging on us.

Model of Personality

Behaviorism is unique in that statements about a view of persons are typically only indirectly made by writers in this tradition. The real focus of the model is on the principles of behavior that apply to all organisms, both animal and human. From the basic philosophical assumptions of behaviorism, to understand persons you only need to understand the laws of learning. Behavioral understandings of the person are generally that the person is a bundle of behavior patterns, reflexes, perceptions and impressions. The self is nothing more, in this view, than the aggregation or composite of the person's empirical characteristics.

In contemporary texts on behavioral assessment (e.g., Bellack & Hersen, 1998; Kazdin, 2001), persons or their personalities are not assessed but rather behaviors and their controlling variables. For example, a primary characteristic of behavioral assessment is that it provides "a hypothesized model of the client" (Haynes, 1998, p.11). This position can be taken to its logical conclusion that "personality is not a real thing" (Bellack & Hersen, 1977, p.12) Behavioral views of the person can rightly be described as atomistic; persons are best understood by looking at the "atoms" of their behavior patterns and how these atoms are arranged and related. These atoms are not seen as being held together by or emanating from any comprehensive core of the person that we might call a self. Rather, at the foundation of personhood, the behaviorist considers classical and operant learning processes as the explanation for all behavior, with a core emphasis on environmental influences on behavior. Early researchers focused on delineating theories of learning and the different mechanisms and principles that could explain learning (Krasner, 1990). So it is to these processes we now briefly turn. (These topics are immensely complex and have generated an enormous literature; thus any brief summary is bound to be misleading due to oversimplification and selective attention.)

Classical conditioning. Classical conditioning is the process by which an involuntary response becomes reflexively associated with new eliciting stimuli. All human beings exhibit reflexive, unlearned (or unconditioned) responses to stimuli that elicit these responses from us, as when the smell of food elicits salivation, a puff of air elicits eye blinking, a burn elicits pain, a noxious odor elicits nausea and so forth. These reactions do not demonstrate learning. Instead, we exhibit these responses without prior training. Pavlov showed that these reactions could be associated with new stimuli that themselves had previously not elicited these responses, which is learning at its most basic.

The classic example of this process is Pavlov's dogs, who learned to salivate at the sound of a bell because of the repeated association of the bell with the presentation of food. In this case the food was the *unconditioned stimulus* that elicited an unconditioned response of salivation. After conditioning trials the previously irrelevant bell became a *conditioned stimulus* (i.e., it became a relevant stimulus only through conditioning trials) that could elicit a conditioned response of salivation even when no food was presented.

The procedures of Wolpe's behavior therapy are based on these principles. Wolpe considered anxiety a central feature of most adult psychopathology. Anxiety can easily be conceptualized in terms of classical conditioning. For example, an intense emotional reaction (such as fear) to a "legitimate" or understandable stimulus (e.g., being bitten by a dog) can become associated through the process of classical conditioning with previously emotionally neutral stimuli (e.g., going out of one's house). In an extreme case a person unfortunate enough to make the associations between being bitten and leaving his house might become agoraphobic, profoundly fearful of being away from home and in situations where escape would be difficult. If, in trying to leave the house and overcome the anxiety, he gave into the fear and did not leave, the agoraphobic response would be further reinforced by the powerful relief from the anxiety gained through avoiding what he feared.

This analysis of the dynamics of the establishment of debilitating fears also leads to some fruitful hypotheses about fear reduction. Pavlov demonstrated that most conditioned responses could be changed or "wiped out" through two means: (1) a new response that was incompatible to the previous conditioned response could be conditioned to the conditioned stimulus, or (2) the conditioned response could be extinguished by presenting the conditioned stimulus repeatedly without pairing it with the unconditioned stimulus.

Wolpe pioneered the technique called *systematic desensitization* based on the former process of pairing a new response with the old stimulus. Wolpe understood the phenomenon of anxiety largely in terms of its physical, observable manifestations and thus reasoned that the response most antithetical to anxiety was muscular relaxation. Desensitization was developed to provide a way for relaxation to become associated with what had previously been an anxiety-evoking stimulus. A therapist would first teach an anxious client physical relaxation and then have the client slowly and gradually imagine closer and closer approaches to the anxiety-provoking stimulus while the client maintains a relaxed state. After the client is able to maintain physical relaxation while imagining a full approach to the previously feared stimulus, the therapist would then guide the client closer to real-life approaches to the feared stimulus.

Behavior therapists may also utilize Pavlov's latter notion of extinguishing the unwanted response. Extinction for the dogs occurred simply by presenting the bell, which had previously been associated with food, over and over again without any presentation of the food. In this way the salivation response to the bell eventually died out. Similarly, some argue that many forms of anxiety are best extinguished by exposing the client to the feared stimulus or stimuli without the feared outcome occurring. Exposure to a feared stimulus can be gradual or all at once. For example, Marks (1981) reported the case of a woman with a longstanding obsessive-compulsive disorder who had previously not responded to either drugs or several forms of psychotherapy, including psychoanalysis. He worked with the formulation that the fears of germs, sickness, death and so forth were generating avoidance behaviors such as compulsive cleaning rituals and avoidance of social contacts. These avoidance behaviors in turn reduced the anxiety, which reinforced the avoidance. Therapy then consisted of exposing the patient to the feared stimuli, which Marks did in an intensive inpatient treatment program. Marks had the woman touch "contaminated" objects (e.g., dirt, shoes, toilet seats, floors and used eating utensils) all while refraining from cleansing herself; she even was asked to put her soiled fingers in her mouth, to rub her clothes before putting them on and to rub her own eating utensils before using them. Within days, since there was no trauma to keep the conditioned fear alive (since the feared disease and death did not occur), the obsessive-compulsive neurosis and the anxiety causing it slowly diminished (extinguished). At follow-up, she maintained her therapeutic gains.

Operant learning. Operant learning, also called instrumental learning, refers to the modification of spontaneously emitted behavior (in contrast to the elicited behaviors we have just been discussing such as salivation or fear). These emitted behaviors are presumed to exist for the purpose of operating on the environment, hence the term *operant behavior.* Operant learning is the process by which this emitted behavior is modified over time by the *consequences* that follow contingently upon the response behavior and by the stimuli that form the context under which the behavior occurs.

The classic example is, of course, the rat in the Skinner box. Lever pressing or other forms of emitted rat behavior are modified by the consequences arranged to follow the behavior. Responses followed by such events as presentation of food or drink, or by the removal of unpleasant noise or shock, are likely to increase in frequency *(reinforcement).* Responses followed by aversive consequences such as a spray of ice water or shock, or by the removal of food or drink, are likely to decrease in frequency *(punishment).* Rats can attend to and learn to respond to stimuli, such as lights, which signal that reinforcement is available (e.g., lever pressing leads to food when only the green light is on) or unavailable (e.g., lever pressing is ineffective when the red light is on). We are more likely to smile at a passing stranger on the sidewalk if we have received smiles in return from the previous people we have passed.

Whereas classical conditioning does not create new behavior, operant conditioning can lead to new and complex behavior. First, new behaviors never before emitted by the organism can be taught through the process of *shaping.* Shaping involves reinforcing closer and closer approximations to a goal response. For example, a chicken can be taught to peck a piano key by first reinforcing the behavior of being nearer and nearer the piano, then the behavior of touching the piano closer and closer to the keyboard, until a peck on the keys can be reinforced. New complex patterns of behavior can be created by chaining, wherein more and more links between specific behaviors are required to occur together for reinforcement to be delivered, until an entire chain of behavior occurs before the final reinforcement (e.g., the chicken now raises a curtain, moves a stool, and then plays a piano).

Those who practice behavior modification posit that human behavior is largely the result of these operant processes. Human problems occur when (1) people learn maladaptive or inappropriate responses, (2) people fail to learn effective or appropriate responses due to their previous learning environments, or (3) the wrong environmental contingencies are provided in response to maladaptive behaviors. Often the cause is described as the combination of all three factors. The disruptive behavior of the aggressive child in the home and classroom may be the result of previous learning of inappropriate responses of hitting, yelling and tantrums in response to conflict. The child may also have failed to learn appropriate anger management skills and appropriate ways of expressing emotion and interacting with others. Finally, the aggressive behavior may be reinforced by peers, parents and teachers who, perhaps unwittingly, pay attention to the child when misbehavior occurs, allow the child to "get her way," and fail to reinforce appropriate behavior and interactions with peers.

Social learning theory. Learning theory approaches were forced to incorporate much more complex phenomena by the recognition that humans, and even relatively simple animals, learn not just by direct but also by observed or vicarious experience. This was behaviorism's first (and forced) engagement with cognitive phenomena, and a key step toward more clinically relevant strategies to complex human difficulties.

Social learning theory as developed by Bandura (1986) highlights the social context and relationships in which these learning processes take place and the social influences on the development of behavior. Further, social learning theory emphasizes the crucial role of cognition in selectively attending to and encoding information in one's environment, the impact of values and expectations on motivation to engage in various behaviors, and, more broadly, the interaction of cognition and the environment to construct behavior. The influence of this theory is reflected in the assessment, conceptualization of behavior and learning processes, and the clinical approaches (e.g., modeling, skill training) of contemporary BT.

Social learning theory provides a perspective on human learning not addressed by classical and operant learning theories. In particular, the concept of *observational learning* helped describe how we are affected by social influences. We learn not just by direct experience but by observing others; such observations impart information and elicit emotional reactions that influence our beliefs, expectations and self-perceptions. The impact of observational learning was described in Bandura's classic experiments on aggression in children, showing that children exposed to aggressive models behaved more aggressively, while children who viewed prosocial behavior performed by others displayed reductions in aggressive behavior.

Other important concepts embedded in social learning theory include self-efficacy and reciprocal determinism. Self-efficacy refers to how a person's beliefs or perceptions regarding his or her own capabilities to act effectively (or not) influence how he or she later behaves. Reciprocal determinism asserts that we are both the product and the creators of our environments; this in contrast to classic determinism, which emphasizes how an environment causes behavior alone. In reciprocal determinism, behavior is explained through the dynamic and reciprocal interaction of the environment with our personal factors (e.g., sex, ethnicity, temperament, beliefs, self-perceptions) and our behavior.

Notably, social learning theory provides for greater human agency than classical and operant learning processes (Bandura, 2001). Though in this view the individual is not free from the effects of the environment, there is some recognition that the individual has the ability to influence one's own behavior and impact his or her environment. According to social learning theory, humans are shaped by their environment, but are also able to be self-reflective and to engage in forethought and self-regulation of behavior. Thus, cognitive processes are given a greater role in determining behavior than in the foundational learning theories of behaviorism.

Model of Psychotherapy

Believing that behavior is caused by its environment, behavior therapy begins with a careful assessment of the factors that seem to exert influence on the problematic behavior. Modern behavior analysis is typically less mechanistic and uses a form of analysis termed *functional behavior analysis* that assesses behavior in light of its interaction with historical, motivational and situational antecedents and its expected consequences (Haynes & O'Brien, 2000). Note that persons are not assessed but behaviors and the functional relationships and contextual variables that affect behavior.

Two contemporary behavior therapy approaches, functional analytic psychotherapy (FAP) and acceptance and commitment therapy (ACT), take it a step further and assess not only the role of contextual variables but also less easily observed subjective cognitive and affective factors (Callaghan, Gregg, Marx, Kohlenberg & Gifford, 2004) in recognition of the role of intrapersonal and interpersonal experiences in the development and maintenance of clients' problems. Yet the premise of this assessment approach continues to be that a "system's" (i.e., not a person's) behavior and psychological events cannot be understood unless objectively evaluated through systematic investigation (Skinner, 1953). In BT, ongoing assessment should include multimethod, multi-informant and multimodal measurements that are aimed at decreasing bias and are interpreted with the understanding that human behavior will change depending on context, time and contingencies for the behavior. Even in FAP, which utilizes the therapeutic relationship to reinforce more adaptive, effective interpersonal behaviors through differentially responding to the client's in-session behaviors, the therapist continually assesses whether his or her contingent responses result in changes in the client's targeted problematic behaviors and distress (Kohlenberg & Tsai, 1994).

As a general example the temper tantrums of a five-year-old may be seen by the parent as caused by disrespect for authority, low self-esteem or a problem of the sinful heart (as some Christian families have described the problem). The behavior therapist, however, would collect data on the events and situational factors (antecedents) that predict the behavior and the events that reinforce it (consequences). By performing a comprehensive behavioral assessment the therapist discovers that the behavior only occurs when one parent is present and not in the presence of the other (more consistent disciplinarian) parent, that the worst misbehavior occurs when the parent uses abrupt and harsh directives (such as yelling for the child to stop what he is doing), and that the parent responds to misbehavior by yelling without any real punishment. Such cycles often escalate over time as the parent worries about "setting off" another tantrum and becomes unsure of his or her parenting. The analysis may also show that the problem behavior occurs when the parents are engaged in a heated argument and that the child's misbehavior causes the parents to cease their argument, thus allowing the child to have some control over the environment. A BT intervention in such a case occurs at the point at which action will be effective (Skinner, 1976), and might include preparing the child for difficult transitions, providing consistent negative consequences for tantrum behavior and positive consequences for cooperative behavior, and altering the family dynamics when in conflict. Intervention does not occur until a clear conceptualization of the behavior is obtained through thorough analysis.

Due to the commitment to the scientific method, behavior therapists emphasize continuing assessment both throughout and after the intervention period to verify that change is occurring and is maintained as expected. Thus, a strength of BT is the evaluation of treatment effectiveness and the subsequent modification of therapy itself. In general, the therapeutic techniques that emerge out of this model are powerful methods for teaching new behaviors and for arranging environments to make desired behavior more likely and to reduce or completely extinguish undesired behavior. Several examples will illustrate these principles and how they have been effectively used.

One of the dramatic successes of BT has been in the treatment of children with pervasive developmental disorders (PDDs), autism in particular. While the causes of these disorders are still uncertain, BT interventions are the most effective treatments for generating social behavior, everyday adaptive skills and independent functioning (Lovaas & Smith, 2003; Schreibman, Koegel, Charlop & Egel, 1990). BT for children with autism involves intensive training provided consistently for many hours per week. The goal is to modify these children's behavior by altering their environment (and thus the antecedents and consequences) and to encourage the acquisition of new skills. Children are first rewarded with tangible rewards for appropriate behavior at their current level of functioning. New, adaptive behaviors and social skills are slowly developed through shaping and chaining. Extremely dangerous behavior such as self-injurious head-banging may have to be directly punished (e.g., with time-out procedures, verbal reprimands or loss of a privilege), but as much negative behavior as possible is simply ignored with the goal of displacing negative behavior with positive response to more appropriate behavior as the child's functioning improves. Progressing from fundamental behaviors, such as language sounds and attending to others, programs reinforce increasingly more complex and socially skilled behaviors. Early, intensive interventions utilizing these strategies of BT have produced astonishing outcomes for many children with PDDs, who after treatment may display behavior and social functioning similar to children without PDDs (Newsom & Hovanitz, 2006).

Parent training and classroom behavior management programs also reflect contemporary BT practice. Skinner and others argued that the best way to manage behavior is to use positive reinforcement, but this is difficult to implement, particularly in the classroom, because misbehavior so often obtains inordinate amounts of attention from the teacher and other students. Many behavioral programs have been developed that involve direct reinforcement of positive behavior through contingency management systems, such as a reward system in the classroom or home in which children can earn tokens which count as points toward obtaining some desired reward (e.g., school supplies, a special role in the classroom, parties, sleepovers, special privileges, etc.). Because each reward is earned through points in this token economy system, teachers and parents can specify desired behavior and reinforce the child frequently. Adults are also trained to provide differential attention to appropriate behavior and to ignore disruptive and inappropriate behavior. Other students can be trained to model appropriate behavior. Such programs are effective in increasing positive social behavior, compliance and academic performance, and have been used to teach children greater self-control (DuPaul & Eckert, 1997; Mc-Mahon, Wells & Kotler, 2006).

A final example of BT is social skills training. Many individuals who report interpersonal difficulties lack critical social skills, and BT teaches clients the social skills necessary to interface more effectively with their social world. Clients are provided with instruction and modeling of specific abilities, as well as support and reinforcement for skill acquisition and practice (i.e., role plays, homework, in vivo practice). The focus is on increasing competence with discrete skills in specific social situations (e.g., enhanced listening, or assertiveness in a job). In general, social skills training with adults and children, in outpatient and inpatient settings, has been found to produce clinically significant effects on outcomes such as social performance, self-esteem and decreased anxiety (Morrison, 1990).

CHRISTIAN CRITIQUE

Philosophical Assumptions

The first philosophical presupposition we mentioned in regard to behavior therapy was naturalism. Obviously, naturalism is at odds with the Christian faith: God exists and is above nature since he is the maker of nature, and therefore dogmatic naturalism is false. There are such supernatural entities as God, angels, the devil and demons. However, this quick dismissal of doctrinaire naturalism is not an endorsement of the opposite belief—that human beings are purely supernatural beings.

Authors such as Boivin (1985) have argued that while Christians must reject a behavioristic worldview that denies the reality of the supernatural, it may be biblical to assert that while there are supernatural entities that interact with the created order, the created order itself (including humanity) is purely naturalistic. Compare the words of Watson (1930), "Man is an animal different from other animals only in the types of behavior he displays" (p.v) with the words of Boivin (1985), "Only our relationship and responsibility to God makes us qualitatively different from animals" (p.83). Boivin asserts that a Christian understanding of the person does not need to posit more than a natural existence for humanity. He supports this view by pointing to the Hebraic notion of the unity of human existence, to the doctrines of embodied life and to the confusion of traditional Christian anthropology about soul and spirit. He suggests, in short, that naturalism is true with reference to human beings.

We agree that there has been at times a misplaced emphasis on doctrines of disembodied souls in the Christian tradition. Nonetheless, the Christian faith seems to require viewing persons as partially immaterial beings. The naturalism of behaviorism does, however, remind us that humans have pridefully underestimated the extent to which our embodied existence conditions, shapes and even determines some aspects of our experience. As suggested by Browning and Cooper (2004), as long as we are careful not to completely swallow the most dogmatic of philosophical assumptions underlying BT, that of pure naturalism with no acknowledgment of a spiritual nature, self-transcendence and freedom, we can and should take seriously how external reinforcement contingencies do influence our behaviors and personhood. The success of BT in clear cases of conditioned anxiety (phobias) belies our creature nature and the forces of learning on us. But in emphasizing only bodily existence, the behaviorist misses a key aspect of human nature—the interplay of body and soul-spirit and the distinctively transcendent aspects of our natures.

The behavioristic rejection of "mentalism" and its view of the mind are also problematic. If thought is merely a behavioral disposition or a byproduct of physical brain events, then humans cannot transcend the physical order of things. This provides a conceptual grounding for the doctrine of determinism. As we shall see in the paragraphs to come, such determinism is not acceptable. Christian belief does not lead to an easy resolution to the brain-mind issue, though it does set up certain parameters within which to choose proper resolutions to the matter (Jones, 1985). One of these parameters, though, must be some notion that thought is more than just an epiphenomenon, as strict behaviorism presupposes. Christians cannot accept a notion that belief and thought are not effectual causes of behavior.

We have already delineated how behaviorists accept determinism and thus reject the concept of freedom and consciousness. Even so, it is common to read of "freely emitted behavior" and even "freedom" in behavioral writings. Zuriff (1985) is helpful here in noting that the language of freedom or action is used in BT to designate behaviors that are not reflexively elicited or coerced. In this view, a certain action (for example, raising a hand) is free if the behavior coincides with one's desires (as when waving bye-bye to a child) but is not free when it is against one's desires (as when one raises both hands during a robbery or in response to stimulation of the motor cortex of the brain during neurosurgery). Note though that all of the actions in these examples would be regarded by the behaviorist as causally determined; the first two by the "laws of learning" and the last one by neurological stimulation.

What makes the first instance of waving "free" for the behaviorist is not that one could have acted otherwise under the same circumstances; in the behavioral analysis one could not have done so given one's learning history and the current context (e.g., interaction with a child). It was "free," in the view of Skinner and others, because the enacting of that behavior was not unpleasant for the actor and it was in accord with the person's causally predetermined desires at the moment. In other words, the actor had the subjective experience of choice, but the choice and the desires that motivated it were really predetermined by learning history. To the behaviorist all behavior is regarded as inevitable; we can never do other than what we do.

In critiquing this view we must first note that not all psychologists engaged in modern forms of BT use mechanistic forms of analysis that are characteristic of this strict behaviorist assumption. In addition, clients who make an active choice to engage in BT and alter a problematic behavior (rather than those "in charge" of behavior modification plans) are in effect acting on their environment, which in turn will act on their behaviors. Indeed, as mentioned in the introduction of this chapter, modern forms of BT utilize "mindfulness" and "acceptance," indicating that the mental and motivational aspects of our personhood cannot be denied in treatment.

The coupling of environmental influences and freedom can be seen within Christianity as well; we are called to make the active choice of putting ourselves in an environment and in conditions (e.g., community, workplace, social and leisure activities) that encourage "a new way" to promote behavior change and spiritual growth (Browning & Cooper, 2004; Lasure & Mikulas, 1996). Some have argued that the commonalities between behaviorism and Christianity should be given more attention, including the emphasis within behaviorism on improving quality of life and Christian strivings of being free from or avoiding sin (e.g., Rom 7:7-25) (Galuska, 2003). It is further argued that BT could offer resolution to these strivings through behavioral techniques (e.g., self-control, reinforcement) (Galuska, 2003). Though we do not deny the utility of behavioral interventions, as Zuriff (1985) stated, at the core behavioristic psychology "is not ... compatible with the notion of a free-willed self-initiating agent" (p.199).

We argued in chapter two that Christian belief requires a rejection of determinism—the view that every human event is the inevitable outcome of preceding events—and requires belief in limited freedom. Though some Christian psychologists (e.g., Bufford, 1981) and some Christian groups embrace such a strong view of God's sovereignty that they could be labeled theological determinists, such a position has not been typical of historic, orthodox Christianity. John Calvin is commonly believed to have denied the freedom of persons, but along with Muller and Vande Kemp (1985), we would argue that his belief in God's sovereignty, divine election, predestination and the depravity of the human will cannot be equated with the philosophical determinism accepted by most behaviorists. Human freedom is even defended in the Calvinistic tradition, as stated in the Westminster Confession of Faith (Leith, 1973): "God hath endued the will of man with that natural liberty, that [it] is neither forced nor by any absolute necessity of nature determined to good or evil."

In most segments of the Christian tradition, human beings are regarded as responsible, as morally culpable. Responsibility for our actions seems to require the capacity to have acted other than we did in a given situation. Thus, from a Christian perspective total determinism is unacceptable and limited freedom is an essential belief (Evans, 1977). The Christian must believe that a person's choices are sometimes the ultimate and deciding factor in the occurrence of an action in order to believe that we are truly responsible beings who can be held accountable for our actions before God.

Yet note that causes do not have to be exclusive. To argue that in a particular instance the person was an ultimate cause does not rule out that other causes also affected the behavioral outcome. Even though we make real choices, we do so as persons with experiences and constraints that exert an effect. Accepting the notion of agent causation does not mean denying the assertion that some or even much of our behavior is determined, or that the true choices of a free agent are shaped, by constitutional or environmental factors.

The Christian concept of limited freedom is not the same as freedom from regularity, freedom from influences on behavior or freedom from finitude. It simply means that the final choices that create behavior were not merely the result of impersonal forces, and the person choosing was not merely a "locus" of influences coming together. Rather, the person decided among real options, influenced by his or her history and constitution. This position has been excellently delineated by Browning and Cooper (2004, p.102):

> The doctrine of the freedom, transcendence and responsibility of humans does not mean that we are totally free and completely unconditioned by either internal impulse or external reinforcements. In fact, it means just the opposite. It means that in spite of our massive conditionedness by these forces, there is still a sufficient modicum of transcendence over them to make it possible for us to alter, to some meaningful degree, the course of our lives.

It would seem that we are stuck with incompatible perspectives on this topic; determinism and limited freedom do not in fact appear to be reconcilable.

Positively, we can learn from behavior modification that our behavior is influenced and shaped by many factors that we are often unaware of. In denying determinism Christians are often in danger of embracing a prideful claim that their choices and actions are totally free and unconditioned by their material existence. We are dangerously close to a self-deifying view that denies our finitude and dependency. It also seems true that human beings are a composite of lower and higher capacities, and that we erroneously want to deny the real role conditioning influences play in our basic psychological makeup.

Model of Personality

We introduced earlier the atomistic view of the person embedded in behaviorist psychology. In this view there are no necessary interrelationships between discrete components of the person's behavior. If interrelationships exist between clusters of behaviors, as when a person tends to lie and to steal, they are thereby the accident of conditioned association or some such process. There is no necessary grounding of any particular behavior or behavior pattern in a self.

A concept of general human responsibility is thus impossible, since each behavioral pattern has its own specific controlling conditions that bear no necessary relationship to the person as a whole. There is no "person" to hold responsible for the behavior exhibited, which is why Skinner (1971) could call for the abolition of our criminal jurisprudence system; there really are no persons to be punished but only response patterns to be modified, and thus behavior modification should replace judicial punishment. Further, one negative behavior pattern (e.g., repeated lying) does not make the person a bad person; rather, the lying is a behavior pattern that needs to be modified. There is, in fact, no "good" or "bad" within our characters, merely behavior patterns that are unrelated to the "person," as the person does not exist.

There is a certain clinical wisdom and utility to such an approach, in that the spurious overidentification by a client with a particular negative aspect of her or his behavior is genuinely problematic. We have known sincere Christians who ignore many positive areas of discipline and maturity in their lives to focus on one negative pattern ("I've not been able to kick this bad habit; I am an evil, unlovable person!"). Thus, religious thinkers can come away from BT with crucial insight: not every behavior pattern is a true index of the state of the self. One person's rudeness in a situation may be an accurate index of their arrogance, pride and selfdeification. The exact same act by another person may be an anomaly related to being inattentive to social cues at that moment. Perhaps even behavior patterns that are good indices of the condition of the heart will have to be changed deliberately after the heart changes. Old, sinful habit patterns do not automatically change when the heart changes.

Even so, Christian thought requires the identification of specific behaviors in some significant manner with the unified person, because a person who commits specific behavioral acts that are sins must be capable of validly being labeled a sinner. In a powerful way, a person's behavioral acts often are diagnostic of the inner condition of the "heart," or unified core of the person. As Christ said, "By their fruit you will recognize them" (Mt 7:16). Behaviors are not atoms unconnected with the heart; they are often (but not always) evidence of what lies in the heart. If we deny that persons are unified beings, then there is no one to hold responsible for sin, no unified person to be redeemed and sanctified or punished, and sins are just behaviors which occur in a person's body or in his or her actions, but are unconnected with the person per se. Atomism is thus unacceptable, though instructive, to the Christian.

Every theory of personality has a view of human motivation, though we have dealt only implicitly with it in BT thus far. The behavioral view is both simple and complex. First, BT is simple in proposing that human survival is the driving, evolutionarily based motivation behind our behavior. As Browning and Cooper (2004) and others have pointed out, there are remarkable parallels between Skinner's environmental reinforcement and Darwin's concept of natural selection. For the Darwinian evolutionist nature "selects" species that successfully adapt to their environmental niche. For the behaviorist the environment "selects" behaviors by reinforcing those responses that aid survival and adaptation to the organism's niche in life.

Looking only at rat behavior in Skinner boxes, we often mistakenly imagine reinforcement to be something that others (behavioral engineers or parents) intentionally do because they deliberately want to change the behavior of the subject (rat or child). Yet in the "real world," reinforcement and punishment occur naturally depending on how good of a match the organism's behavior is to the demands of the environment. For example, a particular type of hunting behavior by a predator may be reinforced by a successful kill because the hunting behavior meshed well with nature. To Skinner, individual adaptation to the environment, and hence greater chance of survival, is the motivation for human behavior. One of the distinctives of behaviorism is that it proposes a small list of inherent motivations or instincts that are themselves critical to survival, including such drives as for food, drink and sex (Herrnstein, 1977).

However, the behavioral view of motivation becomes exquisitely complex when we realize that almost anything can become a reinforcer that motivates performance through its association with more primary or basic reinforcers. Things like money or verbal praise become reinforcement through constant association with primary reinforcers such as food, warmth and sexual outlet. In this way we can be led to value (and hence be motivated by) a diversity of stimuli, including financial reward, the praise of our parents and peers, or interpersonal recognition. Further, response patterns like academic excellence, artistic creativity, physical brutality and psychopathic manipulation can become vehicles for obtaining primary reinforcers and hence the response patterns can come to have a positive value in their own right. So in the behaviorist analysis there is no one core human motivation that is easily appealed to in order to understand human behavior. Rather, human motivation is idiosyncratically organized; each person's motivations may be different from those of others.

Christians may applaud the motivational diversity of behavior therapy, but be rightly troubled by its assumption that all effective motivations ultimately depend on basal drives shared with animals. Additionally, moral concepts of altruism and unconditional love of other become mere behavioral reactions to reinforcement. Christians must claim that human beings are capable of acting out of higher motives, such as the desire to serve God, and that these higher motives cannot always be reduced to the drive for tangible reinforcement.

A Christian judgment that human motivations ought to be more noble and higher may be valid; at the same time, appeals to "higher motives" may be ineffective incentives to change a person's behavior. For instance, Christians often object to token economies for their problem children on the grounds that the children ought to obey their parents and do their chores because "it is the right thing to do," not to earn points to purchase video games. But when a disruptive child is motivated only by the avoidance of punishment and rewards, those appetites may be the best avenue for modification of the child's behavior. Such an initial change may establish the very possibility of the child being motivated by other things, such as a respectful and loving relationship with a parent. Having children obey their parents, improve their school performance and attend church to earn tokens to buy toys may be the best way to expose them to activities which they ought to value more, and thus increase the likelihood that they will come to prefer them. Just because Christianity teaches that people ought to value more than material things does not mean they do, and there is no psychotherapy system more humble and realistic about the depth to which human motivation can sink than BT.

The approach also suggests a technology for the alteration of human values and motives through the acquisition of skills and association of events. As Clouse (1985) put it, "God created us as beings who respond to reinforcers and punishers in our environment" (p.94). Perhaps it is the original sin of human pride and self-reliance more than anything that makes us prone to believe that we supersede all environmental influence. The deliberate structuring of our environments to build up righteous behavior seems a helpful lesson to learn from behavior modification. The New Testament epistles often give instructions not for individual effort and growth, but to the creation of powerful fellowship contexts, which can be effective mechanisms for the modification of individual behavior. Sometimes the best path to personal change is the immersion of the individual into the community, with the person thus being subject to the contingencies of the personal consequences of that community. The behavioral analysis of this influence is, on an ultimate level, unsatisfactory, but it points us to an aspect of personal reality to which we might not otherwise attend.

We can also mention in passing the behavioral view of good and evil (see Browning & Cooper, 2004). For the behaviorist, good and evil as such do not exist, because there are no values that exist outside of human conditioning patterns. Moral codes, to Skinner, are believed to embody codified instructions about how to obtain reinforcement (this is the "good") and avoid punishment (the things that are "bad"). A moral absolute such as "Thou shalt not steal" is behaviorally understood as expressing the normative pattern in a particular culture that persons can generally expect rewards for honesty and diligence, and punishment for theft and cheating. Browning and Cooper (2004) convincingly argue that a close examination of Skinner's work, especially of his famous utopian novel about a behavioristic community, *Walden Two,* shows that beneath Skinner's purportedly purely evolutionary ethic lies a commitment to a radical egalitarian justice ethic that places special emphasis on the "primary goods of liberty and opportunity" (p.99). Because this detailed examination of Skinnerian ethics is more relevant to Skinner's utopian aspirations rather than to behavior modification as a therapy system, we refer the reader to Browning and Cooper for further information.

One of the most frequent criticisms of BT is that its views of the person are simplistic. However, it is not the case that behaviorists think human behavior is simple. They acknowledge that we are capable of exquisitely complex behavior and that we are affected by complex environments. Complex behavior is attributed to the human capacity for enacting complex chains of behavior, for making fine discriminations between stimuli so that our complex behavior is well tailored to our exact circumstances, and for being guided by symbolic rules. These rules are regarded as mere compound stimuli that shape our behavior. Thus, though the basic processes governing behavior are simple, just as simple brushstrokes of color may grow into paintings of the most exquisite sorts, so simple learning processes can yield behavioral patterns of true complexity.

The core of our complaint then must not be that BT sees human behavior simplistically but rather that by reducing human processes to instances of basic learning concepts, it does irrevocable harm to our view of persons. This is reductionism. The danger is that at some point in reductionistic arguments, what is essential for maintaining a holistic view of what it means to be human will be lost. At the point where the human as a self, as a person, disappears and is replaced by conditioned response patterns, reductionism has gone too far. On the other hand, we must remember that to intervene, or to have science at all, some level of reductionism is necessary. At some point we must determine that our assessment is as complete as necessary or possible, and that we are unable to gain a truly full understanding of the complex and unique person whom we are treating. We must choose an intervention that will most likely focus on only a particular component of our conceptualization. If counselors had to understand clients in all their unique and incredible complexity before intervening, no counseling would ever get done.

The issue is whether in the process of simplification too much gets lost. We would argue that this is indeed the case in behaviorism. Even though basic learning processes can yield startling complexity, it still demeans humanity to regard all behavior as resulting from basic learning processes. (It is not demeaning, however, to suggest that some or even much of our behavior may be shaped by such processes.) The fundamental and irrevocable weakness of behavior modification is that in the process of reducing complexity to fundamental processes, all that is recognizably and distinctly human disappears.

We now turn to a further examination of the concepts of consequence and habit. Remember from chapter two that a Christian view of persons asserts that we were created to exercise purposeful dominion over the earth. We might conclude from this that we are intrinsically goal-oriented beings whose actions are meant to produce tangible outcomes in our world. Hence, it is not nonsense from a Christian point of view to expect human beings to be influenced by the consequences of their actions. Scripture is full, if you will, of direct appeals to act in our own welfare, as C.S. Lewis (1980) pointed out so well in his sermon "The Weight of Glory." God through his revealed Word promises us unimaginable and eternal rewards both now and in the hereafter if we will but become his followers, and unimaginable punishment if we do not (see Piper, 1977). As Bufford (1981) effectively argues, one of the primary ways God deals with humanity is through consequences for our actions, and it would be foolish to deny that human behavior is profoundly shaped by the contingencies we perceive and interact with. Thus, behaviorism has something to remind us of.

However, we cannot simply state that behaviorism is true because rewards are discussed in the Bible. First, in BT, reinforcement (not rewards) is used in a technical sense that entails implications about human behavior and nature that Christians cannot accept. The concept of reward, in the Christian view, often implies moral worthiness to receive the reward, not just manipulation by consequences. Second, any psychological theory can make sense of human beings responding to material incentives; so BT is merely unique in the emphasis on this dynamic rather than being the only theory that recognizes it. Nevertheless, it seems true that by emphasizing this human tendency to respond to incentives, unique and effective means of intervening can be developed, especially with specific populations, such as with children and individuals with profound developmental disabilities, for whom verbal methods are less likely to effect change.

Christian thought is also hospitable to the notion of habit. In fact, the biblical counseling method of Jay Adams is actually built in part around the notion that both sinful and righteous behaviors can and do become habits. Adams (1979, chap.14) argues that the core of a Christian counseling approach is contained in Ephesians 4:22-24, where we are instructed to lay aside the old self and put on the new self. Adams argues that these terms of self refer essentially to habit patterns formed out of the choices one has accommodated oneself to. Thus, for Adams, laying aside the old self is "dehabituation" and putting on the new self is "rehabituation" (p.237). Habit is said to be "a great blessing of God that has been misused by sinners" (p.161). The capacity to respond automatically is misused through its adaptation to perform sinful acts out of habit, as when we train our hearts in greed (2 Pet 2:14; see also Jer 13:23). Adams argues that the believer can also develop godly habits with the help of the Holy Spirit (Heb 5:14), and that these habits can be undermined by, for example, "bad company" (1 Cor 15:33). A Christian view of persons recognizes the place of habit in human life, which behavior modification certainly does. However, Adams would distinguish his approach from behavior modification especially in his assertion that real change only happens with the indwelling of the Holy Spirit, and not through human effort alone.

Model of Psychotherapy

Applied behaviorism has often been criticized with reference to how it might be applied in a utopian attempt to shape humanity. For instance, many regard C.S. Lewis's famous science fiction novel *That Hideous Strength* to have been an early antibehavioristic tract (and a thought-provoking one it is!). More directly, Van Leeuwen (1979b, 1979c) and Browning and Cooper (2004) critique and draw implications from *Walden Two,* Skinner's behavioristic utopian novel. It is a recurrent theme among critics of Skinner that in spite of his deterministic assumptions, he often makes pronouncements that demonstrate his implicit ethical commitment of how we should or must implement behavioral control technology on a society-wide basis if we are to see "what man can make from man" (Skinner, 1971, p.206).

His critics point out the contradiction of saying on the one hand that "all behavior is determined, everything happens as it must," while at the same time saying, "we must seize the opportunity now to reform and reshape humanity to save our race and better our plight." Browning and Cooper (2004) are correct in judging Skinner to be endorsing something like societal husbandry to cultivate the types of behavior patterns among the populace that the elite behavior-control experts would judge as being for the common good of our species. Such a system would of necessity become elitist and totalitarian. On the basis of these tendencies many dismiss behavior modification. We will not interact further with how behaviorism might be implemented as social policy and grapple instead with how it is used clinically.

Let us first address what are for many the most troublesome cases in which the recipients of therapy are not able or willing to agree to the change process. What of behavior modification with the developmentally disabled or as applied on inpatient psychiatric wards where patients may be detained against their will? There are some legitimate similarities between behavior modification applied in these situations and the more speculative accounts of how they might be applied in a totalitarian system. First, we must acknowledge that the interventions in these situations are generally applied with the consent of the parent, legal guardian or custodian of the persons in the interest of their best welfare. Second, this particular dilemma is one faced by all coercive applications of therapy methods.

Further, those engaged in BT typically view what they are doing as building necessary behavior changes to equip clients to acquire greater freedom and choice in life. Rebellious adolescents, it could be argued, are actually experiencing diminished freedom because their behaviors are largely being shaped by deviant social cues and reinforcement, and they are missing out on other age-appropriate opportunities. Thus, coercive intervention may be necessary to alter established behavior patterns, as when adolescents engaged in risky or self-injurious behavior must conform to a behavior management system on an inpatient unit or in the home. Hopefully, the new, healthy behavior acquires greater value and the deviant behavior fades. Even highly aversive treatment, such as punishment by shock or physical restraint, may be necessary to disrupt highly destructive behavior such as self-abuse.

Another example of a coercive treatment that demonstrates the effectiveness of BT as well as the values that are implicitly held by this treatment modality is behavioral treatment of children with developmental delays. As described earlier, BT for children with autism and related disorders involves an intensive protocol. As part of the treatment, several coercive techniques might be used to decrease aggressive and self-stimulatory behaviors, including time-out, the shaping of alternative, more socially acceptable behavior, and the provision of a loud "no" or slap on the thigh or hand (Lovaas, 1987). The outcome of these interventions is typically quite good, with the eventual decrease or complete extinction of these unwanted behaviors. BT in this case is used to achieve the goal of creating and enhancing the child's eventual freedom from aggressive and self-stimulatory behaviors, much like the Christian idea of dying to sin in order to experience freedom from sin. To many the outcome of this coercive treatment is desirable and beneficial; however, some argue that this treatment approach is unethical or, at the extreme, that treatment of autism spectrum disorders as a whole are invalid as these individuals (and their behaviors) are inappropriately deemed disordered. Interestingly, the controversy indicates that our view of psychopathology and treatment is ultimately grounded in varying particular beliefs of what good human functioning should resemble.

We can see some legitimacy to the behaviorist's argument that coercive treatment is valid when the suffering person is failing to act in self-enhancing fashions. What compassionate person will accept the strident demands of a twelve-year-old that only her peer group should tell her how to behave? Who will withhold shock punishment from a mentally challenged individual who has a ten-year history of horrible head banging, when this treatment promises to eliminate that behavior in two days?

However, what legitimately frightens skeptical nonbehaviorists is the lack of any sharp and clear delineation in the theory of how practitioners distinguish between incompetent and competent persons, and between adaptive and maladaptive behavior patterns, especially since in the behavioristic view, everyone's actions are determined anyway. Behavior modification is trumpeted as a tool that can be applied to change any behavior. What then will stop abuses such as the application of "behavioral principles" in prisoner-of-war camps where human beings were deprived of sufficient food to make them more responsive to food as a reinforcer for compliance and hard work? The potential for such abuses is frightening.

In the outpatient situation, however, BT is less controversial and has even been referred to as "amoral" (Woolfolk & Richardson, 1984). That is, although behavior modification has values built into its system, as a therapy model it has a much less well-developed notion of human health or perfection than the classic psychoanalytic or humanistic models. Its supporters argue that a less defined ideal allows for greater flexibility of direction and less intrusive influence of the therapy's embedded values. Its application, in other words, is usually put more at the disposal of the client based on the client's values. This argument may be somewhat true, but our concern is that such amorality would simply relocate the influence from a relatively public therapeutic model to a more elusive and idiosyncratic locus (i.e., the personal opinions and values of the therapist). Hence, its techniques can be pointed in many directions, as its abuses show. Without a built-in explicit model of healthy humanness, behavior modification becomes almost a collection of techniques in search of an application, as Tan (1987) has noted.

The fact that behavior modification has developed a diversity of techniques is both a strength and a weakness. On the surface, students of BT often feel they are studying a loosely woven collage of intervention strategies. None of the other therapies rival BT in the degree to which treatment for different persons can be truly individualized because of the many techniques found in the model, and this is a strength. Further, its supporters argue that BT is not a set of techniques but a framework for analysis and modification, based on a purposefully clear and simple approach to theory-development of human behavior (i.e., systematic and ongoing evaluation of behavior and controlling factors). And yet the most frequent complaint against BT is its superficiality, and the appearance of superficiality is certainly strengthened by the chaotic breadth of technologies available. This apparent superficiality may reflect the more profound lack of a central organizing understanding of personhood at the center of the model.

Another reason that BT is judged superficial is that its view of persons is ahistorical; the important determinants of human action (and hence of personality) are almost exclusively in the present. While behavioral therapists use concepts such as learning history, their emphasis is on the current determinants of behavior. The origins of the self-defeating habit pattern are of little intrinsic interest to the therapist; the factors that cue the behavior and currently reinforce it are preeminent.

The issue here is the cause of distress, and the behavior therapists do have a point worth considering, that of how an event from the past can have any causal impact on us now. They argue that past events must be made current in some form to affect us in the present. So if a person is troubled by memories of a traumatic event from the past, the determinants of their current memories must be examined rather than the event in the past. Some Christians might view this present focus as a strength, in that it facilitates accountability and action for growth. Others would view it negatively in that it trivializes a person's sense of history and hence sense of self.

Of all the therapy models the person of the therapist is least important in BT (Tan, 1987). Behavior therapists have been forced by empirical research to admit that the quality of the therapist-client relationship is a powerful determinant of therapeutic outcome, and modern forms of BT reflect their acknowledgment and use of the therapeutic relationship to foster change. BT has evolved with use of the relationship as an important medium through which reinforcement and modeling occur and a source of motivation for the client (Kohlenberg, Hayes & Tsai, 1993). However, this finding has been brought into the model after the fact, and to many behavior therapists, the efficacy of therapy lies in the techniques applied to client problems rather than the relationship being an influential or curative variable in and of itself.

BT corresponds well to the Christian concept of stewardship. Stewardship would dictate that Christian counselors be committed to documenting the effectiveness of their efforts. It is easy for counselors to get a warm feeling that they are helping people, but if hard research would show that the people who talk to those counselors were, three years after the end of therapy, no better off than before entering therapy, then all the warm feelings in the world would not justify the time and expense invested in the counseling.

Behavior therapists are typically more committed than many other practitioners to outcome evaluation, which is actually one of the defining principles that shapes the field. They seek hard documentation for the outcomes they strive for. There exists a large body of evidence from clinical research studies and meta-analyses of the efficacy of BT and cognitive-behavioral therapy for specific psychological problems. On the other hand, there also exist meta-analyses that compare various forms of psychotherapy that have not proven the greater efficacy of BT with general populations or for specific disorders (e.g., Dunn & Schwebel, 1995; Parloff, London & Wolfe, 1986; Smith, Glass & Miller, 1980). BT may be particularly useful for specific populations. For instance, behavior modification has emerged as the most efficacious treatment for children and adolescents (Casey & Berman, 1985; Weisz, Weiss, Alicke & Klotz, 1987; Weiss & Weisz, 1995). Overall, the emphasis on outcome evaluation of psychotherapy in this model should be commended. If counseling were not a profession established on the presumption of effectiveness, this might not matter. But it is built on that presumption, and efforts should be directed at establishing such accountability.

CONCLUSION

The fundamental vision of humanity embedded in the behaviorist tradition is one of humans as temporal beings only, motivated by survival and successful adaption to a challenging environment. Our capacities for learning, which so often serve us well, can go awry with the result that we learn conditioned responses and operant behaviors that interfere with our capacity to deal adaptively with the challenges life throws our way. Despite being determined by our learning histories, human beings can change through their efforts and their interactions with those around them. Through the creative application of techniques based on research in the basic psychology of learning, human problems can be ameliorated.

From a Christian perspective the behaviorist claims of materialism and determinism are easily rejected. Yet the model serves to remind us of our createdness and temporality. While we are transcendent beings, we are not only transcendent. In our temporality and creature nature, the reality of habit, the power of consequences and our environments, and the very "conditionedness" of our existence must be more thoroughly understood and accepted by Christian counselors. Although persons may not be understood as only loose collections of action patterns and potentials, we are beings whose behavior has different degrees of relatedness to the conditions of our hearts. Behavior modification provides effective procedures for dealing with many problems and populations. Nevertheless, though BT may give us a useful account of our creatureliness, it falls far short in appreciating our higher human capacities.

FOR FURTHER READING

Bufford, R. (1981). *The human reflex: Behavioral psychology in biblical perspective.* San Francisco, CA: Harper & Row.

A sympathetic apology for behaviorism by a "Christian behaviorist."

Lattal, K.A., & Chase, P.N. (Eds.). (2003). *Behavior theory and philosophy.* New York, NY: Kluwer.

A recent in-depth exploration of the philosophical roots of behaviorism.

O'Donohue, W.T., Henderson, D.A., Hayes, S.C., Fisher, J.E., & Hayes, L. (2001). *A history of the behavioral therapies: Founders' personal histories.* Reno, NV: Context Press.

An insider's look at the history of behavior therapy as related by the founders.

Woolfolk, R., and Richardson, F. (1984). Behavior therapy and the ideology of modernity. *American Psychologist, 39* (7), 777-786.

A penetrating analysis of how behavior therapy reflects aspects of our Western cultural milieu.

REFERENCES

Adams, J. (1979). *More than redemption: A theology of Christian counseling.* Phillipsburg, NJ: Presbyterian & Reformed.

Bandura, A. (1986). *Social foundations of thought and action.* Englewood Cliffs, NJ: Prentice-Hall.

Bandura, A. (2001). Social cognitive theory: An agentic perspective. *Annual review of psychology,* Vol.52 (pp.1-26). Palo Alto, CA: Annual Reviews.

Baucom, D.H., Shoham, V., Meuser, K.T., Daiuto, A.D., & Stickle, T.R. (1998). Empirically supported couple and family interventions for marital distress and adult mental health problems. *Journal of Consulting and Clinical Psychology, 66,* 53-88

Baum, W.M. (1994). *Understanding behaviorism: Science, behavior, and culture.* New York, NY: HarperCollins.

Bellack, A.S., & Hersen, M. (1977). *Behavior modification: An introductory textbook.* New York, NY: Oxford University Press.

Bellack, A.S., & Hersen, M. (Eds.). (1998). *Behavioral assessment: A practical handbook* (4th ed.). Needham Heights, MA: Allyn & Bacon.

Berry, W. (2001). *Life is a miracle: An essay against modern superstition.* New York, NY: Basic Books.

Boivin, M. (1985). Behavioral psychology: What does it have to offer the Christian church? *Journal of the American Scientific Affiliation, 37,* 79-85.

Brown, H. (1977). *Perception, theory and commitment: The new philosophy of science.* Chicago, IL: University of Chicago Press.

Browning, D.S., & Cooper, T.D. (2004). *Religious thought and the modern psychologies* (2nd ed.). Minneapolis, MN: Fortress Press.

Bufford, R. (1981). *The human reflex: Behavioral psychology in biblical perspective.* San Francisco, CA: Harper & Row.

Callaghan, G.M., Gregg, J.A., Marx, B.P., Kohlenberg, B.S., & Gifford, E. (2004). FACT: The utility of an integration of functional analytic psychotherapy and acceptance and commitment therapy to alleviate human suffering. *Psychotherapy: Theory, Research, Practice, and Training, 41,* 195-207.

Casey, R.J., & Berman, J.S. (1985). The outcome of psychotherapy with children. *Psychological Bulletin, 98,* 388-400.

Clouse, B. (1985). Moral reasoning and Christian faith. *Journal of Psychology and Theology, 13,* 190-198.

Dueck, A., & Parsons, T.D. (2004). Integration discourse: Modern and postmodern. *Journal of Psychology and Theology, 32,* 232-247.

Dunn, R.L., & Schwebel, A.I. (1995). Meta-analytic review of marital therapy outcome research. *Journal of Family Psychology, 9,* 58-68.

DuPaul, G.J., & Eckert, T.L. (1997). The effects of school-based intervention for attention deficit hyperactivity disorder: A meta-analysis. *School Psychology Digest, 26,* 5-27.

Erwin, E. (1978). *Behavior therapy: Scientific, philosophical and moral foundations.* New York, NY: Cambridge University Press.

Evans, C. (1989). *Wisdom and humanness in psychology.* Grand Rapids, MI: Baker.

Evans, C.S. (1977). *Preserving the person: A look at the human sciences.* Grand Rapids, MI: Baker Books.

Eyberg, S.M. (1988). Parent-child interaction therapy: Integration of traditional and behavioral concerns. *Child and Family Behavior Therapy, 10,* 33-46.

Galuska, C.M. (2003). Advancing behaviorism in a Judeo-Christian culture. In K.A. Lattal & P.N. Chase (Eds.), *Behavior theory and philosophy* (pp.259-274). New York, NY: Kluwer.

Gergen, K.J. (2001). Psychological science in a postmodern context. *American Psychologist, 56,* 803-813.

Gorsuch, R.L. (2002). The pyramids of sciences and of humanities: Implications for the search for religious "truth." *American Behavioral Scientist, 45,* 1822-1838.

Hayes, S.C. (2004). Acceptance and commitment therapy and the new behavior therapies. In S.C. Hayes, V.M. Follette & M. Linehan (Eds.), *Mindfulness and acceptance: Expanding the cognitive-behavioral tradition* (pp.1-29). New York, NY: Guilford Press.

Hayes, S.C., Follette, V.M., & Linehan, M. (Eds.). (2004). *Mindfulness and acceptance: Expanding the cognitive-behavioral tradition.* New York, NY: Guilford Press.

Hayes, S.C., Strosahl, K.D., & Wilson, K.G. (1999). *Acceptance and commitment therapy: An experiential approach to behavior change.* New York, NY: Guilford Press.

Haynes, S.N. (1998). The changing nature of behavioral assessment. In A.S. Bellack & M. Hersen (Eds.), *Behavioral assessment: A practical handbook* (4th ed.). Needham Heights, MA: Allyn & Bacon.

Haynes, S.N., & O'Brien, W.H. (2000). *Principles and practice of behavioral assessment.* New York, NY: Kluwer/Plenum.

Hembree-Kigin, T.L., & McNeil, C.B. (1995). *Parent-child interaction therapy.* New York, NY: Plenum Press.

Herrnstein, R. (1977). The evolution of behaviorism. *American Psychologist, 32,* 593-603.

Jacobson, N.S., & Christensen, A. (1996). *Integrative couple therapy: Promoting acceptance and change.* New York, NY: Guilford Press.

Jacobson, N.S., Christensen, A., Prince, S.E., Cordova, J., & Eldridge, K. (2000). Integrative behavioral couple therapy: An acceptance-based, promising new treatment for couple discord. *Journal of Consulting and Clinical Psychology, 68,* 351-355.

Jones, S. (1985). Mind-brain relationship. In D. Benner (Ed.), *Baker encyclopedia of psychology* (pp.712-715). Grand Rapids, MI: Baker.

Jones, S.L. (1994). A constructive relationship for religion with the science and profession of psychology: Perhaps the boldest model yet. *American Psychologist, 49* (3), 184-199.

Kazdin, A.E. (2001). *Behavior modification: In applied settings* (6th ed.). Belmont, CA: Wadsworth.

Kohlenberg, R.J., Hayes, S.C., & Tsai, M. (1993). Radical behavioral psychotherapy: Two contemporary examples. *Clinical Psychology Review, 13,* 579-592.

Kohlenberg, R.J., & Tsai, M. (1994). Functional analytic psychotherapy: A radical behavioral approach to treatment and integration. *Journal of Psychotherapy Integration, 4,* 175-201.

Krasner, L. (1990). History of behavior modification. In A.S. Bellack, M. Hersen & A.E. Kazdin (Eds.), *International handbook of behavior modification and therapy* (pp.3-26). New York, NY: Plenum Press.

Kuhn, T.S. (1996). *The structure of scientific revolutions* (3rd ed.). Chicago, IL: University of Chicago Press. (Original work published 1962).

Lasure, L.C., & Mikulas, W.L. (1996). Biblical behavior modification. *Behavior Research and Therapy, 34,* 563-566.

Leith, J. (1973). *Creeds of the churches: A reader in Christian doctrine, from the Bible to the present.* Atlanta, GA: John Knox Press.

Lewis, C.S. (1980). *The weight of glory and other addresses.* New York, NY: Macmillan. (Ed. by W. Hopper; originally published 1949).

Lovaas, O.I. (1987). Behavioral treatment and normal educational and intellectual functioning in young autistic children. *Journal of Consulting and Clinical Psychology, 55,* 3-9.

Lovaas, O.I., & Smith, T. (2003). Early and intensive behavioral intervention in autism. In A.E. Kazdin & J.R. Weisz (Eds.), *Evidence-based psychotherapies for children and adolescents* (pp.325-340). New York, NY: Guilford Press.

Marks, I. (1981). *Cure and care of neuroses.* New York, NY: Wiley.

McMahon, R.J., Wells, K.C., & Kotler, J.S. (2006). Conduct problems. In E.J. Mash & R.A. Barkley (Eds.), *Treatment of childhood disorders* (3rd ed, pp.137-268). New York, NY: Guilford Press.

Morrison, R.L. (1990). Interpersonal dysfunction. In A.S. Bellack, M. Hersen & A.E. Kazdin (Eds.), *International handbook of behavior modification and therapy* (pp.503-522). New York, NY: Plenum Press.

Muller, R., & Vande Kemp, H. (1985). On psychologists' uses of Calvinism. *American Psychologist, 40,* 466-468.

Newsom, C., & Hovanitz, C.A. (2006). Autistic spectrum disorders. In E.J. Mash & R.A. Barkley (Eds.), *Treatment of childhood disorders* (3rd ed., pp.455-511). New York, NY: Guilford Press.

Parloff, M., London, P., & Wolfe, B. (1986). Individual psychotherapy and behavior change. *Annual Review of Psychology, 37,* 321-349.

Piper, J. (1977, March). How I became a Christian hedonist. *His,* 1, 4-5.

Schreibman, L., Koegel, R.L., Charlop, M.H., & Egel, A.L. (1990). Infantile autism. In A.S. Bellack, M. Hersen & A.E. Kazdin (Eds.), *International handbook of behavior modification and therapy* (2nd ed., pp.763-789). New York, NY: Plenum Press.

Skinner, B.F. (1953). *Science and behavior.* New York, NY: Free Press.

Skinner, B.F. (1971). *Beyond freedom and dignity.* New York, NY: Bantam.

Skinner, B.F. (1976). *About behaviorism.* New York, NY: Vintage Press.

Smith, M., Glass, G., & Miller, T. (1980). *The benefits of psychotherapy.* Baltimore, MD: Johns Hopkins University Press.

Tan, S.Y. (1987). Cognitive-behavioral therapy: A biblical approach and critique. *Journal of Psychology and Theology, 15,* 103-112.

Tsai, M., et al. (2009). *A guide to functional analytic psychotherapy: Awareness, courage, love, and behaviorism.* New York, NY: Springer.

Van Leeuwen, M. (1979a). The behavioristic bandwagon and the body of Christ (Part 1): What is behaviorism? *Journal of the American Scientific Affiliation, 31,* 3-8.

Van Leeuwen, M. (1979b). The behavioristic bandwagon and the body of Christ (Part 2): What is behaviorism? *Journal of the American Scientific Affiliation, 31,* 88-91.

Van Leeuwen, M. (1979c). The behavioristic bandwagon and the body of Christ (Part 3):

What is behaviorism? *Journal of the American Scientific Affiliation, 31,* 129-138.

Van Leeuwen, M. (1982). *The sorcerer's apprentice: A Christian looks at the changing face of psychology.* Downers Grove, IL: InterVarsity Press.

Watson, J. (1930). *Behaviorism* (3rd ed.). Chicago, IL: University of Chicago Press.

Weiss, B., & Weisz, J.R. (1995). Relative effectiveness of behavioral versus nonbehavioral child psychotherapy. *Journal of Consulting and Clinical Psychology, 63,* 317-320.

Weisz, J.R., Weiss, B., Alicke, M.D., & Klotz, M.L. (1987). Effectiveness of psychotherapy with children and adolescents: A meta-analysis for clinicians. *Journal of Consulting and Clinical Psychology, 55,* 542-549.

Wolpe, J. (1978). Cognition and causation in human behavior. *American Psychologist, 33,* 437-446.

Wolpe, J., & Rachman, S. (1960). Psychoanalytic "evidence": A critique based on Freud's case of little Hans. *Journal of Nervous and Mental Disease, 131,* 135-148.

Woolfolk, R., & Richardson, F. (1984). Behavior therapy and the ideology of modernity. *American Psychologist, 39,* 777-786.

Zuriff, G. (1985). *Behaviorism: A conceptual reconstruction.* New York, NY: Columbia University Press.

6

COGNITIVE THERAPY

Mark R. McMinn, Stanton L. Jones, Michael J. Vogel and Richard E. Butman

***

If choosing an approach to psychotherapy were based simply on popularity in the scientific literature, then cognitive therapy would be the clear choice. Robins, Gosling and Craik (1999) evaluated scientific trends for four major schools—psychoanalysis, behavioral psychology, cognitive psychology and neuroscience—and concluded that psychoanalysis was virtually absent from psychological science over the previous several decades, behaviorism had waned dramatically from its heyday in the 1950s and 1960s, and neuroscience has shown only a slight increase in the scientific psychology literature.[6] But cognitive psychology showed

6 The popularity of the neuroscience school may have changed since Robins et al. reported their findings in 1999. We suspect neuroscience will be an area of rapid growth in the future. Also, though psychodynamic therapies have been underrepresented in the scientific literature, it is

a striking and consistent increase over the last fifty years of the twentieth century, and was clearly "the most prominent school" (p.117). The ascendance of cognitive therapy in scientific psychology corresponds with a growing number of Christian adaptations (Backus, 1985; Backus & Chapian, 2000; Cloud & Townsend, 1995; Crabb, 1975, 1977; Johnson & Ridley, 1992; Mc-Minn, 1991; McMinn & Campbell, 2007; Propst, 1988; Schmidt, 1983; Thurman, 2003). But popularity does not ensure orthodoxy, so the astute Christian has good reason to question some assumptions of contemporary cognitive therapies.

DESCRIPTIVE SURVEY

Describing cognitive therapy is challenging because history has rendered it a moving target, with its emphasis changing from one decade to the next. When the first edition of *Modern Psychotherapies* was published in 1991, the predominant paradigm was shifting from what Hayes (2004a) describes as the first wave to a second wave in behavioral and cognitive therapies. That is, traditional behavioral therapies were giving way to a form of cognitive

---

important to note that scientific evidence supports the usefulness of psychodynamic interventions (see Shedler, 2010).

therapy that emphasized identifying and changing disturbing thoughts. Because another chapter in this volume is devoted to behavioral therapies, we do not attempt to describe the first wave here. The therapies in this chapter differ from the behaviorist approaches considered in chapter five in that cognitive therapists believe some human behavior is caused by internal or mental events. For the true behaviorist all the ultimate causes of behavior are external to the person; internal events are real but ineffectual epiphenomena, mere temporary conduits for environmental forces. In cognitive therapy internal events are seen as powerful in their own right, and not ultimately reducible to environmental events. In sum, thought is judged to be real and important.

The second wave of cognitive therapy focuses on understanding and changing these internal events. Much of what is still offered in contemporary psychotherapy is second-wave cognitive therapy. Second-wave cognitive therapy involves intervening by helping clients evaluate and change their thoughts, beliefs and assumptions. For example, two skiers of equal experience stand at the top of a difficult slope. One is exuberant about the trip down the mountain; the other is terrified. A cognitive therapist assumes the difference is related to appraisal. One skier is thinking, *This will be great fun,* and the other is thinking about life insurance benefits. One perceives pleasure, the other risk. Cognitive therapy helps people gain perspective and control over negative thought patterns so they can also have greater flexibility with their feelings and behaviors. Prototypes of second-wave cognitive therapy can be seen in the work of Albert Ellis (1962, 1978), Aaron Beck (e.g., Beck, 1976, 1993; Beck, Rush, Shaw & Emery, 1979) and Donald Meichenbaum (1977, 1985). Ellis's model is known as rational emotive behavior therapy (REBT), Beck's as cognitive therapy, and Meichenbaum's as cognitive-behavioral therapy. Collectively, we will call these approaches "cognitive therapy."[7]

Within the past two decades a third wave of therapies has emerged. This movement, though in its infancy, is rather broad and tends to draw from many sources of influence, including contextualism, postmodernism and spirituality (see Hayes, 2004b, for a review). It builds

---

7 In the first edition of Modern Psychotherapies, Jones and Butman referred to these as cognitive-behavioral therapy. The change in nomenclature reflects the movement of the cognitive therapies toward incorporating constructivist and interpersonal approaches to therapies (see McMinn & Campbell, 2007; Ryle, 1990; Safran & Segal, 1990; Safran, 1998; Segal, Williams & Teasdale, 2002).

on the foundations of traditional behavior and cognitive therapies (the first and second waves, respectively) while incorporating aspects such as mindfulness and acceptance (Hayes, 2004a). This third wave can be grouped into at least three distinct approaches: acceptance and commitment therapy (ACT; Hayes, 2005; Hayes & Strosahl, 2004; Hayes, Strosahl & Wilson, 1999); mindfulness-based cognitive therapy (MBCT; Segal, Williams, Teasdale, 2002; Williams, Teasdale, Segal & Kabat-Zinn, 2007); and dialectical behavior therapy (DBT; Linehan, 1989, 1993a, b).

Second-wave approaches focus on changing internal mental events—appraisals, meanings, solutions and otherwise—in order to gain greater control over unwanted emotions and behaviors. The third-wave theorists, on the other hand, tend to deemphasize the traditional, mainstream aspects of cognitive focus and instead underscore the significance of attentional and metacognitive processes. They are less concerned with the accuracy of perception and prefer to accentuate contextual and functional aspects of thoughts and behaviors. In other words, they are more interested in the interactional processes—the how—than in content of thoughts or behavior—the what (see Dobson, 2010). The anxious skier atop a steep hill might learn to dispute automatic thoughts in a second-wave therapy. Instead of thinking, *I'm going to die,* the skier might learn to say, *I've skied tough slopes before, and I have never died yet; this will be fun!* In a third-wave intervention the therapist might help the client accept and understand the context of anxious thoughts rather than fighting them. So the skier at the top of the slope may reflect on how these anxious thoughts seem to come whenever something unpredictable lies ahead, then to accept the anxiety as part of living in an uncertain world, while still choosing to ski down the hill.

As evidenced by the relatively rapid shift from first- to second- to third-wave therapies, the cognitive therapies do not have a unifying personality theory that provides stability and theoretical coherence.

> Despite the increasing popularity of cognitively oriented theorizing in psychotherapy, there is no single, uniform, cognitive theory of personality development, psychopathology, and change, only a host of differing cognitive concepts, many of which appear to be independent and lacking in cohesion. (Safran & Segal, 1990, p.44)

Cognitive therapy's lack of personality theory is both troublesome and helpful for the Christian clinician. It is troublesome because assessment and interventions can sometimes

seem haphazard and lack a coherent rationale. It also makes it difficult to critique cognitive therapy because assumptions made by one therapist may or may not be held by other cognitive therapists. However, there is also some benefit in cognitive therapy not having a systematic personality theory because it leaves a void that can be filled in with a Christian view of persons. McMinn and Campbell (2007) have recently attempted such a venture, using a Christian view of persons as the foundation for an integrative psychotherapy that relies heavily on contemporary cognitive therapy treatment strategies.

One thing that characterizes academic clinical psychology today is the relative neglect of grand personality theories in favor of what might be called "microtheories" of specific phenomena. Researchers today tend to be eclectic about the grand theories they draw inspiration from, being strongly wedded to none of them. Their goal is to develop well-articulated smaller-scale theories about specific phenomena (such as altruism, panic, depression or social skills), not about persons as whole beings. The hope is thus to make these theories more accurate than the grand theories by making the universe of phenomena they attempt to explain smaller. For example, cognitive therapy began as an attempt to understand and treat depression, and then broadened to an approach for dealing with all affective disorders, bringing under its umbrella anxiety as well. It is a theory about pathological emotions and a proposal for effective change methods for altering maladaptive emotional reactions. It is important to note, however, that even microtheories must make general assumptions about human beings that exhibit the phenomenon of study, and thus these approaches are necessarily embedded in grand theories of human personality, though they are often less explicit about those assumptions. This complicates the evaluation of their approaches.

To understand the multifaceted origins of the cognitive therapies, we need to consider the confluence of four factors. The first is the social cognitive approach to human personality of Bandura (1986) and Mischel (1973), which evolved out of traditional behaviorism—what Hayes (2004a) considers the first wave leading to today's cognitive therapy. Whereas behaviorism emphasizes a deterministic relationship between environmental contingencies and human behavior, the social cognitive approaches introduced the possibility of reciprocal determinism (Bandura, 1978). That is, not only does the environment influence the person, but the person also influences the environment. Unlike radical behaviorists, who reduce the person to a set of behaviors, social cognitive theorists acknowledge both behavior and internal factors as important in human personality. Thus the environment, behavior and internal factors are in constant interplay. This "softening" of radical behaviorism created a climate in the scientific psychological community for a cognitive psychology that focused on internal events and mental representations of reality, though a close alignment between social cognitive theory and the clinical practice of cognitive therapy has not materialized. Perhaps this is because most of the major social cognitive theorists are not clinicians, which has prevented a clear and cogent connection between social cognitive theory and clinical application, or perhaps it is due to the growing influence of interpersonal theories on the practice of cognitive therapy.

Cognitive science is a second factor to consider in evaluating the theoretical roots of the cognitive therapies. Cognitive scientists study mental processes such as perception, memory, recall and reasoning. Prevailing paradigms in cognitive science have often paralleled technological advances, so it is not surprising that today's cognitive science is strongly influenced by computer technology and information processing models of understanding human cognition. In an information processing system, certain information is put into the system through the sensory systems (e.g., vision, hearing), then the information is organized, stored and later retrieved. At some point the information emerges out of the system and is expressed through verbal or nonverbal behavior. Information processing theory poses many problems as a philosophical foundation for cognitive therapy (McMinn & Campbell, 2007; Safran & Segal, 1990).

A third factor is what might be considered clinical pragmatism. Both Ellis and Beck were trained in psychoanalytic therapy. They became frustrated with an approach they perceived to be slow and ineffective, and so developed alternative approaches based on their observations of the change process in psychotherapy. In other words, they developed an approach to therapy that removed symptoms quickly, but without doing much theoretical or philosophical work first. Unlike many other psychotherapies, which are built atop a theoretical foundation, Beck's and Ellis's cognitive therapies began with a set of practice behaviors that helped people change. At best, they developed the theory simultaneous to the practice. At worst, the theory was filled in later, after the practice techniques were established. But again, the possibility of filling in a theoretical foundation after practice techniques are established also

creates the possibility that a Christian foundation can be established while retaining some of cognitive therapy's effective change strategies.

Fourth, the cognitive therapies have been influenced by constructivist forces in psychology (Mahoney, 1993, 2003; Safran & Segal, 1990; Safran, 1998). Once cognitive therapists wrestled the domain of thoughts away from the behaviorists, so that internal events were deemed important in their own right, it was only a matter of time before psychologists realized that these thoughts are socially constructed—influenced in profound ways by gender, ethnicity, culture and interpersonal relationships. As a result, some of the recent approaches to cognitive therapy reflect a growing distance from behavior therapies and rapprochement with object relations and interpersonal approaches to psychotherapy. As third-wave cognitive therapies have gained momentum, this contextual influence has become more explicitly spiritual, especially related to Buddhist ideas (e.g., Hayes, 2002; Linehan, 1993a). Mindfulness, radical acceptance of one's emotions and openness to suffering are common elements of third-wave cognitive therapies. Hathaway and Tan (2009) note that "these strategies can be found in many cultural contexts, but are highly developed in Eastern spiritual traditions, such as Buddhist Vipassana meditation" (p.160). Whereas the second-wave therapies were developed apart from religious considerations and then religious adaptations emerged (most often Christian), many of the third-wave therapies have been developed by individuals with training in both psychology and Eastern spirituality.

Philosophical Assumptions

Each of the influencing factors just described comes with philosophical assumptions, though the first two and the third and fourth are similar enough that they can be considered together. The first two overlap substantially with assumptions of behaviorism and the third and fourth with assumptions of relativism.

Social cognitive approaches, cognitive science and assumptions of behaviorism. Social cognitive and cognitive science views share some of the assumptions of behaviorism. This seems reasonable when considering that social cognitive perspectives emerged out of behaviorism, and both cognitive science and behaviorism share a materialistic scientific worldview.

Overlapping assumptions include materialism and atomism, both of which deserve critical evaluation from a Christian worldview. Materialism denies the existence of the spiritual realm and posits that matter is all that matters.

Though materialism contributes to spiritual obliviousness, it also serves to remind us of the physicalness and finitude of our existence and the way this conditions all aspects of our being. Historically, Christians have sometimes erred by ignoring the material, veering toward a gnostic understanding of the world, and so it behooves us to consider the inescapably material nature or dimension of existence. Atomism suggests that each person is a loose collection of behavioral and cognitive habits and predispositions. While this undermines notions of personal responsibility (since the person behind the behavior is not necessarily viewed as a moral agent), atomism helps us not to overidentify with our actions.

Some other assumptions of behaviorism can be seen in cognitive therapy, but in muted tones. These include reductionism, determinism and antimentalism. Reductionism is present in cognitive therapy, though the steps of reducing a phenomenon do not seem to go so far in the direction of basic processes as with behavior modification. Instead of reducing all events to operant learning, human phenomena are understood in terms of expectancies, thoughts, assumptions and so forth. Still, this is not a holistic view of persons.

Determinism is modified substantially in cognitive therapy. Remember that the classic behaviorist believes that events outside the person, operating through the laws of learning, totally determine all behavior. We cannot do other than what we do. Bandura (1978) has taken this issue on indepth with his views of reciprocal determinism, and other cognitive theorists and therapists have typically endorsed his formulation of this matter enthusiastically. (Bandura's softer form of determinism is discussed in more detail later in this chapter.)

The antimentalism of behavior modification is altered in an interesting way in cognitive therapy. The view that thoughts are noncausal epiphenomena gives way to the notion of thought patterns being powerful determinants of behavior. At the same time, thoughts are typically regarded as being the result of naturalistic processes. Since these thought patterns are not presumed to operate by the rules of operant and classical learning, cognitive therapists can remain materialists who do not believe in mentalism (in the sense of believing in an immaterial mind or soul), but at the same time can believe that human thought is a complex and causally efficacious phenomenon that is not a simple result of reinforcement. For the behavior modifier, the thought *I should study for my calculus exam tonight* is presumed to be a mere byproduct of the external reinforcement contingencies that produce studying

behavior (such as reminders by a professor, the past history of grades and praise, and so on). In cognitive therapy such a thought is seen as an important contributor to studying behavior occurring; it is a causal force in its own right. That is why cognitive therapists are often called "mentalists" by behavior modifiers; this is perhaps the highest insult the behavior modifier can inflict.

Following recent developments in cognitive science and neurobiology, some cognitive theories now borrow from the assumptions of evolutionary theory. This position often overlaps substantially with the above mentioned assumptions, but it seems to have a decidedly more developed, prescribed metaphysical framework. Insofar as evolutionary theory posits a view of the universe in totality, proponents tend to endorse an extreme form of materialism. In doing so they generally assume a monistic, reductionist position wherein the physical universe is all that exists. Anthropological claims from evolutionary theory often follow that the individual is merely a combination of physical elements that comprise the brain, body and emotion, all governed by various physical mechanisms promoting selfpreservation and fitness. Human activity is generally considered within a context predicated on biological causation, and therefore adherents to evolutionary theory tend to assume a form of antimentalism and determinism. For Christians the assumptions of evolutionary theory generally, and as they relate to cognitive therapies specifically, deserve careful scrutiny. While some have argued that theistic evolution is amenable to a biblical worldview (e.g., Collins, 2006), others in the Christian community seem to have responded to all evolutionary theory with wholesale rejection, if not contempt. It is daunting for thoughtful Christians to take this on as an integration task, where both science and Scripture are affirmed and valued. Yet this is the task we are called to, which suggests that one needs to understand the scientific foundations of materialistic perspectives while still recognizing that a Christian worldview both affirms the material world and demands a spiritual dimension that cannot be fully explained by materiality.

Clinical pragmatism, constructivism, and assumptions of relativism. The third and fourth influencing factors described earlier—clinical pragmatism and constructivism—also come with philosophical assumptions, one of which McMinn and Campbell (2007) call functional relativism. In most forms of cognitive therapy, the veracity of a client's thoughts are evaluated based on slippery relativistic criteria that are selected because they bring about enhanced mood and functioning. The major tasks of second-wave cognitive therapies are helping the client identify, evaluate and alter irrational thoughts, but who determines what is rational or irrational?

There appears to be three ways to answer this question, each associated with one of the pioneers of cognitive therapy and all heavily steeped in relativism. First, some clinicians define rationality themselves and then pronounce their values to clients. This produces a form of relativism that is highly vulnerable to error because it emerges out of one person's worldview and remains unaccountable to larger systems of determining truth from untruth. Albert Ellis (1962, 2000) used this approach when crafting various lists of irrational beliefs.

A second approach is what Aaron Beck calls collaborative empiricism. Beck often has his clients conduct "experiments" in which they collect data to determine the validity of their thoughts. But in looking closely at these experiments one realizes they are far from objective, and are mostly based on what makes the client feel better; a thought that adds to depression or anxiety is deemed irrational, whereas a thought that leads to greater peace of mind is deemed rational.

A third approach is found in social constructivist views of rationality. Though Donald

Meichenbaum's early writings were steeped in behavioral language, he soon moved to an information processing perspective and then to constructive narrative perspective where "humans actively construct their personal realities and create their own representational realities of the world" (Meichenbaum, 1993, p.203). The job of the therapist, then, is to help the client construct a story that brings a certain degree of peace and hope. This is not necessarily as individualistic and haphazard as it may seem at first glance. Most social constructivists embed an understanding of truth in cultural and community values, thereby broadening the base of accountability beyond the personal values of the client and therapist. The constructivism of second-wave cognitive therapy naturally leads to the contextual, acceptance-based approaches found in third-wave cognitive therapies. From a Christian perspective, social construction is not fully adequate as a basis for truth because it overlooks the possibility of a transcendent God defining and revealing truth.

Model of Personality

Ideally, psychotherapies are connected to personality theories that are, in turn, embedded in well-reasoned metaphysics and supported by scientific findings. Conversely, the most useful personality theories are connected with effective models of psychotherapy. Unfortunately, the connection between personality theory and cognitive therapy is disappointing in both directions.

Here we can make a distinction between bottom-up approaches and top-down approaches. Bottom-up approaches are developed by psychologists with strong philosophical or research interests and then clinical applications are worked out later. Top-down approaches come from clinicians with strong applied interests; the theoretical underpinnings are developed to support new methods of intervention. There is a traditional bottom-up theory by Walter Mischel (1973) that warrants consideration, but it has not reached very far up. In other words, it has not influenced the actual practice of cognitive therapy very much. Similarly, the third-wave work of Steven Hayes (e.g., Hayes et al., 1999) has progressed from a bottom-up approach, though its influence is only budding, and it also has not yet made a grand impact on cognitive therapy. Many of the remaining models of cognitive therapy, both second and third wave, have been developed with a top-down approach, but the theories have not reached very far down. That is, many of the theoretical models developed to describe the work of cognitive therapists are relatively shallow and unsophisticated with regard to metaphysics and connections with psychological science. Nonetheless, they hold core assumptions on which a model of personality could essentially be based. Here we briefly outline the development of these approaches, beginning with their origins and concluding with their contributions to personality theory.

Mischel. Walter Mischel (1973) has suggested that rather than understanding personality from the perspective of universal dispositions or traits, people are better suited to "idiographic analysis" where each person is analyzed individually without reducing individual differences to measurements of universal traits (such as the big five traits of McRae & Costa, 2003). Each person's personality is unique and must be understood as such.

Mischel organizes his idiographic approach to understanding persons around five person variables. These are not traits or psychological structures (such as the id, ego, superego of psychoanalysis), but are categories of processes that can develop differently in different persons. Though Mischel is associated with the social cognitive approach, his person variables also show clear connections with an information processing approach.

The first variable is *cognitive encoding strategies.* All persons sort the raw data of their sensations of the world in different ways. Our encoding strategies transform a perception of a mouth movement of another into either a warm, accepting smile or a judgmental grimace of condescension, for example. Some Christians might look at others in the church and categorize a small group as "real believers" and all others as "hypocrites," while another person may sort persons according to maturity judged by how gracious and loving they seem to be. Persons with sophisticated, broad, adaptable ways of sorting or encoding their experiences will be more adjusted and adaptable than persons with simplistic, rigid and narrow encoding strategies.

Second, Mischel describes *cognitive and behavioral construction competencies.* In response to the raw data we take in through our senses and our encoded perceptions, we must figure out our world by constructing a cognitive model of it and then go on to construct actions for responding to it. Once we have given a label to experience, we put bits of experience together in a way that seems to make sense. These models may vary from highly accurate and productive (such as the insightful understanding of the politically astute employee in an organization) to highly inaccurate and destructive (such as the paranoid delusions of the psychotic). On the basis of that model and utilizing the skills available, the person then acts. People differ widely in the actions they are capable of exhibiting. For example, married persons differ widely in their capacity to be emotionally sensitive and responsive to their spouses. We all differ in terms of the ways we make sense of our world and the capacities we possess for acting in response to it.

Third, Mischel postulates *subjective stimulus values.* Another dimension on which persons differ is what they value and hence what motivates them. According to Mischel, people build up from the few basic motivations that Skinner allowed (need for food, warmth, water, pleasure, etc.) to almost an infinite array of valued stimuli, which then become incentives for behavior or a focus for motivation. People can then differ immensely on what are motivations for them because of their very different learning histories.

Fourth is *operant and classical conditioning.* Though he has moved beyond traditional behaviorism, Mischel believes that basic learning processes are still influential in human behavior. He does not understand these in the mechanistic manner of a Skinnerian, but believes them to be operative at a cognitive level. For instance, operant learning (changes in behavior based on reinforcement patterns) is understood not as the mechanistic conditioning of operant behavior but as the influencing of choice behavior by the alteration of expectations of reward.

Fifth, Mischel describes *self-regulatory systems and plans.* One of the major contributions of Bandura (1978) and Kanfer (1979) in moving beyond traditional behavioral conceptions of persons was the proposal that persons typically internalize control of their behavior as they develop. Skinner may believe that our environment controls all, but these theorists argued that through memory, expectancy and language we take our environment inside us, and thus the thoughts we engage in become as powerful determinants of our actions as the external environment. While the exam-preparation behavior of a student may be partially due to external contingencies, such as social praise from dorm associates, availability of other activities and so forth, the student can also create alternative forces that influence behavior through, for example, self-statements such as *I must study now or I will flunk out of school,* or *Imagine how my boyfriend will be impressed when I get an A in this course!* The image of the boyfriend conjured up at will can be as powerful a determinant of behavior as the real person. People then differ in their capabilities to regulate their own behavior. People differ according to what behavior they pay attention to in themselves, how they judge that behavior (e.g., stringent versus generous standards of judgment) and how effectively they give overt consequences *(No video games for me tonight; I didn't do my housework!)* or covert consequences (self-statements such as *I did a great job!* or *I'm a hopeless case!)* to themselves.

Mischel's understanding of personality has not resulted in a formal therapy approach per se, but his model provides a framework for understanding the connections between social cognitive approaches, information processing theory and potential therapeutic interventions. His work on self-regulatory systems and plans is related to Bandura's work on self-efficacy. This is the concept that it is not just past consequences of an action that determine its occurrence (as Skinner might argue) or even the expectation of a future consequence (a cognitive event which Skinner would deny the importance of), but it is also our evaluation of our own competency or effectiveness in behaving that determines action. For example, a Skinnerian would say a shy person's reluctance to interact with others is a function of having not been rewarded for such activities in the past and of receiving ongoing rewards for shy behavior. As treatment, the Skinnerian would implement a learning strategy that would positively reinforce outgoing behavior. To this

Bandura would add that the shy person must not only expect reinforcement for outgoing behavior, but must also manifest a sense of personal efficacy for those types of behaviors, a sense on confidence about interacting effectively with others.

Ellis. Rational emotive behavior therapy does not have a comprehensive theory of personality per se, but focuses more on a view of emotional disturbance and health. The core assertion of REBT is that a person's *thoughts* are central to understanding that person. Ellis formulated this relationship in an A-B-C format. People often come for therapy because *consequent emotions* (C) are disturbing them (e.g., feeling depressed). It is common for people to attribute their emotional or behavioral consequence to activating events (A), as if there were some necessary and invariant causal relationship between A and C (e.g., "My car is wrecked and I am broke, so I'm depressed"). According to Ellis, people are not really disturbed by events themselves, but by the *beliefs* (B) they hold about those events. So in order for a car accident to result in depression, Ellis postulated that an intervening belief must be brought into play. For example, "It is terrible and awful that I have no money to repair my car." In therapy, Ellis taught clients to *dispute* (D) these irrational thoughts in order to achieve a more hopeful cognitive *effect* (E).

The A-B-Cs of REBT are the core of its approach to personality. As mentioned earlier, a full-fledged theory of personality usually attempts to predict and explain behavior in all or most areas of life. Ellis's A-B-C theory could be pressed to do so, but this would most likely result in weak, ambiguous explanations or predictions such as "my thinking and beliefs led me to act this way." Such loose explanations are largely useless in the scientific study of personality, and so REBT has spawned no serious scientific hypotheses or research regarding the broader aspects of human personality. But for clinical purposes, where the focus is less on predicting or explaining behavior generally and more on the focal explanation and modification of distress, the simplicity of REBT is regarded by its proponents as a virtue, in that simplicity increases the utility of the theory.

The simplicity of REBT has benefited those committed to developing Christian versions (Hauck, 1972; Johnson, 1993a; Johnson & Ridley, 1992). Though Ellis himself was a rather staunch atheist and hedonist (Ellis, 1980), the theoretical shallowness of his approach means that REBT interventions need not be rooted in the worldview assumptions of its founder. One can use Christian principles instead of hedonistic principles to discern what is rational—something Ellis (2000) eventually acknowledged. One religious adaptation of REBT was even coauthored by Ellis himself (Nielsen, Johnson & Ellis, 2001).

Meichenbaum. Meichenbaum's early work (1977), which goes back as far as his doctoral dissertation, was to develop a method for understanding the impact of cognitions on behavior and emotion, and a method for changing the nature of that impact. He proposed a three-stage process for effective change. First, a person must become aware of thoughts relevant to the problem being experienced. Next, therapist and client must determine alternative thoughts (self-statements) that can believably replace thoughts that are causing the person trouble. Finally, the person must implement thought changes and begin to enjoy the benefits of nondestructive cognition.

For example, some of Meichenbaum's work has been with impulsive, hyperactive children. In this population it is assumed that the problems are due in part to a failure to establish the cognitive skills that normal children have to manage their own behavior. Thus impulsive children might be taught initially to define their task and continually remind themselves what to do ("I'm in class and my job here is listening to the teacher"), to use thoughts to cope with distractions or less than optimal performance ("Oops. My mind wandered! Back on track; just pick up where you left off") and to use positive thoughts to reward good performance and perhaps negative thoughts to punish unwanted performance ("Great! I'm doing better. I paid attention for ten minutes in a row!"). Meichenbaum's methods have been applied to such populations as children, schizophrenics, adults with anxiety disorders or chronic pain, and those with explosive tempers (see Meichenbaum, 1985).

Later, Meichenbaum (1993) described three metaphors for his work, progressing from his early career to present. Interestingly, his three metaphors correspond closely with the three waves of cognitive therapy described by Hayes (2004a). The first, just described, represents Meichenbaum's earliest work when cognitive-behavioral therapy was based on the behavioral paradigm of conditioning. Next, Meichenbaum moved toward an information processing paradigm. Here the client is not merely learning new thought processes to modify behavior, but is seen as an active agent in interpreting and reinterpreting life events. From an information processing perspective, people are constantly engaging in transactions with the environment—perceiving, interpreting, remembering, recalling, attributing and so on. Often these transactions involve cognitive errors that cause a person to misperceive a situation. So a depressed person may perceive a minor illness as an awful catastrophe, where someone not prone to depression simply sees it as an unfortunate event. In the third and longest stage of Meichenbaum's career, he has turned toward constructive narrative to understand the change process. This is rooted more in existentialism and hermeneutics than in behaviorism. Each person is living out a story, and the way the story is interpreted and told has powerful effects on how it is lived. The therapist becomes a conarrator, helping clients retell their story in ways that bring hope and meaning to life. These changes in Meichenbaum's perspectives reflect general trends in cognitive therapy—moving away from its behavioral roots toward more existential and interpersonal models of personality.

Beck. Whereas Meichenbaum has moved from a behavioral perspective to information processing and then constructivist narrative, Aaron Beck's model has always been based on an information processing perspective. Over time, Beck's model has become increasingly sophisticated, both as a result of his own work and because of others who have suggested additions and modifications to his theory. Beck has applied his ideas to many different clinical problems, including depression (Beck et al., 1979), anxiety disorders (Beck, Emery & Greenberg, 1985), substance abuse (Beck, Wright, Newman & Liese, 1993), bipolar disorder (Newman, Leahy, Beck, Reilly-Harrington & Gyulai, 2002), personality disorders (Beck, Freeman & Davis, 2003), and marital problems (Beck, 1988). Beck has been a productive clinician and researcher. His work differs from REBT in more fully utilizing cognitive and behavioral methods, in being less doctrinaire in what he regards as rational and irrational (using instead the labels "adaptive" and "maladaptive" beliefs) and most importantly in encouraging a therapeutic style less combative and rigid than Ellis's in favor of a gentler, though direct, Socratic questioning style known as *guided discovery.*

Beck proposes that pathological levels of depression and anxiety are the result of dysfunctional automatic thoughts. It is commonly noted that depressed and anxious people report thoughts that are clearly inaccurate. A depressed man says, "Everything I've ever done has been a failure"; yet friends who know him well reveal that he has done and still is doing many things satisfactorily. An anxious woman says, "There is no way I can handle that situation; it will destroy me"; yet family members disclose that she has in fact handled situations like what she is afraid of in the past, and that what she fears cannot destroy her. Other approaches to counseling view these thoughts as symptomatic of other problems (low self-esteem, projection of unacceptable impulses) and thus see no benefit in directly changing the thoughts. In Beck's model the distorted thinking is not the symptom of the problem, it is the cause of the problem. In a direct fashion, most clearly reflective of the Socratic philosophical tradition, Beck uses persistent but gentle logic and persuasion to alter the person's thinking, and he uses collaborative empiricism—involving the client in collecting evidence to support or undermine beliefs ("Please gather all your employee reviews for the last five years; if you really are a complete failure, there shouldn't be a single positive statement on them").

Beck's model has been criticized for being superficial and overly intellectual, and indeed it is often presented this way by instructors in introductory counseling classes and by clinicians with minimal training in cognitive therapy. In actuality, Beck's model has developed far beyond the superficiality he is accused of. One of the most helpful developments in recent years has been the introduction of *schemas* to the cognitive therapy model (Needleman, 1999; Young, Weinberger & Beck, 2001; Young, Klosko & Weishaar, 2003). A schema is a structure that contains a representation of reality that functions beneath conscious awareness. Whereas dysfunctional automatic thoughts are responses to particular situations, schemas contain more general rules and assumptions about the world. A socially anxious person may have a dysfunctional thought such as, *I am going to turn red and get all flustered when I give my class presentation, and I may even faint and make a fool of myself.* This automatic thought is situation specific, quite accessible to consciousness and easily changed by looking at the evidence (e.g., *I have never fainted before, and it's not terrible to blush when presenting, so I guess it will be okay).* But beneath these automatic thoughts are intermediate beliefs that are more general, less conscious and not so easily changed (e.g., *I must always impress people with my poise and preparation).* Intermediate beliefs are shaped by the deepest and most general beliefs of all, often referred to as core beliefs. Core beliefs are typically unconscious and emerge out of a person's developmental past (e.g., *I am only loved if I perform well).* These various beliefs and related cognitive processes are all part of a person's cognitive schema.

Schemas can be activated and deactivated, depending on life circumstances. A student with a fear of class presentations may function well on a day-to-day basis, but as the date of the presentation comes closer, the fear and apprehension begins to grow as the schema is activated more and more. Schemas can be deactivated in one of two ways: either the circumstances change (e.g., the professor cancels the presentation) or the person learns to exercise conscious control to deactivate the schemas. This, of course, is the point of therapy—to help people gain the necessary self-awareness and skills to deactivate their troublesome schemas.

Cognitive schemas do not function alone. They are also connected with motivational, affective, behavioral and physiological schemas. As the date of the presentation approaches, the anxious student will be more motivated to prepare (motivation), and may spend many hours researching the topic in the library (behavior). A sense of fear also grows (affect) and causes the person to tremble and feel nauseated (physiology). All these can be altered by changing the associated cognitions. Beck (1996) understands cognitive, affective, physiological, motivational and behavioral schemas to exist in packages he calls *modes.* So a person will behave quite differently from one situation to another (note the similarity with Mischel's model here), depending on what modes are functioning. Walking in the wilderness and seeing a poisonous snake is likely to trigger one mode. Sitting next to a close companion at a beautiful symphony is likely to trigger another.

Some of those who criticize Beck for not considering emotions and developmental issues have not kept up with his theoretical developments. Schema theory helps account for the influences of early childhood, and Beck's notion of modes helps explain the connection between emotions and cognitions.

Still, there are inadequacies with Beck's model (McMinn & Campbell, 2007). Any thorough personality theory should account for motivation, and Beck's system does not do this satisfactorily. Though he suggests that motivational schemas exist within modes, he does not explain how motivation affects one's progress through life. Beck's model may help us understand why a person who encounters a deadly snake is motivated to run away, but it does not explain why one loves nature and goes hiking in the first place. It accounts for why a student wants to avoid class presentations, but not for why one attends college, seeks new knowledge, pursues intimate relationships and finds a career (unless these are motivated by dysfunctional beliefs).

Hayes. Steven Hayes (e.g., Hayes, 2004a, 2005; Hayes et al., 1999) developed acceptance and commitment therapy (ACT), a bottom-up approach grounded in functional contextual philosophy (see Hayes, 1993), to explain human suffering and direct the processes of change. Unlike his predecessors in the first and second waves, Hayes deemphasizes some of the mechanistic and formal assumptions dominant in behaviorist and information processing approaches (Hayes 2004a, b; Hayes et al., 1999). In doing so, he dismisses the mechanist's notion of the world as preorganized into an objective and predictable reality; his approach to therapy is no longer about understanding the true elements, relations and forces at work in the lives of clients—the cogs in a machine. Instead, Hayes focuses his attention on the functions of actions (whether behavioral, cognitive, emotional or other), looking to provide a pragmatic, holistic account of events in order to guide the process of therapy—the contexts in which the machine operates. His functional emphasis also departs from the formal considerations at the heart of information processing approaches, so therapy shifts from changing the kind of action to altering its role in a client's context. For instance, modifying an irrational thought is not the clinical focus in ACT, but rather the aim of therapy is to understand and then alter the contexts in a client's life, both internal and external, that permit the thought to function negatively. Thus, by mindfully observing the irrational thought, a shift of internal contexts, its problematic functions loosen and it then becomes acceptable.

Context is king from the perspective of ACT. An initial goal of this approach is therefore to understand the contextual factors that have led an individual to experience suffering, especially those embedded in language and learning (Hayes et al., 1999). Hayes (e.g., 2004a, b) suggests that when these processes go awry they foster psychological inflexibility, the result of which is indiscriminant aversion, cognitive fusion and experiential avoidance. A subsequent goal of ACT is to diffuse the influence of these responses through various metacognitive and attentional strategies (e.g., mindfulness), all of which are in the service of acceptance. When, for example, a client admits to thinking, *I am worthless,* the ACT practitioner might have the client dispassionately repeat aloud the metacognitive observation, "I am having the thought that I am worthless," until it loses its negative effects. Again, the goal is not to replace the cogs and, for instance, substitute worthy for worthless, but instead it is to shift the contexts, this time internal, where the thought *I am worthless* operates in order to undermine its influence. As an eventual goal in ACT, clients are encouraged to construct their values and desired life consequences to function as a dependable guide for future activities (Hayes, 2004a, b; Hayes et al., 1999). In other words, ACT helps clients build a personalized set of guiding beliefs, important to their true sense of self, from which goals can be specified and responsible actions carried out—the commitment aspect. This rightfully may serve to raise the brow of any believer concerned about relativism.

As a theory of personality, ACT is limited. Hayes bases his approach on the *assumption of destructive normality* and tends to suggest that the ordinary state of human psychological processes is dysfunctional. In particular, ACT proposes that human beings are inborn with unique mechanisms for language and learning that form the bases of evaluative knowledge. While originally intended for flourishing, these mechanisms have become corrupted and been misused over time such that the natural state of humankind is now one of fear, self-criticism and deception. In other words, ACT assumes that within language and learning processes lie the origins of pain and despair. The ubiquity of human suffering is not too unlike the Christian doctrine of original sin, and Hayes is quick to draw similarities between his approach and the Bible (e.g., Hayes et al., 1999), even as he also draws comparisons between ACT and Buddhism (Hayes, 2002).

At a grander level ACT assumes that human beings have developed into linguistic, meaning-making (although he calls it "sense-making") organisms through the process of evolution. And although Hayes begins to consider the interactions between biological predispositions, sociocultural influences, environmental pressures and sources of individual motivation, this is the closest that ACT comes to a comprehensive theory of personality. Needless to say, ACT is not based on a comprehensive personality theory. However, its lack of specificity in the area of personality theory may actually appeal to the Christian community, who are now free to establish a more sophisticated, theologically informed view of humankind.

Segal and colleagues. Struck by the need to reduce relapse after cognitive therapy for depression, Zindel Segal, Mark Williams and John Teasdale (2002) set out to provide a modified form of cognitive therapy known as mindfulness-based cognitive therapy (MBCT)—a top-down endeavor. Their quest initially led them to the work of Beck and his colleagues (e.g., Beck, 1976; Kovacs & Beck, 1978), which suggested that individuals acquired persistent attitudes and assumptions following an episode of depression, making them vulnerable to relapse (Segal et al., 2002). However, this rather linear conceptualization, with persistent negative and self-critical thinking patterns giving way to depressed moods, did not seem to adequately explain recurrence for Segal, Williams and Teasdale. They then began to reconsider how activating depressive symptoms (i.e., mood, body, thought) might elicit learned responses and cause relapse (Segal et al., 2002; Williams et al., 2007). A new understanding of the vulnerabilities to depressive relapse began to emerge out of their work, indicating that previous episodes had imprinted particular modes of thought, mood and bodily sensation that were capable of reactivation when only a single element was triggered. (Notice the similarities between this and Beck's notion of modes.)

For example, as an individual with a history of depression feels some sad or unpleasant moods, experiences that were part of previous depressive episodes, associated bodily sensations and thoughts might also become reactivated. Segal and colleagues maintain that once these symptoms reemerge, the individual will likely begin to ruminate on the negative aspects of self and situation *(What is wrong with me? I have nothing to be upset about, so why am I feeling this way?).* By appraising unwanted emotional and bodily experiences as problematic and in need of immediate resolution or avoidance, the ruminative mind then redirects mental attention from the external world toward the internal problem in a critical, judgmental manner *(I need to stop feeling this way. I must be really messed up inside.).* Segal et al. (2002) suggest this ruminative state of mind might act as a catalyst for relapse. In sum, they drew from Beck's cognitive theory of depression (e.g., Beck et al., 1979) to develop an anatomy of depressive relapse, and then began to explore possible treatment strategies to prevent or disrupt the cycles of rumination and experiential avoidance.

Segal and colleagues enlisted the help of Jon Kabat-Zinn, whose early work in mindfulness-based stress reduction (e.g., 1990) seemed to offer a promising solution for depressive relapse. With the subsequent integration of cognitive therapy and mindfulness, MBCT began to incorporate features of Western and Eastern thought into its core assumptions, especially those related to personality (Segal et al., 2002; Williams et al., 2007). From this perspective the individual evolved into a bipartite mind comprising two broad modes for experiential processing: the doing mode and being mode (see Crane, 2009, for a review). The doing mode, which includes the ruminative mind, emerged as the goal-oriented, problem-solving dimension, narrowly directing attention away from momentary sensations to thoughts about past and future experiences. The advantage of this mode is its analytical prowess within the external world, enabling individuals to detect discrepancies between actuality and desire in order to maximize gains and minimize losses (Segal et al., 2002; Williams et al., 2007). In contrast, the being mode is a psychological mechanism that developed to process momentary sensations rather than to strive toward achievement; it is metacognitive, intentional, experiential and nonjudgmental. Its major advantage is in being able to provide perceptual feedback from events in the immediate sphere of awareness through an attitudinal tone characterized by acceptance, compassion and curiosity.

Distilled from this microtheory is a vague set of materialistic assumptions, not least of which is that humans have emerged through the process of evolution. As mentioned, psychological mechanisms, particularly the doing and being modes, developed and were retained for the advantages they afforded throughout the course of evolutionary history. The bipartite mind exists now because it once promoted fitness and self-preservation, motivations assumed to underlie the whole of human activities. MBCT also assumes that sociocultural influences are at least partially responsible for the prevalent overreliance on the doing mode in Westernized communities. As a theory of personality, MBCT is limited in focus and lends very little to any comprehensive model. As with other theories, Christians are encouraged to view this as an opportunity to thoughtfully plunder the riches in MBCT and incorporate them into a biblical worldview.

Linehan. Marsha Linehan (e.g., 1987, 1989, 1993a, b) originally developed dialectic behavior therapy (DBT) to more effectively treat individuals with chronic suicidality, particularly women with borderline personality disorder (BPD) (Dimeff & Linehan, 2001). Over the next two decades, however, DBT was adapted to serve the needs of various other populations and treatment settings, though it managed to remain the choice treatment for individuals with BPD (see Lieb, Zanarini, Schmahl, Linehan & Bohus, 2004; and Robins & Chapman, 2004, for a review). The clinical versatility of this approach is almost certainly linked to its conceptual sophistication and integrated foundations, which have drawn influence from several diverse approaches to therapy, behavioral science, mindfulness and dialectical philosophy (Dimeff & Linehan, 2001; Koerner & Dimeff, 2007). We focus here, however, on the origins of

DBT and its top-down assumptions about personality.

Clinical observations, it would seem, led Linehan to the initial conclusion that BPD was at its core a pervasive disorder of the emotional regulation system (Koerner & Dimeff, 2007; Linehan, 1993a). As such, she saw the problematic behaviors indicative of BPD (e.g., suicidality, dissociation) as failed attempts to self-regulate and tolerate distress. Situating her approach to case conceptualization in biosocial theory, Linehan then suggested that these behaviors had developed from and were maintained by biological and environmental factors; problems arose from an interaction between inborn vulnerabilities and pervasively invalidating environments (Dimeff & Linehan, 2001; Koerner & Dimeff, 2007; Linehan, 1993a, b). Among other things, these experiences inhibited individuals with BPD from effectively managing their cognitive and emotional responses, rendering them easily overwhelmed and incapable of effective self-validation (Robins, Schmidt & Linehan, 2004). In approaching these needs with the traditional cognitive therapies, however, Linehan quickly noticed a therapeutic dilemma: individuals with BPD became suddenly flooded with cognitive and emotional arousal when change was emphasized (as in traditional cognitive therapies), but when change was deemphasized, and suffering in the present situation was accepted, they felt invalidated, enraged and hopeless (Robins et al., 2004). In other words, treatment with an exclusive focus on change was too much, and treatment with an exclusive focus on acceptance was too little.

Dialectic behavior therapy emerged out of this context, firmly rooted in a dialectical philosophy that provided Linehan with both a method of persuasion and a set of worldview assumptions with which to tackle the challenges inherent in the treatment of BPD (Koerner & Dimeff, 2007; Robins et al., 2004). While a comprehensive discussion is beyond the scope of this chapter, the essential idea of dialectics is that each proposition or thesis also contains a contradictory proposition or antithesis. From a dialectical perspective, progress occurs not as a single proposition triumphs over another, but rather it comes from the resolution of opposites—thesis and antithesis blend together to form a synthesis. Linehan (e.g., 1989, 1993a, b) allowed this philosophy to guide her approach in DBT, believing that with enough perspective and the right skills, individuals with BPD might learn to grow—self-regulate, tolerate distress and otherwise—as they begin to synthesize their dialectically opposed experiences, particularly of acceptance and change. The practice of mindfulness seemed to offer just such a synthesis, teaching individuals with BPD the skills to simultaneously observe and engage their experiences—to accept and to change them (Robins et al., 2004). Through a series of training modules DBT incorporates these skills with traditional cognitive and behavioral strategies for emotional regulation, distress tolerance and interpersonal effectiveness.

In terms of personality, DBT offers very little to any normative conceptualization of development; it is a microtheory about disorder. BPD follows a diathesis-stress model, where biological predispositions interact with toxic life circumstances and lead to pathology. At a metaphysical level the emphasis on biology and genetics offers some theoretical rationale for the material dimensions of personality development from the perspective of DBT. However, what relationship, if any, the immaterial dimensions have with the material processes is rather unclear in this approach. It would seem that the incorporation of dialectical philosophy into DBT all but demands the existence of immaterial in direct opposition to the material. The resolution or synthesis of the tension between dualism and monism (as exemplified in the mind-brain dilemma) is of particular interest, though none is offered in DBT. This is curious because Linehan herself studied both contemplative Christianity and Zen Buddhism, both of which demand exploration of the immaterial in relation to the material world. In sum, this approach has strong metaphysical implications for a theory of personality development, but more needs to be done before DBT can offer a complete or satisfying picture of personality.

Models of Health and Abnormality

Because cognitive therapy lacks a comprehensive personality theory that accounts for human motivation, it also tends to be sketchy about defining normalcy and abnormality. Nonetheless, three assumptions about health and abnormality warrant attention—two from traditional approaches and one from the third wave. First, cognitive therapy assumes normalcy is defined by society and by a person's own assessment of his or her level of distress and functioning. Thus cognitive therapy is characterized by what Woolfolk and Richardson (1984) call "amorality," a tendency to go along with the individual's definitions of normalcy and abnormality. If a client comes into a clinic complaining that a pattern is a problem, then for that person it is a problem. This usually meshes well with common sense; no one is going to disagree that agoraphobia or suicidal depression is abnormal. But it leaves open to the individual decision of the therapist and client the normalcy or abnormality of various adjustment problems.

A perhaps extreme example is Lazarus's (1980) work with a woman who reported having married her husband only for the financial rewards he gave her. She had had numerous sexual affairs. She came to therapy because of a developing aversion to sexual relations with her husband. Lazarus's response was not to confront the obvious narcissism of the client or to urge her to work on the marriage. Rather he deemed her aversion to sex in a loveless and pragmatic marriage a worthwhile target for therapy and taught her cognitive techniques to allow her to "turn herself off emotionally" so that she could continue to tolerate sex with her husband while continuing to enjoy her adulterous affairs. While this is an extreme example, it points to the risks of an obscure definition of normalcy.

Second, cognitive therapy assumes that normalcy is achieved by thinking more rationally than the thinking that occurs in an abnormal state. This also fits well with common sense. No one would question that a highly functioning person free from psychological distress is thinking more clearly than a person in the throes of a psychotic episode or profound depression. But what seems obvious when considering this extreme example becomes more troubling when considering the underlying assumption that daily health is achieved through proper thinking and compromised through sloppy thinking. McMinn and Campbell (2007) demonstrate various reasons why this assumption needs to be questioned. We will return to their analysis later in this chapter.

These seem directly tied in with a final assumption, this time offered by third-wave theorists, which suggests cognitive processes, and not merely their contents, can sometimes lead to abnormality. In other words, from this metacognitive,thinking-about-thinkingperspective, it is not so much that the substance of thoughts is problematic, but rather it is the activity of thought itself that is disruptive. Health comes by dislodging oneself from socio-culturally and individually held truths, rules and requirements, thereby becoming free to step back, take stock and choose a direction that best suits a person. It is also about finding balance between rationality and other forms of experiencing the world. However, a danger of this assumption is that the accountability embedded in communities and shared truth claims is discredited, leaving individuals with the task of constructing relativistic forms of functional truth and reality.

Model of Psychotherapy

In the 1960s, 1970s and early 1980s, cognitive therapy in clinical practice tended to be characterized by short-term interventions targeted at specifically defined problems. Problems were attacked as directly as possible, in a manner some belittled as mere "symptom reduction." The A-B-Cs of Ellis, Beck's early model of change and Meichenbaum's link to behaviorism all lent themselves to rapid, symptom-focused methods of change. Then in the late 1980s and early 1990s more intensive cognitive therapy interventions began emerging. Ellis's model waned in deference to Beck and Meichenbaum—perhaps due to its superficiality or maybe to Ellis's abrasive interpersonal style. (Meichenbaum once quipped that Ellis could only get away with his style because he practices in New York City.) Meanwhile, Beck's model deepened theoretically with the development of schema theory (Young, 1990), which allowed therapists to use cognitive therapy with disorders other than depression and anxiety. Cognitive therapy was extended to more intractable problems such as substance abuse (Beck et al., 1993) and personality disorders (Beck, Freeman & Associates, 1990;

Linehan, 1993a; Young, 1990). At the same time, Meichenbaum (1993) and others (Mahoney, 1993) became increasingly intrigued with constructivist, narrative models, which often required lengthier, more in-depth treatment, typically calling the client back to childhood events in order to make sense of present circumstances.

Progress toward interpersonal and contextual considerations in cognitive therapy suffered a setback in the late 1990s when the Society of Clinical Psychology, which is Division 12 of the American Psychological Association (APA), launched an ambitious and controversial project of identifying empirically supported treatment procedures (Chambless & Hollon, 1998). In order to be included on the Division 12 list, a therapy needed at least two double-blind studies demonstrating its effectiveness, and the therapy needed to be manualized to assure that it be delivered in similar ways by various research centers. The longer-term cognitive therapies were dealt a damaging blow as a result, both because they were too new to have a strong research base and because they did not lend themselves to manualization. Vigorous debate followed (e.g., Garfield, 1996; Havik & VandenBos, 1996; Messer, 2004; Silverman, 1996; Wampold & Bhati, 2004), eventually resulting in a more open understanding of evidence-based practice than what initially guided the Division 12 task force (e.g., Norcross, Hogan & Koocher, 2008).

The third-wave therapies have created a useful bridge between the research support garnered for cognitive therapy in early days and the emphasis on contextual factors that began with the constructivist cognitive therapy movement. A number of the third-wave therapies have been evaluated empirically, and though most do not meet the Division 12 criteria exactly (Öst, 2008), they show a reasonable level of efficacy.

McMinn and Campbell (2007) distinguish between symptom-focused, schema-focused and relationship-focused therapy. Symptom-focused therapies rely heavily on therapeutic techniques and are best suited for treating uncomplicated anxiety disorders. Current treatments for anxiety disorders almost always involve a combination of behavioral and cognitive interventions, with a heavy emphasis on the behavioral. Treating panic disorder, for example, involves both exposure to early symptoms of the panic cycle and cognitive restructuring (Craske & Barlow, 2001). Similarly, treating obsessive-compulsive disorder involves cognitive restructuring plus exposing the client to fearful, obsessive thoughts without allowing the corresponding behavioral rituals

(Foa & Franklin, 2001). Many symptom-focused interventions are completed within ten to fifteen sessions.

Some other disorders—most notably clinical depression—have a high relapse rate with traditional symptom-focused interventions, and so cognitive therapists are turning to longer-term schema-focused interventions (Young et al., 2001). The first part of these interventions is almost identical to some aspects of symptom-focused interventions as the therapist helps the client evaluate and restructure dysfunctional automatic thoughts. Treatments for depression may also involve behavioral techniques, such as increasing the number of pleasant events in a person's daily routine or learning assertive skills, but there is relatively greater emphasis on cognitive methods than behavioral methods (Young et al., 2001). Unlike symptom-focused treatment, schema-focused treatment does not end once the symptoms are treated. Rather, the therapist and client explore the deeper cognitive structures and the developmental issues that may have given rise to maladaptive schemas. Schema-focused interventions typically require twenty to forty sessions.

Relationship-focused interventions go beyond traditional cognitive therapy, moving in the direction of interpersonal and object-relations therapy and away from the behavioral tradition from which cognitive therapy emerged. The emphasis shifts to the therapeutic relationship more than the specific therapeutic methods the therapist uses.

CHRISTIAN CRITIQUE

The earliest forms of cognitive therapy were closely related to behaviorism, so many of the points made in chapter five also relate to cognitive therapy. But the lack of a comprehensive personality theory has resulted in a drift away from behaviorism to other theoretical perspectives making today's cognitive therapy a loose connection of ideas from behaviorism, contemporary psychodynamic theory, humanism, existentialism, social constructivism and generic forms of spirituality. This makes the task of a Christian critique rather daunting, but it also demonstrates a theoretical flexibility that makes cognitive therapy adaptable to a Christian worldview.

Philosophical Assumptions

As stated in chapter five, the behavioristic presuppositions of materialism, naturalism, atomism, reductionism and scientism are unacceptable for Christians because they exclude God and supernatural activity, and they strip humanity of its God-given rationality and dignity. Let us then turn to the matter of determinism.

As Christians we must believe in limited freedom, as developed in chapter two. And we must reject the kind of materialistic determinism espoused by Skinner. But is reciprocal determinism, as developed by Bandura, adequate as an understanding of limited freedom?

Bandura (1989) says explicitly that "freedom ... is defined positively in terms of the exercise of self-influence.... Self-generated influences operate deterministically on behavior the same way as external sources of influence do.... The self is thus partly fashioned through the continued exercise of self-influence" (p.1182). Note several things about this statement. First, Bandura defines freedom positively rather than negatively, presumably meaning that freedom does not mean the absence of causes. Second, it is clear that Bandura conceives of the working of the self in a mechanical way, suggesting that it develops by universal laws of behavior and is activated by external influences that impinge on the person. For Bandura, human beings are free in the sense that their behavior has an effect on their environment and hence on the changing of their own behavior (which he calls the development of the self). Further, these self-systems are not mere way stations for environmental influence but contribute something to behavior beyond the influence of environment.

Bandura's view can best be understood in terms of the distinction between hard and soft determinism (as discussed in chap.5; Evans, 1989). Both forms of determinism share the belief that behavior is determined and thus could not have occurred otherwise. Where the two views differ is that the hard determinist (e.g., Skinner) explicitly acknowledges that his view is incompatible with freedom while the soft determinist redefines freedom in such a way as to make it compatible with determinism, thus creating the illusion of freedom. Bandura engaged in just such a redefining move in the previous reference by defining freedom not as the capacity to have acted other than the causal forces dictated but as the exercise of self-influence, even when the exercise of self-influence is itself causally determined to occur! In other words, we have freedom whenever the self exercises its influence, even though the self-system operates by determined rules and thus could not have behaved otherwise. Bandura is clearly a soft determinist.

In Bandura's view we are not free in the sense of having any choices over which we exercise ultimate control as responsible agents. Bandura (1978) himself stated that there is no "psychic agent that controls behavior" (p.348).

For example, according to Bandura honesty may be described as an ability to resist external temptations to steal or lie, but that personality disposition is itself caused by something other than the decision of the person. At a descriptive level Bandura would agree that the person has the perception of making decisions to be honest. But ultimately the development of the characteristic of honesty is caused by factors over which the person has no control. The person learned to define honest and dishonest behavior, to value honesty and to regulate his or her own behavior to be able to resist external temptation by the standard laws of learning. Moral choice becomes just another behavior that is acquired the way all behaviors are acquired. This is why Wren (1982) described the social-learning understanding of persons as "paramechanical." The person never escapes the closed circle of determined acts.

In none of the behavioristic conceptions of the person do we have true limited freedom. All of these models are thus dangerous in that they propose a view of human persons in which we are mechanisms of some sort or another, beings which always do what they must do. This is as true for Bandura's conception of the person as for Skinner's. In the latter, we are noncognitive machines; in the former, we are thinking machines. Such views demean our true nature and undermine our sense (which reflects reality) of our responsibility for our actions.

As cognitive therapy has moved away from its moorings in behavioral theory, it has also moved away from Skinner's hard determinism and even Bandura's soft determinism. Beck's notion of a conscious control system suggests a degree of limited freedom, though Beck himself seems less interested in articulating philosophical presuppositions than making sense of what he observes as a clinician. It is possible that Beck sees the conscious control system as a metaphor for soft determinism, but he gives no reason to suspect this. Ellis and Meichenbaum also seem to assume human freedom—Ellis identifying more with a humanistic understanding of autonomous freedom and Meichenbaum with a postmodern constructivism understanding where one's perceptions influence reality just as surely as reality shapes one's perceptions. All cognitive therapists—perhaps especially those involved in third-wave approaches—emphasize metacognition, which is the ability to think about one's thinking. The very idea of metacognition assumes some degree of human freedom.

Of course, moving away from deterministic views brings other challenges. Ellis's model carries many of the same risks as the humanistic therapies (see chap.7) where individual freedom and personal happiness are elevated to such a priority that they leave no room for the universal realities assumed in Christianity. For example, the doctrine of sin is central to Christian orthodoxy. To some extent, sin is inescapable and therefore determinative. In Romans 7:14-25, the apostle Paul describes his battle with sin—how he desires freedom in Christ but fights against his sin nature despite his noble wishes.

> So I find this law at work: When I want to do good, evil is right there with me. For in my inner being I delight in God's law; but I see another law at work in the members of my body, waging war against the law of my mind and making me a prisoner of the law of sin at work within my members. (Rom 7:21-23)

This passage implies a degree of determinism, just as the following passage in Romans 8 implies a degree of freedom to choose right over wrong through the transforming power of Christ. Early in his career Ellis (1960) singled out the notion of sin to be the cause of virtually all psychopathology, calling people to rise above these guilt-inducing religious ideas in order to experience true freedom and happiness. He later argued that many religious doctrines, with their confining views of human freedom, are contrary to mental health (Ellis, 1971). Though

Ellis (2000) eventually reversed his earlier views of religion, this seemed more a concession to ideological trends in psychology and scientific data that demonstrated his earlier views to be wrong than any real philosophical change in REBT.

Other cognitive therapists have tried to look beyond behavioral assumptions to find explanations for dysfunctional automatic thoughts. This trend has pushed cognitive therapy closer to contemporary psychodynamic thought (Jones & Pulos, 1993; Ryle, 1990; Safran, 1998). A person may be troubled by the thought, *My boyfriend seems distant, and that is terrible.* A relationally oriented cognitive therapist will want to help this person reevaluate how terrible a distant boyfriend really is (i.e., dispute the automatic thought) while also looking deeper to see where the automatic thought originates. Perhaps this person has an intermediate belief: *I must always have a boyfriend to be a complete person.* But where does this intermediate belief come from? Perhaps it springs forth from a core belief, *I am defective and unlovable,* which emerged from childhood years with an enraged alcoholic mother and a passive, distant father. Notice how looking to childhood helps explain the origin of automatic thoughts while also introducing the same deterministic assumptions found in psychodynamic theories. Childhood experiences are determining psychological functioning later in life. Just as linking cognitive therapy with behavioral theory yields a deterministic view of persons, so also does linking cognitive therapy with psychodynamic theory.

On first look the third-wave therapies seem to resist the deterministic impulses found in other forms of cognitive therapy. The emphases on constructing one's own path in life and on mindfulness, for example, seem to suggest a good deal of individual freedom in choosing how one appraises and accepts a situation. Still, the underlying assumptions of evolutionary psychology rest on the deterministic notion that survival dictates human behavior and experience.

Nonetheless, of all the various psychotherapies perhaps the cognitive therapy view, faulty as it is, comes closest to a Christian view of freedom. Most cognitive therapists avoid the radical suggestion of autonomous freedom embraced by the humanistic psychologies, and they stop short of the suffocating determinism of classical psychoanalysis and behavior modification. It fails because only a theistic view of persons which asserts that we are created for moral accountability has an adequate grounding for a full conception of limited freedom.

Cognitive therapists are distinctive among the psychotherapy approaches for being open with clients about the change process and trying to enlist the client as a collaborator, a concept that carries with it a high view of the client's powers of choice and freedom. Compared to psychoanalysis, person-centered therapy and family-systems approaches, which seem to have a low view of the person's capacity for meaningful change apart from expert intervention, cognitive therapy has a high view of the person's capacity for change through self-control and related processes.

Although Beck appears to have no Christian intent, there are similarities between his notion of conscious control and the writings of the apostle Paul, who instructs his readers to transform their identities by the renewing of their minds (Rom 12:1-2) and to form a new identity in Christ (Rom 6:1-14; see also Roberts, 2001). Both Beck and the apostle Paul assume humans can develop self-awareness and the ability to change their views of self in relation to the world. Some Christian psychologists have taken these similarities too far, implying an intrinsic consistency between cognitive therapy and Christianity. But the similarity is limited to how the change process is perceived; their fundamental goals are still different. The goal of cognitive therapy is to help people feel and function better on their own terms and by their own definitions, whereas the apostle Paul's goal was to help people form an identity in Christ regardless of the immediate psychological consequences, and to make progress toward growth in holiness and manifesting Christlikeness as defined by God.

As noted previously, Hayes's assumption of destructive normality bears some resemblance to the Christian notion of original sin. Both have a certain deterministic quality that is viewed alongside the hope of human agency. We are mired in something destructive, but we are also able to gain freedom. How we gain freedom over destructive normality is the place where Christian orthodoxy and ACT part ways, with ACT being informed more by Buddhist spirituality than Christian thought.

Let us now move from the assumption of determinism to the cognitive therapy view of mind. There is no one cognitive therapy view of mind, but the general approach to the mind-brain problem is consistent with that of cognitive science and behaviorism in embracing an implicitly materialistic theory, viewing thought as a naturalistic process rooted in our neurology. But there are options in thinking about the mind-brain distinction that take the physical bases of thought seriously but do not leave us trapped in a deterministic framework. In particular, we can look at the emergentist view of Nobel Prize winner Roger Sperry.

Sperry's (1980) view of mind-brain interaction, in much too brief summary, is that human thought is founded on but transcends in limited ways physical determination. He suggests that human thought, characterized by limited freedom, emerges from the complex neurological building blocks of brain processes, which are fundamentally dependent on their physical substrates yet capable of transcending that physical programming. One of the analogies he uses is that of a rubber tire. By being formed into a tire shape, the rubber molecules behave in ways not predictable from knowledge of just their physical properties. Rolling freely is a property of wheels, not of rubber. Similarly, Sperry argues that thought emerges from—and has properties based on but not completely predictable from—the physical functioning of the brain. This view is intriguing, in that it proposes real freedom (a transcendent property), but not a freedom that ignores or is independent from the physical realities of our created natures.

Problems can occur at different levels of functioning. One person may have an existential crisis (a problem at the highest level of transcendence), which is manifested as anxiety, while another can have a biologically mediated anxiety problem (perhaps as a bad reaction to a prescription medication, a "purely" chemical problem). But most human concerns are multiple-level problems. An example would be a person with a phobia who is biologically predisposed to emotional overreactivity and who is unfortunately exposed to some powerful classical-conditioning experiences with phobic objects and develops distorted thinking patterns and expectancies based on past experience and finally responds to these proclivities in an existentially inauthentic manner (Evans, 1986). This view suggests that we can validly learn from the behavioral approaches in spite of their reductionism, as they give some perspicacious understandings of more primitive aspects of human psychological functioning.

Cognitive therapy does not fully embrace an emergentist view of mind, but it moves in that direction in suggesting that the rules governing the behavior of cognition are not the same rules of learning that govern lower-order animal behavior. And the movement of cognitive therapy toward constructivism (Mahoney, 2003) and mindfulness (Segal et al., 2002) seems to be moving it closer to emergentism. Segal et al. (2002) describe mindfulness training as an important part of cognitive therapy, likening changing one's frame of mind to changing gears on a car:

> We can think of the task of mindfulness training as teaching individuals ways to become more aware of their mode of mind ("mental gear") at any moment, and the skills to disengage, if they choose, from unhelpful modes of mind and to engage more helpful modes. We can describe this process as learning how to shift mental gears. (p.70)

Clearly implied in this description is a sense of transcendence over material processes. Mindfulness and constructivism hold other problems, such as relativism, but they also bring an autonomous view of the mind that makes cognitive therapy more acceptable to Christians as an integrating view of persons.

Sperry's view suggests that distinctly human characteristics are built on but not wholly reducible to the more basic processes we share with animals. A complicated human phenomenon such as religious conversion can involve basic processes, such as operant and classical conditioning; middlelevel phenomena, such as expectancies, encoding strategies and stimulus values; and highest-level processes, such as human responsibility and existential authenticity. Today's cognitive therapy spans much of the gap between operant learning at one extreme and existential choice at the other, reflecting the gamut of processes that are at play in human experience, from the naturalistic to the transcendent.

Finally, the assumptions of relativism found in each of the major models of cognitive therapy warrant consideration. A Christian view differs from the modern psychotherapies in that Christianity asserts that truth is established and revealed by God. Thus, the task of a Christian is to learn the truth and live accordingly; one makes meaning of life because God first ordained that life is meaningful and good. Furthermore, God reveals particular ways of living that maximize life's meaning and goodness. Christians are called to discern God's will and live accordingly—not because God is a cosmic sadist who wants people to plod through lives of joyless obedience, but because God desires people to experience an abundant life now and through all eternity, and knows how this is best accomplished.

In contrast, virtually all cognitive therapies assume that truth and meaning are not revealed by God but are human constructions. One of the most dangerous examples of this can be found in early forms of REBT when Ellis apparently perceived himself capable of determining what thoughts were rational and irrational. For example, Ellis (1962) considered it irrational to become upset over other people's problems. One wonders what he might say of the apostle Paul's instruction to "weep with those who weep" (Rom 12:15 ESV). Even more, one wonders how and why he determined sympathy to be irrational. When truth is defined by a particular clinician, it is vulnerable to the whims of personal circumstances and contemporary trends. Early in Ellis's career he deemed virtually all dogmatic religious thought to be irrational (Ellis, 1971).

Beck's approach may be slightly more responsible in that he collaborates with clients to set up "experiments" which help determine the veracity of a thought. In this way he is grounding rationality in at least two people's ideas (client and therapist), but it often seems that the goal of helping the client feel better becomes the standard of distinguishing rational and irrational thoughts. This may lead to symptom relief, and relieving suffering is a good and high calling, but a Christian worldview does not allow the luxury of defining rationality or truth on the basis of personal comfort.

The most responsible form of relativism is to ground reason in larger communities and cultures. Rather than one person or one therapeutic dyad determining rationality, the values of a larger group are used to define truth. It might be a contemporary community, such as an extended family or an ethnic group, or a historical community, such as a religious tradition. Today's psychology, with its emphasis on multicultural awareness, often draws on this socially constructed view of rationality. Both Meichenbaum's constructivist approach and contemporary third-wave approaches to cognitive therapy emphasize contextual factors more than previous forms of cognitive therapy. At best, this interest in social constructivism and cognitive therapy fits with a collectivist understanding of truth. At worst, in the hands of less responsible clinicians, it can devolve into an individualistic relativism where each person "writes" his or her own story with little regard for the large social values surrounding the person.

Though Christians ultimately reject relativism, it is important to look for a degree of wisdom in social constructivism that values culture and context. For example, not many decades ago it was considered morally unacceptable for Christians in the United States to attend movies, have a glass of wine with dinner or use playing cards. Most Christians now recognize that these were not biblical truths but socially constructed phenomena peculiar to a particular time and culture. More significantly, in centuries past

Christians have used the Scripture to justify atrocities such as slavery and oppressive versions of patriarchies, apparently thinking they were following God's truth, without recognizing how they were constructing views of truth according to social and economic values. Some recognition of social construction as a descriptive truth about the impact of our culture on our beliefs is important for thoughtful Christians, but constructivism should not substitute for believing in absolute truth. However imperfect our ability to perceive God's truth may be, Christianity is built on the assumption that reality is bigger and more than social construction.

Believing that God ordained absolute truth still does not guarantee that each individual Christian can interpret that truth correctly. In our fallen state each of us is blinder than we know (Moroney, 2000), and we need the help of a historical and contemporary community to correctly discern truth. A thoughtful Christian worldview calls us to dig deeply and find value in contemporary cultures and historical perspectives, and to do so not because truth is socially constructed but because social communities help us better understand aspects of God's revealed truth that might otherwise slip past our attention.

Models of Personality, Health and Abnormality

Because of the propensity of practitioners in this school of psychology to focus on microtheories of the specific pathologies, there is little we can comment on from a Christian perspective regarding the discipline's overall approach to defining personality, health and abnormality. There are no grand postulates about ultimate human ideals or about motivations among the prominent cognitive therapies.

However, McMinn and Campbell (2007) have recently proposed a model of integrative psychotherapy that is grounded in a Christian view of persons. They begin with three major theological views of the *imago Dei* (image of God; see Gen 1:26). Functional views focus on humans being created as managers over creation, given responsibility to behave in particular ways in relation to themselves, other humans and nature. Structural views of the *imago Dei* emphasize that humans have substantive capacities that allow us to live differently than the rest of creation. Most often these structural capacities have been deemed to be rationality and morality, though many more capacities could be named. Relational views suggest that humans do not carry the image by themselves, but that God's image is evident in relationship. The language of Genesis 1:27 seems to connect God's nature as a triune being with humans being created male and female. Just as God is complete in communion between Father, Son and Spirit, so also humans are complete in relation to one another. Though some debate about which of the three views of the *imago Dei* is best, most theologians find value in each view. McMinn and Campbell build their theory of motivation and change on these three views of the *imago Dei,* noting the similarity between these three views and major paradigms in psychology: behavioral, cognitive and relational. The therapy they propose has three levels of intervention that can be applied in varying degrees depending on the client's needs and commitment to therapy: symptom-focused intervention, schema-focused intervention and relationship-focused intervention.

McMinn and Campbell's (2007) model is relatively new, empirically untested and built on a Christian view of persons that places it outside mainstream psychology. Thus, we need to turn our attention back to critiquing the mainstream cognitive therapies discussed throughout this chapter. But before we do it is worth noting that McMinn and Campbell emphasize that being made in God's image is a multifaceted phenomenon. A popular defense of psychodynamic theory offered by Christians is to pronounce that God is relational and so humanity—made in God's image—is also relational. This is partly right, but it is also partly wrong by limiting God's image to a single dimension. God is also rational and moral and functional (and much more), and so being made in God's image involves more than just being relational.

Thus, there is some compatibility between Christianity and any system that places a high premium on human rationality. Cognitive therapy would say that what we believe has tremendous implications for our personal well-being. This certainly resonates with biblical themes, such as the words of Paul in Philippians 4:8-9: "Whatever is true, whatever is noble, whatever is right, whatever is pure, whatever is lovely, ... think about such things.... And the God of peace will be with you." According to cognitive therapy and the Bible, our thoughts are events over which we have control, and these thoughts have implications for the quality of our lives. A failure to believe the right things can lead to spiritual impoverishment, as we fail to appropriate God's resources. We see this especially in the area of suffering. When we view our temporal lives as primary and have as our highest goals comfort and prosperity, then suffering will be a misery-producing and faith-undermining experience. But if suffering is viewed as an opportunity for testimony for the gospel, as a means for fellowship with Christ in his sufferings, as preparation for eternal glory through learning to loosen our ties to this life, and as an opportunity to learn to better comfort others, suffering can be transformed into a meaningful path that one treads for the sake of God's love (Kreeft, 1986).

Some have drawn parallels between the Christian process of sanctification and the ways people change in cognitive therapy (Edwards, 1976; Pecheur, 1978). For example, Romans 8:5 reads, "Those who live according to the sinful nature have their minds set on what that nature desires; but those who live in accordance with the Spirit have their minds set on what the Spirit desires." This view of sanctification is one that fits well with many of the directive messages of Scripture that tend to be cognitive and behavioral in character; that is, they urge a dual emphasis on changing thoughts and actions (as Pecheur, 1978, ably points out). Further, this view meshes well with the methods advocated to promote spiritual growth by many conservative Christian groups, such as rigorous Bible study, Bible memorization, disciplined prayer and attention to good deeds.

We would agree that the processes and means for accomplishing sanctification are perhaps the most powerful parallel in the

Scriptures to the therapeutic process of growth. We would not, however, assert a fundamental identity between sanctification and therapy generally or cognitive therapy particularly. Cognitive and behavioral change does not mesh well with the more charismatic understandings of spiritual growth, which emphasize direct experiences of God's grace, nor with the more socially oriented Anabaptist traditions, which emphasize corporate life, the dynamics of life together, and the imperative to pursue peace and justice as the route to growth (Foster, 1998; Propst, 1988; Dueck & Reimer, 2009).

Further, the emphasis on cognitive change does not thoroughly comport with a relational understanding of spirituality, wherein spiritual growth is more a function of an alive relationship with the personal God than anything else. As Tan (1987) says, "Cognitive-behavioral therapy may overemphasize the rational thinking dimension of human functioning and undermine the experiential, and even mystical aspects of the Christian life and faith" (p.106; Tan cites 1 Cor 1:18-31; 2 Cor 2:12-16; 5:7 to support his contention). While the cognitive therapy emphasis on rationality is a positive, it cannot be made an absolute.

McMinn and Campbell (2007) note a number of limitations to cognitive therapy's optimistic views of rationality. First, cognitive therapists seem to assume that the fundamental human problem is irrationality, but such a view is not fully compatible with Christianity. The basic problem facing humanity is sin—both personal acts that cause damage to self and others and the state of brokenness in which our world languishes (Rom 8:20-25). Sin touches much more than our rationality; it reaches into every aspect of human nature (Berkouwer, 1971; McMinn, 2008). If sin is indeed the problem, then "the vision of calm reason is only ultimately possible with a faith in the providence of God" (Browning & Cooper, 2004, p.233).

Second, cognitive therapists seem to assume that healthy people are basically rational, but a great deal of scientific and historical evidence demonstrates otherwise. Even the healthiest individuals have distorted perceptions of themselves and the world around them (Moroney, 2000).

Third, such an optimistic view of rationality does not account for human motivation. What causes a person to grow and change throughout life; is it really an urge to become more logical and rational? A Christian view of human motivation emphasizes one's yearning for restored relationship with God and others. McMinn and Campbell (2007) go on to suggest that many of the cognitive irrationalities that emerge in therapy are connected to strained or ruptured relationships in the person's past or present. Human rationality and irrationality is often motivated by an intrinsic desire for relationship. It is worth noting that cognitive scientists are also noting connections between thought processes and human relationships (Andersen & Chen, 2002).

Fourth, some approaches to cognitive therapy tend to elevate cognition to a place of preeminence while dismissing emotions as trivial or undesirable postcognitive phenomena. Woolfolk and Richardson (1984) make this same point, noting that in cognitive therapy emotion is often treated as an add-on, a nuisance variable that must be controlled, modified or explained. Emotion is not conceived as a human capacity that enriches life or as a source of knowledge and growth. Just as in many evangelical circles, emotion in cognitive therapy is treated as a nuisance, as in: "Get your beliefs and your actions straight, and the emotions will just fall in line." This is a demeaning view of emotion, and it is not consistent with a Christian perspective. All through Scripture we see that God experiences various emotions, including those we deem positive and those we deem negative. Jesus, the "image of the invisible God" (Col 1:15), certainly experienced and expressed a diverse array of emotions—joy, sadness, anger, dread, grief, to name a few—and so Christians ought to value emotions as an important part of God's image revealed in humanity.

Fifth, some cognitive therapists seem to prioritize the techniques of rational change above the therapeutic relationship, as if the change occurs only through cognitive awakening. Throughout Scripture we see the importance of both rationality and relationality in how people change, and the two are almost always intertwined. In Romans 12:1-2 Paul teaches his readers to renew their minds (rationality) so that they can present themselves in purity to God (relationality). In Ephesians 4:23 Paul again writes of renewing one's mind, and then gives a relational reason why Christians should do so: "Be imitators of God, therefore, as dearly loved children and live a life of love, just as Christ loved us and gave himself up for us as a fragrant offering and sacrifice to God" (Eph 5:1-2). We could go on and on with examples, but the point is clear: both rationality and relationality are important, and they are intertwined in the healthy life.

Sixth, cognitive therapy's emphasis on rationality can be quite insensitive to culture and context. What seems rational to a therapist of one culture and gender may seem less rational to a client of a different background. Although the Christian message contains universal truths for all people in all time, we also see examples in Scripture of Christ and his followers understanding and respecting the cultural context in which they lived and taught.

Perhaps the greatest danger in cognitive therapy is that of embracing a distorted standard of rationality. Since the goal of therapy is the eradication of pathological emotional reactions, the beliefs or cognitions of the client tend to be judged by their utility rather than by their truthfulness. (We introduced this problem earlier in this chapter when discussing the philosophical assumption of functional relativism.) For example, suppose that the continual recurrence of the thought *I am a sinner whose righteousness is as filthy rags before the Lord; I am wholly without merit before him* brought substantial distress to its thinker, including loss of sleep and loss of enjoyment of worldly success. With only a pragmatic standard to guide the therapist, the most expeditious course would be to attempt to undermine the belief by whatever means available with the goal of either eradicating or modifying the client's thought. Questions such as, What evidence is there that God exists or that God cares about your behavior at all? might be pursued by the secular therapist. The goal would be to eradicate the thought because it bothers the client. The religious counselor, on the other hand, might judge the negative emotional reaction appropriate because of the validity of the thoughts themselves, and other explanations for the emotional agitation possibly sought. A time of true repentance and grieving over our sinfulness is a healthy part of the Christian life, and might be a rational response under these conditions.

But it is also true that it does not seem to be God's wish that we all be paralyzed by our grief over our sin, and there should come a time where believers come to see their sinfulness in the context of the marvelous provision of salvation from God, and where our remorse becomes secondary to our love for this marvelous redeeming God who desires us to worship him and serve him, and to our celebration of his grace. So in the case of a protracted and overly severe preoccupation with one's own sinfulness, the Christian cognitive therapist would regard the thoughts as true but perhaps not in their proper context among other Christian beliefs, and hence might see the emotional response as problematic. Thus the Christian counselor would not be using the pragmatic standard for judging beliefs. The therapist's method would not be to undermine the belief, but to put it in proper perspective among other beliefs.

Another issue worth addressing is the underlying assumption that humans are fundamentally motivated to enhance their own welfare. For example, most cognitive and behavioral considerations of interpersonal behavior use the organizing conception of competency to evaluate interpersonal action. This concept suggests that human behavior is primarily directed at obtaining desired goods from the personal and impersonal environment. Competent responses are most often defined as those that are "effective" or "competent" at getting what we want or at accomplishing a specific task (see McFall, 1982). Behavioral theories and concepts direct our attention inexorably to the functional value of any human behavior; that is, *what it does for the organism.* This seems to be a holdover from the Skinnerian understanding that sees all significant behavior as operant—designed to operate on the environment to produce a desired outcome.

This orientation manifests itself in the cognitive therapy understanding of love and altruism. Cognitive therapists have been active in developing clinical models of marriage therapy, typically beginning with the assumption that individuals are motivated to maximize rewards for themselves—something Stuart (1980) has called the best bargain principle.

Whereas this assumption is explicit for many behavioral therapists (e.g., Jacobson & Margolin, 1979), it is more subtle but equally pernicious in cognitive therapy. For example, Epstein and Baucom (2002) write, "We propose that adults seek to meet a variety of important human motives and needs, both communal and individual, within the context of their intimate relationships" (p.15). Though this is a reasonable statement reflecting humans' desire for relationship, Epstein and Baucom are still assuming that each person in a relationship behaves based on motives to meet personal needs and desires. This assumption has its parallels in other social sciences as well, such as in rational choice theory in economics.

So even in the most giving of human relationships—marriage—persons are assumed to be attempting to maximize their own receipt of personal satisfactions. This is also true of cognitive therapy's view of altruism (doing good for another for no apparent reason). Kanfer (1979), for example, suggested that altruism is a form of behavior where one delays personal and immediate reinforcement for the sake of long-term outcomes: "[The] task, as in self-control, is to train persons to act for the benefits of another because it is in their own self-interest" (p.237). They take for granted that people are basically out for themselves. People are seen as having their own welfare as their only ultimate concern.

In some ways Christian theology is similarly pessimistic about humanity. Seeing self-enhancement as a core motivation should not be a surprise for persons who believe in human depravity. But we are not just depraved, selfish beings; we are also all created in the image of God, the God of all love, the giving and self-sacrificing God. Thus it would seem that all humans have some capacity for transcending their human egocentrism and that Christians should have a special capacity for self-transcendence through God's grace, for compassion and self-sacrificing love. The love described in 1 Corinthians 13 is definitely not a self-interested love devoid of personal sacrifice. Love is a foundational human capacity created in us from the beginning, as when the first humans in the creation story were told to cleave to one another and that the two would become one flesh. Descriptively, the Christian Scriptures and tradition seem to take human selfishness into account, appealing, for example, to the rewards we will personally receive in heaven to motivate good behavior here on earth. But the Scriptures never stop at that point, going on to call persons to a life wherein our desires conform evermore to God's purposes without regard for our own welfare.

With God's help, we are capable of such a transition.

Just as with behavior modification, cognitive therapists often emphasize competence and skill development. For example, the person with panic disorder can learn skills to escape the vicious cycle of rapid breathing and runaway thoughts. By learning calming self-talk the person regains control over breathing patterns and returns oxygen–carbon dioxide ratios to normal levels. Common competencies taught in cognitive therapy include self-efficacy, schema deactivation, assertive communication and countering automatic thoughts.

If we believe that the task of mastery is consistent with a biblical understanding of persons and that we are each to be about some dimension of a dominion work, then competence seems an important concept in human life. If self-efficacy (the idea that we are motivated by our beliefs in our own effectiveness) is equated with human pride, it will be viewed negatively by Christians, but it need not be viewed as such. Rather, our actions seem to have been meant by God to matter, to be effective. We are beings designed for meaningful work and effective interactions with our world. Christianity is not wedded to prescribing that each of us feel or perceive ourselves to be incompetent, as if the feeling of helplessness were a virtue. Propst (1988) correctly reminds us that Christianity is not merely a religion of the afterlife but one that endorses a certain spirituality of everyday life. As we submit our day-to-day lives to God, he redeems them and allows us to live to his glory. But we continue to live in this world and must have effective and righteous ways of dealing with it.

Thus it would seem that helping clients achieve meaningful mastery over their lives is a goal compatible with Christian faith. As Tan (1987) suggested, though, an overemphasis on self-efficacy can lead to pride. In our effectiveness we seem to have been meant to live in a dynamic tension of delight in our competencies and realization of our utter dependence on God. Perhaps the best summary of this dynamic is the statement of Paul in Philippians 4:13: "I can do everything through him who gives me strength."

A Christian view of will and self-control also has some broad compatibilities with the view expressed by cognitive therapy. The Christian view of will is that it is a capacity that can be developed, as opposed to it being an all-or-nothing, static personality trait. Hebrews 12, for instance, discusses at length the notion of discipline from God, noting that we are disciplined for our good (Heb 12:10; note the appeal to personally desirable consequences) and that discipline is often unpleasant. Hebrews 12:12-13 ("Strengthen your feeble arms and weak knees. 'Make level paths for your feet'") are especially interesting, in that they provide a practical agenda for strengthening weak spots in our personal discipline. The injunction to "make level paths for your feet" clearly means to choose a course that puts minimal stress on an area of personal weakness, as when a person consumed with envy might refrain from obtaining any knowledge about the performance and possessions of others in order not to open a window of opportunity for sin to occur. A voluntary refraining from opportunity for sin may give time for growth in strength to withstand sin.

Compare this view to that of cognitive therapy's view of self-regulation (as did Bufford, 1977). Self-regulation involves developing awareness of the external factors that are powerful determinants of one's behavior and altering them deliberately to produce desired change (for instance, avoiding temptation situations and surrounding oneself with encouraging, strengthening influences), and also developing effective internal or cognitive control capacities through more effective self-observation and administration of consequences to the self (e.g., naming God's commandments, instructing and exhorting oneself). In this view, will is developed as a skill, and thus growth in self-control is possible, rather than being an unalterable personality trait caused by toilet-training practices, as in classical psychoanalysis. In this area there are meaningful compatibilities between cognitive therapy and the biblical view of persons.

As with all the secular therapies, there is a danger in cognitive therapy that the therapist will focus only on psychological change without any spiritual emphasis at all. The focus of cognitive therapy is limited only to temporal aspects of personhood. Spiritual and religious matters have no intrinsic or integral part in the model. Reading a standard cognitive therapy work, one would think that religion only existed as one rather unusual category of belief that occasionally crops up with a client, or as a nuisance variable that affects what a client values. Despite some recent concessions that religion may not be as destructive as previously thought, religious beliefs—except perhaps for Buddhist beliefs in some third-wave approaches—are still not viewed as life-enhancing or intrinsically important in this approach.

One final positive attribute of this approach is its idiographic emphasis. Cognitive therapy embodies a high view of human uniqueness. Persons are not regarded as reducible to five scales on a personality inventory but are seen as individuals with unique abilities, interests, struggles and wounds. This idiographic method allows for some understanding of persons developmentally, and the current trends toward schema-based and constructivist cognitive therapies have made developmental exploration a legitimate part of cognitive therapy. Of course it is possible for a therapy to be too idiographic, making no use of common models for understanding human development, such as the psychosocial development model of Erikson. The extreme embrace of uniqueness can mean that no two persons' experience is comparable and that their development cannot be understood in common terms. This is perhaps a good example of how the idiographic tendencies can be a curse as well as a blessing. Historically, this extreme idiographic perspective has been a fault of cognitive therapy, but it appears to be changing. For example, Needleman (1999) demonstrates how Erickson's psychosocial stages correspond with various core beliefs contained in maladaptive cognitive schemas. Similarly, Young et al. (2003) have identified a taxonomy for early maladaptive schemas and a corresponding assessment device known as the Young Schema Questionnaire (www.schematherapy.com).

Model of Psychotherapy

Perhaps no other therapy approach so closely mirrors a biblical balance of cognitive and action orientation as cognitive therapy. Even a superficial reading of the pastoral exhortations of the New Testament epistles yields a clear theme of obedience in actions and in thoughts as the way to maturity. If one looks at Philippians 3–4 or Ephesians 4, one sees clearly an exhortation to think new thoughts and engage in new deeds to germinate the seed of faith into full spiritual maturity. Perhaps the reason why Adams's (1973) early versions of nouthetic counseling and Crabb's (1977) early model of biblical counseling have enjoyed some continuing popularity is that both embody a combined behavioral and cognitive emphasis that parallels the theme of direct change expressed in Scripture. The real issue is whether this is the exclusive or dominant theme of Scripture. In any case, cognitive therapy shares this focus.

One of Beck's earliest interventions for depression involved helping people plan daily goals and activities, to set goals and then experience the accomplishment of reaching those goals. Many other cognitive therapy techniques have been developed since Beck's early work, and a common theme is providing tools for clients to gain mastery over their thoughts and behaviors. To the extent that this represents a God-honoring development of the capacity to exercise better stewardship over the portion of creation God has placed us in, this can certainly be a worthwhile set of procedures for Christians to embrace. To live effectively, we must be able to order the practical challenges of daily life by managing time and setting goals as well as knowing how to pray, how to communicate our feelings to our spouses and so on. The cognitive approach assumes that many people experiencing problems of living lack one or more of these basic living skills and that therapy can help correct these deficits.

But just as we discussed with behavior modification, the *amorality* of cognitive therapy is problematic. Cognitive therapists seem content to have their clients' values dictate the course of therapy, as we noted earlier (Woolfolk & Richardson, 1984). To some extent it could be argued that all the modern psychotherapies are governed by clients' goals and values, but it is complicated in cognitive therapy because there is no clear theoretical vision for who a person should become. Because cognitive therapy has a less well-developed notion of the ideal human state than such theories as person-centered therapy, it is difficult for cognitive therapy to be a growth psychotherapy—there is no built-in compass pointing out the direction of growth.

From a Christian perspective the lack of prescriptive focus of cognitive therapy actually can allow for a more comfortable utilization of the system by the Christian than some other systems. The techniques of cognitive therapy seem less value-encrusted and thus the system might be more effectively adapted for use by the religious therapist. However, this requires intentional effort. Uncritical acceptance of prevailing cognitive therapy assumptions leads to shallow views of healing and growth. To read some cognitive therapy literature, one would get the constricted impression that growth means the absence of anxiety, depression and the major forms of discomfort; hence, to be fully human is to be without pain. This is a superficial and anemic view of human maturity. Cognitive therapists, consequently, seem proficient at eliminating suffering (about which clients have focused goals) but less capable at producing growth. But this raises the provocative question of whether psychotherapy should be properly limited to healing or problem solving, leaving promotion of growth to such traditional resources as the church.

Healing versus growth in psychotherapy is a topic of much discussion these days, illustrated by two opposing trends. The first is health care reimbursement, which has moved decisively toward symptom-reduction models of psychotherapy. It is more cost effective for an insurance company to pay for twelve sessions of therapy aimed at symptom alleviation than fifty sessions of growth-oriented therapy, even if the briefer therapy may make a person more prone to relapse. The second theme, much smaller in scope, is seen in the growing interest in spiritual direction and psychotherapy. Various Christian psychotherapists are looking back to ancient soul-care traditions and attempting to integrate healing and growth with spiritual and psychological methods (Benner, 2005).

There are risks with both of these trends, which call for caution and discernment. Though it makes sense from an economic perspective to prefer short-term symptom-focused therapy, for a Christian the goals of psychotherapy are inevitably more complex than helping a person feel better. As cognitive therapy models have evolved, they now offer clients ways to explore factors underlying their symptoms in order to gain a degree of self-understanding and to prevent the high rates of relapse associated with the symptom-based treatments. Cognitive therapy will never offer the depth of exploration evident in psychodynamic models, but it can still provide a degree of uncovering that encourages clients to confront their values and beliefs and to leave therapy having asked important questions about character issues, spiritual matters and the directions their lives are heading. It would be a loss for Christian therapists to be so influenced by economic forces that they fail to explore newer depth-oriented models of cognitive therapy.

But it is also worth considering risks of emphasizing spiritual growth as a primary goal for psychotherapists. Christian therapists attempting to blend psychotherapy and spiritual direction face a number of ethical challenges. For example, does the therapist bill the client's insurance company for psychotherapy if part or all of the session is used for spiritual direction? And there are questions of training. Is it legitimate to assume that an advanced degree in psychology, along with spiritual fervor and some experience with spiritual direction, sufficiently qualifies a person to provide spiritual direction services? Perhaps most important, what are the long-term consequences of removing spiritual direction from the authority of the church, where it has always been, and making it a privatized endeavor associated with psychotherapy? For these reasons and more, it seems important to be cautious about the extent that spiritual growth is an explicit goal in Christian versions of therapy.

Somewhere between the extremes of symptom-focused therapy and blending spiritual direction with therapy there is a balance where a Christian psychotherapist helps clients look beneath immediate symptoms to see their deeper wounds and questions about life, and yet the therapist does so in a way that remains within the bounds of training in psychotherapy.

Christian models of cognitive therapy have sometimes used imagery as a method to bring healing and promote spiritual growth. These range from approaches developed by scientifically grounded psychologists (Propst, 1988) to popularized Christian healing-of-memory approaches, such as theophostic ministry (Smith, 2002). It is beyond the scope of this book to critique theophostic ministry, though we recommend that those interested read the hard-hitting critiques that have been offered (e.g., Entwistle, 2004a, b). Our attention here will be limited to formal psychotherapy approaches, such as the model described by Propst (1988).

Propst rightly points out that often the cognitions troubling a client are not in verbal propositional form (such as a wrong doctrinal belief) but are better described as troublesome images, such as a sexually abused woman experiencing fragmentary memories of her childhood abuse as she interacts with men. Propst urges the explicit incorporation of religious imagery, specifically images of Christ. She discusses different imagery interventions, such as the use of the image of surrendering our thoughts, emotions and experiences to Christ. This example would seem acceptable to almost all Christians, in that such surrendering seems an implication of the concept of the lordship of Christ.

Propst (1988) then moves on to examples that may be more troublesome to some Christians, examples that involve the person imaging Christ doing or saying things judged to be therapeutic but which may or may not fit his real character. The imagery examples that Propst shares include the image of Christ telling a woman that it is okay to be scared of breast cancer, of Christ rescuing and comforting a client when as a child she was being abused, and of Christ expressing acceptance and encouraging a woman who had experienced gang rape to touch him. The problem here is that we are making the Christ of our image do what we want or expect him to do, to do what the therapist deems therapeutic, in situations where his (Jesus') response may not be clear.

We have talked with clients who on their own have used even more troubling images for comfort in situations where some Christians would believe that Christ would speak rebuke.

For example, a man who had just left his wife because of his agony due to being "trapped" in a marriage with no love imagined Christ lovingly saying, "I understand. I have experienced unbearable agony too." In other words, he imagined Christ supporting his decision to desert his wife. Some would argue that in that situation Christ would really say, "Take up your cross and go back to your wife; follow me in obedience and I will sustain you." We risk twisting God into the shape we desire when we imagine specific responses on his part. At the same time, perhaps in many circumstances we can understand his character sufficiently to know with confidence what he would do. It will require real spiritual maturity and wisdom to understand when we are on firm ground in projecting the nature of his responses to us, and perhaps will require accountability to the church as well.

Finally, we turn to the question of effectiveness. In general, most psychotherapies have about equal effectiveness in reducing the symptoms assessed by outcome measures: approximately 80 percent of those receiving treatment do better than the average person who does not receive treatment (Asay & Lambert, 1999). As with other therapies, cognitive therapy is deemed to be effective with a variety of disorders. Butler and Beck (2001) reviewed fourteen meta-analyses in the scientific literature, involving over 300 studies and 9,000 clients, concluding that cognitive therapy is useful in treating depression and various anxiety disorders. Some studies have also shown cognitive therapy to be slightly more effective than other treatment approaches with particular disorders and populations (Ehlers & Clark, 2003; Barrowclough et al., 2001), though some of this may be due to the fact that cognitive therapy lends itself to research protocols better than some of the other approaches.

Only a few research studies have compared Christian versions of cognitive therapy with mainstream versions (Johnson, 1993b; McCullough, 1999), and all of these have focused on the treatment of depression. In general, no differences between the effectiveness of Christian and mainstream versions have been reported. Though Propst, Ostrom, Watkins, Dean and Mashburn (1992) found a religious form of cognitive therapy to be slightly better than a nonreligious form in helping religious clients recover from depression, interpreting their results is difficult because they found the most favorable outcome when nonreligious therapists delivered the religious form of therapy.

Various challenges face researchers interested in evaluating Christian forms of cognitive therapy. Most forms of cognitive therapy are relatively superficial adaptations of mainstream approaches, perhaps adding religious imagery or Scripture verses to a therapy that is otherwise unchanged. A more interesting project would be to develop and test a cognitive therapy based on a Christian view of persons. McMinn and Campbell (2007) have proposed such a model, but have not done empirical research to test its effectiveness. A related problem is how to measure outcome. Most researchers and cognitive therapists assume that symptom reduction is the primary outcome variable to consider, but Christians may have cause to question this. Perhaps some clients grow in depth of character and maturity through suffering even if they do not show dramatic decreases in symptom patterns. Conversely, some clients may show striking reductions in symptoms while avoiding the deeper issues of character development that need to be addressed. Finally, research demonstrating that a therapy works does not necessarily reveal how it works. One of the most provocative studies regarding cognitive therapy suggests that it may work because it emulates some of the same therapeutic processes that are used in psychodynamic therapy (Jones & Pulos, 1993). Though cognitive therapists tend to emphasize how to apply particular techniques to help people change, increasing attention is being given to the importance of the therapeutic relationship itself in promoting good outcomes (Lambert & Barley, 2002).

CONCLUSION

Cognitive therapy has at least the following strengths when evaluated from a Christian perspective: It posits limited freedom for the person, though the formal understanding of that freedom is incompatible with a Christian understanding of human responsibility. Cognitive therapy appreciates the embodied, human aspect of our existence and has a well-articulated understanding of at least some of the person variables and processes that seem foundational to human action. The ideographic assumptions seem respectful of human uniqueness. An appreciation of the influence of the environment on behavior (though not environmental determinism) seems appropriate from a Christian perspective. The humbling and broad understanding of human motivation as basically selfish but complex is a strength. Cognitive therapy's high view of rationality is a plus, though the standards of rationality must be modified for the Christian. The view of the centrality of habits of thought and action to making life adjustments seems realistic. The relatively shallow view of personality, as reflected in its amorality and lack of a vision of maturity, makes it a somewhat more adaptable tool for the Christian therapist than some other approaches to therapy. New adaptations of cognitive therapy are sensitive to childhood and cultural issues, yet without going as far toward developmental determinism as psychoanalysis. Finally, cognitive therapy emphasizes empirical accountability in all aspects of its practice, and, for Christians, this accords well with a commitment to good stewardship of time and energies, and with a commitment to honesty.

In spite of all these positives, one is left with a clear sense that there is much more to human beings than cognitive therapy would lead us to believe. Where is transcendence and spirituality? How do we understand self-deception or evil? Does this view really plumb the profound depths of relationships and the terrific impact we have on one another? Isn't emotion more than the output of cognitive habits? What about conflict within the person; isn't this inevitable and indeed helpful to our understanding what it means to be truly human? How are we to grow? Are there any important regularities to the way we develop as human beings? Cognitive therapy's silence on each of these questions is disconcerting.

It seems likely that we are what cognitive therapy depicts us as being: thinking and acting creatures who act on and are acted on by our environments for the purpose of obtaining that which we value. But it also seems clear to the Christian that we are more than this. Nevertheless, given its many strengths, cognitive therapy is likely to be one of the more fruitful models for Christians to explore for its integrative potentials.

FOR FURTHER READING

Barlow, D.H. (Ed.). (2001). *Clinical handbook of psychological disorders: A step-bystep treatment manual* (3rd ed.). New York, NY: Guilford Press.

An excellent reference book for contemporary cognitive and behavioral treatments.

Dobson, K.S. (Ed.). (2010). *Handbook of cognitive-behavioral therapies* (3rd ed.). New York, NY: Guilford Press.

An informative contemporary professional handbook for this approach.

McMinn, M.R., & Campbell, C.D. (2007). *Integrative psychotherapy: Toward a comprehensive Christian approach.* Downers Grove, IL: IVP Academic.

This is an attempt to provide a Christian foundation for cognitive therapy.

Young, J.E., Klosko, J.S., & Weishaar, M.E. (2003). *Schema therapy: A practitioner's guide.* New York, NY: Guilford Press.

A helpful introduction to schemas and how they relate to cognitive processes.

REFERENCES

Adams, J. (1973). *The Christian counselor's manual.* Grand Rapids, MI: Baker.

Andersen, S.M., & Chen, S. (2002). The relational self: An interpersonal socialcognitive theory. *Psychological Review, 109,* 619-645.

Asay, T.P., & Lambert, M.J. (1999). The empirical case for the common factors in therapy: Quantitative findings. In M.A. Hubble, B.L. Duncan & S.D. Miller (Eds.), *The heart and soul of change: What works in therapy.* Washington, DC: American Psychological Association.

Backus, W. (1985). *Telling the truth to troubled people.* Minneapolis, MN: Bethany.

Backus, W., & Chapian, M. (2000). *Telling yourself the truth: Finding your way out of depression, anxiety, fear, anger and other common problems by applying the principles of misbelieve therapy.* Minneapolis, MN: Bethany House.

Bandura, A. (1978). The self system in reciprocal determinism. *American Psychologist, 33,* 344-358.

Bandura, A. (1986). *Social foundations of thought and action.* Englewood Cliffs, NJ: Prentice-Hall.

Bandura, A. (1989). Human agency in social cognitive theory. *American Psychologist, 44,* 1175-1184.

Barrowclough, C., et al. (2001). A randomized trial of the effectiveness of cognitive-behavioral therapy and supportive counseling for anxiety symptoms in older adults. *Journal of Consulting and Clinical Psychology, 69,* 756-762.

Beck, A.T. (1976). *Cognitive therapy and the emotional disorders.* New York, NY: Meridian.

Beck, A.T. (1988). *Love is never enough.* New York, NY: Harper & Row.

Beck, A.T. (1993). Cognitive therapy: Past, present, and future. *Journal of Consulting and Clinical Psychology, 61,* 194-198.

Beck, A.T. (1996). Beyond belief: A theory of modes, personality, and psychopathology. In P.M. Sakovskis (Ed.), *Frontiers of cognitive therapy* (pp.1-25). New York, NY: Guilford Press.

Beck, A.T., Emery, G., & Greenberg, R.L. (1985). *Anxiety disorders and phobias: A cognitive perspective.* New York, NY: Basic Books.

Beck, A.T., Freeman, A., & Associates. (1990). *Cognitive therapy of personality disorders.* New York, NY: Guilford Press.

Beck, A.T., Freeman, A., & Davis, D.D. (2003). *Cognitive therapy of personality disorders* (2nd ed.). New York, NY: Guilford Press.

Beck, A.T., Rush, A.J., Shaw, B.F., & Emery, G. (1979). *Cognitive therapy of depression.* New York, NY: Guilford Press.

Beck, A., Wright, F.D., Newman, C.F., & Liese, B.S. (1993). *Cognitive therapy of substance abuse.* New York, NY: Guilford Press.

Benner, D.G. (2005). Intensive soul care: Integrating psychotherapy and spiritual direction. In L. Sperry & E.P. Shafranske (Eds.), *Spiritually oriented psychotherapy* (pp.287-306). Washington, DC: American Psychological Association.

Berkouwer, G.C. (1971). *Studies in dogmatics: Sin.* Grand Rapids, MI: Eerdmans.

Browning, D.S., & Cooper, T.D. (2004). *Religious thought and the modern psychologies* (2nd ed.). Minneapolis, MN: Fortress Press.

Bufford, R. (1977). *The human reflex: Behavioral psychology in biblical perspective.* San Francisco, CA: Harper & Row.

Butler, A.C., & Beck, J.S. (2001). Cognitive therapy outcomes: A review of meta-analyses. *Tidsskrift for Norsk Psykologforening, 38,* 698-706.

Chambless, D.L., & Hollon, S.D. (1998). Defining empirically supported therapies. *Journal of Consulting and Clinical Psychology, 66,* 7-18.

Cloud, H., & Townsend, J. (1995). *Twelve Christian beliefs that can drive you crazy:*

Relief from false assumptions. Grand Rapids, MI: Zondervan.

Collins, F.S. (2006). *The language of God: A scientist presents evidence for belief.* New York, NY: Free Press.

Crabb, L. (1975). *Basic principles of biblical counseling.* Grand Rapids, MI: Zondervan.

Crabb, L. (1977). *Effective biblical counseling.* Grand Rapids, MI: Zondervan.

Crane, R. (2009). *Mindfulness-based cognitive therapy.* London: Routledge.

Craske, M.G., & Barlow, D.H. (2001). Panic disorder and agoraphobia. In D.H. Barlow (Ed.), *Clinical handbook of psychological disorders* (3rd ed., pp.1-59). New York, NY: Guilford Press.

Dimeff, L.A., & Linehan, M.M. (2001). Dialectical behavior therapy in a nutshell. *The California Psychologist, 34,* 10-13.

Dobson, K.S. (Ed.). (2010). *Handbook of cognitive-behavioral therapies* (3rd ed.). New York, NY: Guilford Press.

Dueck, A., & Reimer, K. (2009). *A peaceable psychology: Christian therapy in a world of many cultures.* Grand Rapids, MI: Brazos.

Edwards, K. (1976). Effective counseling and psychotherapy: An integrative review of the research. *Journal of Psychology and Theology, 5,* 94-107.

Ehlers, A., & Clark, D.M. (2003). Early psychological interventions for adult survivors of trauma: A review. *Biological Psychiatry, 53,* 817-826.

Ellis, A. (1960). There is no place for the concept of sin in psychotherapy. *Journal of Counseling Psychology, 7,* 192.

Ellis, A. (1962). *Reason and emotion in psychotherapy.* New York, NY: Lyle Stuart.

Ellis, A. (1971). *The case against religion: A psychotherapist's view.* New York, NY: Institute for Rational Living.

Ellis, A. (1978). The theory of rational-emotive therapy. In A. Ellis & J. Whitely (Eds.), *Theoretical and empirical foundations of rational-emotive therapy* (pp.33-60). Monterey, CA: Brooks/Cole.

Ellis, A. (1980). Psychotherapy and atheistic values: A response to A.E. Bergin's "Psychotherapy and religious values." *Journal of Consulting and Clinical Psychology, 48,* 635-639.

Ellis, A. (2000). Can Rational Emotive Behavior Therapy (REBT) be effectively used with people who have devout beliefs in God and religion? *Professional Psychology: Research and Practice, 31,* 29-33.

Entwistle, D.N. (2004a). Shedding light on theophostic ministry 1: Practice issues. *Journal of Psychology and Theology, 32,* 26-34.

Entwistle, D.N. (2004b). Shedding light on theophostic ministry 2: Practice issues. *Journal of Psychology and Theology, 32,* 35-42.

Epstein, N.B., & Baucom, D.H. (2002). *Enhanced cognitive-behavioral therapy for couples: A contextual approach.* Washington, DC: American Psychological Association.

Evans, C. (1986, January 17). The blessings of mental anguish. *Christianity Today,* pp.26-30.

Evans, C. (1989). *Wisdom and humanness in psychology.* Grand Rapids, MI: Baker.

Foa, E.B., & Franklin, M. (2001). Obsessive-compulsive disorder. In D.H. Barlow (Ed.), *Clinical handbook of psychological disorders* (3rd ed., pp.209-263). New York, NY: Guilford Press.

Foster, R. (1998). *Streams of living water: Celebrating the great traditions of the Christian faith.* San Francisco: HarperSan-Francisco.

Garfield, S.L. (1996). Some problems associated with "validated" forms of psychotherapy. *Clinical Psychology, 3,* 218-229.

Hathaway, W., & Tan, E. (2009). Religiously oriented mindfulness-based cognitive therapy. *Journal of Clinical Psychology: In Session, 65,* 158-171.

Hauck, P.A. (1972). *Reason in pastoral counseling.* Philadelphia, PA: Westminster Press.

Havik, O.E., & VandenBos, G.R. (1996). Limitations of manualized psychotherapy for everyday clinical practice. *Clinical Psychology, 3,* 264-267.

Hayes, S.C. (1993). Goals and varieties of scientific contextualism. In S.C. Hayes, L.J. Barnes, T.R. Sarbin & H.W. Reese (Eds.), *The varieties of scientific contextualism* (pp.11-27). Reno, NV: Context Press.

Hayes, S.C. (2002). Buddhism and acceptance and commitment therapy. *Cognitive and Behavioral Practice, 9,* 58-66.

Hayes, S.C. (2004a). Acceptance and commitment therapy and the new behavior therapies: Mindfulness, acceptance, and relationship. In S.C. Hayes, V.M. Follette & M.M. Linehan (Eds.), *Mindfulness and acceptance: Expanding the cognitive-behavioral tradition* (pp.1-29). New York, NY: Guilford Press.

Hayes, S.C. (2004b). Acceptance and commitment therapy, relational frame theory, and the third wave of behavior therapy. *Behavior Therapy, 35,* 639-665.

Hayes, S.C. (2005). *Get out of your mind and into life: The new acceptance and commitment therapy*. Oakland, CA: New Harbinger.

Hayes, S.C., & Strosahl, K.D. (Eds.). (2004). *A practical guide to acceptance and commitment therapy.* New York, NY: Springer.

Hayes, S.C., Strosahl, K.D., & Wilson, K.G. (1999). *Acceptance and commitment therapy: An experiential approach to behavior change.* New York, NY: Guilford Press.

Jacobson, N., & Margolin, G. (1979). *Marital therapy.* New York, NY: Brunner/Mazel.

Johnson, W.B. (1993a). Christian rational-emotive therapy: A treatment protocol. *Journal of Psychology and Christianity, 12,* 254-261.

Johnson, W.B. (1993b). Outcome research and religious psychotherapies: Where are we and where are we going? *Journal of Psychology and Theology, 21,* 297-308.

Johnson, W.B., & Ridley, C.R. (1992). Brief Christian and non-Christian rational-emotive therapy with depressed Christian clients: An exploratory study. *Counseling and Values, 36,* 220-229.

Jones, E.E., & Pulos, S.M. (1993). Comparing the process in psychodynamic and cognitive-behavioral therapies. *Journal of Consulting and Clinical Psychology, 61,* 306-316.

Kabat-Zinn, J. (1990). *Full catastrophe living: Using the wisdom of your body and mind to face stress, pain, and illness.* New York, NY: Dell Publishing.

Kanfer, F. (1979). Personal control, social control, and altruism: Can society survive the age of individualism? *American Psychologist, 34,* 231-239.

Koerner, K., & Dimeff, L.A. (2007). Overview of dialectical behavior therapy. In L.A. Dimeff & K. Koerner (Eds.), *Dialectical behavior therapy in clinical practice* (pp.1-18). New York, NY: Guilford Press.

Kovacs, M.B., & Beck, A.T. (1978). Maladaptive cognitive structures in depression. *American Journal of Psychiatry, 135,* 525-533.

Kreeft, P. (1986). *Making sense out of suffering.* Ann Arbor, MI: Servant.

Lambert, M.J., & Barley, D.E. (2002). Research summary on the therapeutic relationship and psychotherapy outcome. In John C. Norcross (Ed.), *Psychotherapy relationships that work* (pp.17-32). New York, NY: Oxford University Press.

Lazarus, A. (1980). Treatment of dyspareunia. In S. Leiblum and L. Pervin (Eds.), *Principles and practice of sex therapy* (pp.147-166). New York, NY: Guilford Press.

Lieb, K., Zanarini, M.C., Schmahl, C., Linehan, M.M., & Bohus, M. (2004). Seminar section: Borderline personality disorder. *Lancet, 364,* 453-461.

Linehan, M.M. (1987). Dialectical behavior therapy: A cognitive behavioral approach to parasuicide. *Journal of Personality Disorders, 1,* 328-333.

Linehan, M.M. (1989). Cognitive and behavior therapy for borderline personality disorder. In A. Tasman, R.E. Hales & A.J. Frances (Eds.), *Review of psychiatry* (Vol.8, pp.84-102). Washington, DC: American Psychiatric Press.

Linehan, M.M. (1993a). *Cognitive-behavioral treatment of borderline personality disorder.* New York, NY: Guilford Press.

Linehan, M.M. (1993b). *Skills training manual for treating borderline personality disorder.* New York, NY: Guilford Press.

Mahoney, M.J. (1993). Introduction to special section: Theoretical developments in the cognitive psychotherapies. *Journal of Consulting and Clinical Psychology, 61,* 187-193.

Mahoney, M.J. (2003). *Constructive psychotherapy: A practical guide.* New York, NY: Guilford Press.

McCullough, M.E. (1999). Research on religion-accommodation counseling: Review and meta-analysis. *Journal of Counseling Psychology, 46,* 92-98.

McFall, R. (1982). A review and reformulation of the concept of social skills. *Behavioral Assessment, 4,* 1-33.

McMinn, M.R. (1991). *Cognitive therapy techniques in Christian counseling.* Waco, TX: Word.

McMinn, M.R. (2008). *Sin and grace in Christian counseling: An integrative paradigm.* Downers Grove, IL: IVP Academic.

McMinn, M.R., & Campbell, C.D. (2007). *Integrative psychotherapy: Toward a comprehensive Christian approach.* Downers Grove, IL: IVP Academic.

McRae, R.R., & Costa, P.T., Jr. (2003). *Personality in adulthood: A five-factor theory perspective.* New York, NY: Guilford Press.

Meichenbaum, D. (1977). *Cognitive-behavior modification.* New York, NY: Plenum.

Meichenbaum, D. (1985). *Stress inoculation training.* New York, NY: Pergamon.

Meichenbaum, D. (1993). Changing conceptions of cognitive behavior modification: Retrospect and prospect. *Journal of Consulting and Clinical Psychology, 61,* 202-204.

Messer, S.B. (2004). Evidence-based practice: Beyond empirically supported treatments. *Professional Psychology, 35,* 580-588.

Mischel, W. (1973). Toward a cognitive social learning reconceptualization of personality. *Psychological Review, 80,* 252-285.

Moroney, S.K. (2000). *The noetic effects of sin.* Lanham, MD: Lexington Books.

Needleman, L.D. (1999). *Cognitive case conceptualization: A guidebook for practitioners.* Mahwah, NJ: Erlbaum.

Newman, C.F., Leahy, R.L., Beck, A.T., Reilly-Harrington, N.A., & Gyulai, L. (2002). *Bipolar disorder: A cognitive therapy approach.* Washington, DC: American Psychological Association.

Nielsen, S.L., Johnson, W.B., & Ellis, A. (2001). *Counseling and psychotherapy with religious persons: A rational emotive behavior therapy approach.* Mahwah, NJ: Erlbaum.

Norcross, J.C., Hogan, T.P., & Koocher, G.P. (2008). *Clinician's guide to evidence-based practices: Mental health and the addictions.* New York, NY: Oxford University Press.

Öst, L-G. (2008). Efficacy of the third wave of behavioral therapies: A systematic review and meta-analysis. *Behaviour Research and Therapy, 46,* 296-321.

Pecheur, D. (1978). Cognitive theory/therapy and sanctification. *Journal of Psychology and Theology, 6,* 239-253.

Propst, R. (1988). *Psychotherapy in a religious framework: Spirituality in the emotional healing process.* New York, NY: Human Sciences Press.

Propst, L.R., Ostrom, R., Watkins, P., Dean, T., & Mashburn, D. (1992). Comparative efficacy of religious and nonreligious cognitive-behavioral therapy for the treatment of clinical depression in religious individuals. *Journal of Consulting and Clinical Psychology, 60,* 94-103.

Roberts, R.C. (2001). Outline of Pauline psychotherapy. In M.R. McMinn & T.R. Phillips (Eds.), *Care for the soul: Exploring the interface of psychology & theology* (pp.134-163). Downers Grove, IL: InterVarsity Press.

Robins, C.J., & Chapman, A.L. (2004). Dialectical behavior therapy: Current status, recent developments, and future directions. *Journal of Personality Disorders, 18,* 73-89.

Robins, C.J., Schmidt, H., & Linehan, M.M. (2004). Dialectical behavior therapy: Synthesizing radical acceptance with skillful means. In S.C. Hayes, V.M. Follette & M.M. Linehan (Eds.), *Mindfulness and acceptance: Expanding the cognitive-behavioral tradition* (pp.30-44). New York, NY: Guilford Press.

Robins, R.W., Gosling, S.D., & Craik, K.H. (1999). An empirical analysis of trends in psychology. *American Psychologist, 54,* 117-128.

Ryle, A. (1990). *Cognitive-analytic therapy: Active participation in change.* New York, NY: Wiley.

Safran, J.D. (1998). *Widening the scope of cognitive therapy: The therapeutic relationship, emotion, and the process of change.* Northvale, NJ: Aronson.

Safran, J.D., & Segal, Z.V. (1990). *Interpersonal process in cognitive therapy.* New York, NY: Basic Books.

Schmidt, J. (1983). *Do you hear what you're thinking?* Wheaton, IL: Victor Books.

Segal, Z.V., Williams, J.M.G., & Teasdale, J.D. (2002). *Mindfulness-based cognitive therapy for depression: A new approach to preventing relapse.* New York, NY: Guilford Press.

Shedler, J. (2010). The efficacy of psychodynamic psychotherapy. *American Psychologist, 65,* 98-109.

Silverman, W.H. (1996). Cookbooks, manuals, and paint-by-numbers: Psychotherapy in the 90s. *Psychotherapy, 33,* 207-215.

Smith, E.M. (2002). *Healing life's hurts through theophostic prayer.* Ventura, CA: Regal.

Sperry, R. (1980). Mind-brain interactionism: Mentalism, yes; dualism, no. *Neuroscience, 5,* 195-206.

Stuart, R. (1980). *Helping couples change.* New York, NY: Guilford Press.

Tan, S. (1987). Cognitive-behavior therapy: A biblical approach and critique. *Journal of Psychology and Theology, 15,* 103-112.

Thurman, C. (2003). *The lies we believe.* Nashville, TN: Thomas Nelson.

Wampold, B.E., & Bhati, K.S. (2004). Attending to the omissions: A historical examination of evidence-based practice movements. *Professional Psychology, 35,* 563-570.

Williams, J.M.G., Teasdale, J.D., Segal, Z.V., & Kabat-Zinn, J. (2007). *The mindful way through depression: Freeing yourself from chronic unhappiness.* New York, NY: Guilford Press.

Woolfolk, R., & Richardson, F. (1984). Behavior therapy and the ideology of modernity. *American Psychologist, 39,* 777-786.

Wren, T. (1982). Social learning theory, self-regulation, and morality. *Ethics, 92,* 409-424.

Young, J.E. (1990). *Cognitive therapy for personality disorders: A schema-focused approach.* Sarasota, FL: Professional Resource Press.

Young, J.E., Klosko, J.S., & Weishaar, M.E. (2003). *Schema therapy: A practitioner's guide.* New York, NY: Guilford Press.

Young, J.E., Weinberger, A.D., & Beck, A.T. (2001). Cognitive therapy for depression. In D.H. Barlow (Ed.), *Clinical handbook of psychological disorders* (3rd ed., pp.264-308). New York, NY: Guilford Press.

7

PERSON-CENTERED THERAPY

Terri Watson, Stanton L. Jones and Richard E. Butman

***

It is especially difficult to get beyond mere intuitive and emotional appeal when evaluating person-centered therapy. Indeed, a counselor in this tradition would strike many as a good model of what it means to be a wise and patient friend, a person with an enormous capacity to listen attentively and respectfully. In a culture like ours where interpersonal contact and intimacy can be lost to absorption in the tasks of everyday living, few would find these qualities unattractive. Perhaps one reason why Carl Rogers's theory and technique has been so warmly embraced within significant portions of the religious community is that it appears to give us valuable clues and guidance on how to respond to those in misery and distress, or how to concretely "love the brothers and sisters."

While only a small percentage of clinicians practice from a purely person-centered perspective, over one-third of "eclectic" therapists integrate Rogers's person-centered therapy and other experiential techniques with their orientation (Norcross & Prochaska, 1988, as cited in Bohart, 2003). During his career Rogers conceptualized what many believe to be the most comprehensive humanistic theory of personality (Bozarth, Zimring & Tausch, 2001). He is considered to be the father of psychotherapy outcome research (Bozarth et al., 2001), and his emphasis on the primary role of the therapeutic relationship in therapy outcomes has received wide support. Kirschenbaum and Henderson (1989) assert that Rogers is "the most influential psychologist in American History" (p.xi).

An ever-evolving approach since the early 1940s, humanistic and person-centered therapies have experienced a noticeable renewal of late as evidenced by the recent publication of two handbooks of humanistic therapy (Cain & Seeman, 2001; Schneider, Bugental & Pierson, 2001). The recent interest in empirically supported therapy relationships (Norcross, 2002), an attempt to counterbalance focus on empirically supported techniques (ESTs) in psychotherapy, had resulted in renewed interest in Rogers's original "necessary and sufficient conditions" for the therapeutic relationship, and compels the Christian student of psychology to take another look at this important historical figure.

DESCRIPTIVE SURVEY

Philosophical Assumptions

Probably no theory of counseling and psychotherapy more fully manifests the humanistic spirit in contemporary psychology than does person-centered therapy, and perhaps no single individual better embodied its essence than its founder, Carl Rogers. For that reason, an understanding of the philosophical assumptions of person-centered therapy must start with a deeper look at the person of Carl Rogers.

It is surprising to many Christians that Rogers grew up in a fundamentalist Christian home and was intent on pursuing full-time ministry during his college years. In fact, excerpts from Rogers's journal during his freshman year paint a picture of a young man fervently seeking God's will in his life:

> I'll try and keep my life in tune with God, so that He can guide me. I have plenty of ambition, in fact I sometimes think I'm too ambitions, but if I can only keep that terrible swelling force within me in the right path, I know all will be well.... Lord, I ask Thy guidance; I am seeking the

> kingdom of Heaven; and the door at which I knock Thou alone knowest beside myself. Lord help me to see in the right spirit that I may obtain. Amen. (Kirschenbaum, 1979, p.20)

During a trip to China as a youth delegate to the World Christian Federation Conference, Rogers encountered liberal Christian thinking and rejected the faith of his parents in favor of liberal humanism (Van Belle, 1985b, p.1016). Following his trip, Rogers wrote: "I have changed to the only logical viewpoint—that I want to know what is true, regardless of whether that leaves me a Christian or no" (Kirshenbaum, 1979, p.25). Rogers pursued theological training at Union Theological Seminary, to the dismay of his parents who felt Union was one of the more liberal seminaries in the country. After attempting full-time ministry as the pastor of a church, Rogers decided to leave the ministry and pursue education in psychology at Teachers College at Columbia University. There, he was influenced by John Dewey, a humanist and pragmatist. Rogers spoke very little about spiritual and religious themes during his teaching and practice of psychology until the later years of his life, where he made increased reference to mystical experiences (Thorne, 2002).

It is quite clear that person-centered therapy is a reaction against what Rogers perceived as the dogmatism of "prescriptive" religion and the elitist and rationalistic tendencies of classical psychoanalysis. In stark contrast to the strongly biological and deterministic assumptions of the early Freudian model (chap.3), Rogers stressed a highly personal, phenomenological and positive view of human experience. Person-centered therapy is often said to embody the permissive and pragmatic mindset of the contemporary North American milieu (Van Belle, 1980). Person-centered therapy emphasizes the primacy of the individual and is often criticized for contributing to modern narcissism and the erosion of any shared sense of meaning or value in contemporary society (Vitz, 1977).

The heritage of person-centered therapy is rooted in phenomenology. Edmund Husserl, often called the "father of phenomenology," strongly influenced this distinctive approach to philosophy. Phenomenology (as summarized by Carver & Scheier, 2004) contends that what we are and what we do is a reflection of our subjective experience of the world and ourselves. External reality can only be known through the inner reality of personal experience. All persons are viewed as unique and possessing a unique perspective or "frame of reference." Self-determinism, the ability to exercise free will in decision making, is also an important tenant of phenomenology that influenced Rogers's development of person-centered therapy. Finally, phenomenology maintains the optimistic perspective that human beings are moving toward health, perfection, goodness and self-sufficiency. Clear evidence of the influence of phenomenology is evident in Rogers's views of personality and human functioning.

As Van Belle (1985a) has observed, Rogers had a profound respect for the client's perception of reality since this inner reality was ultimately the means for promoting development and growth in the individual. Indeed, Rogers is dogmatic in asserting that experience is the ultimate authority in life: "It is to experience that I must return again and again; to discover a closer approximation to truth as it is in the process of becoming in me. Neither the Bible nor the prophets, neither Freud nor research, neither the revelations of God nor man, can take precedence over my own direct experience" (Rogers, 1961, pp.23-24). Person-centered therapy boldly asserts that the client, not the therapist, should be at the heart of psychotherapy (and hence, it is person centered) since only the client has the resources by which to become more aware of and remove his or her obstacles to personal growth.

Rogers's philosophical assumptions were influenced by his historical and cultural milieu. North American values of individualism versus conformity, equality of all persons and rejection of the class system, aversion to authoritarianism, and the primacy of the individual and her freedom in society are all clearly reflected in Rogers's model of personality and health.

Model of Personality

Consistent with Rogers's pragmatic and phenomenological method of therapy, he developed his theory of therapy first, and then a theory of personality emerged from his clinical work.

Perhaps the core assertion of this personality theory is that there is but one motivational force for all humanity: the tendency toward self-actualization. All persons have an inherent tendency to develop their capacities to the fullest, in ways that will maintain or enhance their own well-being. Rogers believes this motivational force is present at birth. Inherent to all living things, Rogers suggests, is the tendency toward growth without any conscious effort. This growth is toward autonomy, away from dependence or control by external forces.

Detractors of person-centered therapy often equate self-actualization with selfishness, but this is not strictly true. Actualization is the realization of our potential, and our potential certainly includes the capacity to love. Thus, Rogers would believe that out of the fully actualized, fully functioning individual would come acts of charity and kindness that would be a free and loving expression of the person's true inner state. Profound narcissism would actually be one mark of a failure to actualize one's potential. Contemporary person-centered therapists view this self-actualizing tendency not as an indication that humans are basically "good," rather they suggest that we all possess an inherent capacity for growth and the ability to change, or a "self-righting tendency" (Bohart, 2003).

While this motivation produces our movement, the direction for the movement comes from the *organismic valuing process*—an inherent capacity to choose that which will enhance us and reject that which does not. The actualization drive creates in us an urge for fulfillment, and the organismic valuing process tells us what will provide that fulfillment. The organismic valuing process is presumed to be an infallible and instinctive compass or guide for choice and action.

Model of Health

What then is the ideal course for human development according to person-centered therapy? The child, blessed with a drive toward actualization and an inerrant organismic valuing process to guide her, still needs the acceptance and positive regard of her parents. If the parents provide this positive regard unconditionally, the child grows up always exquisitely aware of her natural urges and awareness (her self-experience). As consciousness of self emerges, the person will begin to define herself (develop her self-concept) in accord with her own experience of herself and not in terms of how others see her or expect her to be. Further, she has no aspirations to be other than what she is, and her *ideal* self, the perception of what she should be, then perfectly matches the self-concept, which in turn perfectly matches the self-experience.

As we develop and mature, our self-concept increasingly shapes and directs the organismic valuing process. Thus, a self-concept unpolluted by distortions caused by other persons' judgments of us allows the organismic valuing process to continue to operate as an infallible guide. Health, then, is seen as a congruence between what one wants to become, what one perceives one's self to be and what one actually experiences or is. To quote Rogers (1961) on the fully functioning person:

> He is more able to experience all of his feelings, and is less afraid of any of his feelings; he is his own sifter of evidence, and is more open to evidence from all sources; he is completely engaged in the process of being and becoming himself, and thus discovers that he is soundly and realistically social; he lives more completely in this moment, but learns that this is the soundest living for all time. (p.192)

The healthy person then is one who has an intact and functioning organismic valuing process and who completely trusts the valuing process. That person is fully aware, honest, personally satisfied and spontaneous. Health reflects trust of self, openness to experiencing and existential living in the present. Ideally, person-centered therapy posits, this will lead to a new kind of freedom whereby the person chooses to direct his or her life from within rather than by the dictates of the external world. Such "centeredness" (in the sense of balance, not self-centeredness) will release enormous potential to further oneself even more. There will be no need to deny or distort the information that is received perceptually since a strong sense of self has emerged that is consistent with deeply internalized conditions of worth. The chief Rogerian virtues are to be fully alive to the moment, completely self-accepting and strongly committed to an ongoing process of personal growth. Rogers (1961), quoting Kierkegaard, suggests the goal of personhood is to "be that self which one truly is" (p.166).

For contemporary person-centered therapists this includes "listening" to all of the different "voices" residing in the self, including thoughts, feelings and "including any internalized 'voices' from parents and society" (Bohart, 2003). While clients are encouraged to "listen" to their feelings, there is acknowledgment that feelings are not the best guide to decision making. "Person-centered theorists believe that fully functioning people use *all* their faculties. They use both their ability to think rationally and problem-solve with their ability to experientially sense what is personally meaningful to the self" (Bohart, 2003, p.114).

Contemporary person-centered therapists recognize that Rogers's emphasis on independence and autonomy as health is a reflection of masculine, North American cultural values, and thus limited (O'Hara, 1994; Bohart, 2003). They propose a view of self as developing in the context of relationships with fluid boundaries and influences from the environment. These contemporary theorists are sensitive to the cultural difference in the way people construct a sense of self, and suggest that it is necessary to work within the "perceptual universe" of individuals (O'Hara, 1994). This relational view of the self-in-context increases the cultural competency of person-centered therapists in working with disadvantaged people groups both within and outside of North America (Bohart, 2003).

Model of Abnormality

Unfortunately, few of us get through childhood so unscathed. Most of us are subjected to conditions of worth, are loved conditionally; that is, we are expected to act in accord with the expectations of parents or significant others rather than by our instincts in order to receive acceptance. Christian discipline and instruction would, for Rogers, be a prime example of disrespect for the child's self-directedness. The child is confronted with the need to deny certain aspects of his experience and act according to rules or judgments of authority figures *(God wants me to honor my parents; I guess I'm not really angry at Daddy).* He then develops an ideal self, dictated by parental wishes, which does not fit who he really is *(Good boys love their parents and don't get angry with them)* and develops a self-concept that is formed in part by what the child genuinely experiences of himself and partly of what the child feels he must be *(I'm a good boy who doesn't get angry at Mom and Dad).* The distorted self-concept quickly warps the organismic valuing process, resulting in impaired perceptions of himself and his world and of the choices he can make.

In person-centered therapy problems in living are seen primarily in terms of incongruence between different dimensions of the self. Psychopathology results when we become more externally oriented than internally oriented, trying to manufacture feelings or behavior that others demand we exhibit before we can be acceptable. The incongruence between what we really are and what we are trying to be creates psychological pain, rigidity and anxiety. The distortions in the self-concept warp the functioning of the organismic valuing process, so that the person makes more bad (incongruent) choices about what would further his or her personal actualization.

The symptoms of abnormality are seen as signs or symbols of ways that we prevent threatening experiences from becoming more accurately represented in our conscious and subjective awareness. As the symptoms become more pronounced, our informational and perceptual processes become increasingly inadequate and rigid. In short, psychopathology is a split or incongruence between self and experience.

Contemporary person-centered therapists also acknowledge the role of psychological problems stemming from real environmental stressors such as economic or physical hardship, dysfunctional relationships or situations that are beyond one's inherent problem-solving capacities (Bohart, 2003).

Model of Psychotherapy

If external conditions of worth result in the distortion of the self, what can be done about this condition formally in the context of counseling and psychotherapy, or more informally in the setting of everyday interactions? Person-centered therapy suggests that positive self-regard, and thus congruence between self-concept and the person's experience, can be encouraged by relating to the individual with *congruence, empathy* and *unconditional positive regard.*

This will, according to Rogers, encourage the person to more fully trust the organismic valuing process and move toward greater self-actualization. The major task of the therapist is to provide a climate of safety and trust, one that will encourage clients to reintegrate their self-actualizing and self-valuing processes. The therapist accomplishes this through encouraging the psychotherapeutic conditions (the "therapeutic triad") of accurate empathic understanding, congruence or genuineness, and unconditional positive regard, which are seen as the necessary and sufficient conditions for effective counseling (Bohart, 2003).

Empathy has received considerable attention in contemporary psychological literature and is so widely accepted as a key component of therapist effectiveness that nearly all approaches to psychotherapy explicitly value therapist empathy (Bohart, 2003). Empathy is not sympathy; rather, it is the therapist's capacity to experience with the client and accept the client's subjective inner world. It does not mean "agreeing with" the client's perspective; rather, it describes the ability to "intuit oneself inside the client's perceptual universe" (p.127). Some person-centered therapy proponents contend that empathy is *the* key therapist attitude and response to foster the therapeutic relationship (Bozarth, Zimring & Tausch, 2001).

Congruence or genuineness is the therapist's capacity to truthfully and accurately perceive her or his own inner experiencing in response to the client and to allow that inner experience to affect the counseling relationship in a healthy way; it is the capacity to be fully oneself while fully relating to the client. Person-centered therapists distinguish between congruence and transparency, which refers to open sharing of thoughts and feelings on the part of the therapist. In contrast, congruence refers to "attending inwardly to one's experience and working to sort out its meanings" (Bohart, 2003, p.128). Person-centered therapists attend to their reactions to the client, but only share with the client what is in her or his best interest.

Unconditional positive regard is an unyielding acceptance of, respect for and prizing of the client's experience, actualizing tendencies and organismic valuing process. Each of these qualities are seen by Rogerians as being rooted in the personhood of the therapist, and not as mere techniques. They can be learned as practical skills (one can learn lists of empathic responses, genuine responses, etc.), but to be used effectively they must take root in the very being of the counselor. Person-centered therapy never involves advice giving, shaming, teaching, giving interpretations, manipulation or other ingenuine interactions. These, it is argued, are based on a fundamental disrespect of others; they foster dependency and thwart the development of any meaningful sense of autonomy.

Understandably, for the person-centered therapist, the therapeutic relationship is of utmost importance. Unlike other approaches that see therapy as the therapist "doing something to" the client, person-centered therapy is best understood by an analogy to gardening: It is the provision of the right interpersonal soil in which the client's hidden drive to grow and develop can finally be released. Only through the proper characteristics and competencies of the therapist can the client move toward greater congruence and release of his or her own innate capacities.

As coparticipants in a process of change and discovery, the client-therapist relationship is egalitarian, informal and nonauthoritarian. Formal assessment of the presenting concerns or underlying dynamics in the forms of psychological testing or psychiatric diagnosis are seen as inappropriate and unnecessary. Techniques, of which there are few in person-centered therapy, are secondary to the therapist's attitudes, sensitivities and skills. Active listening, clarification and reflection of feelings, personal presence and coparticipation are seen as the only necessary tools in the repertoire of the person-centered therapist, coupled with a profound respect for process and inner-directedness. It is assumed that the client will freely choose to translate the changes experienced in the intimate context of therapy to outside relationships with others.

Change occurs in person-centered therapy when new understandings of self and others emerge from the "creative process" of therapy. Described as "more of a process of creation than of repair" (Bohart, 2003, p.131), person-centered therapy allows the client to creatively explore his or her thoughts, feelings and perceptions in a supportive, empathic relationship, and to "try on" new behaviors (Bohart, 2003).

While many person-centered therapists continue to be purists in their commitment to nondirectivity and trust in the client's growth direction, some person-centered therapists provide an empathic, genuine, egalitarian relationship, but utilize more directive techniques from other approaches to therapy (Bohart, 2003). Emotion-focused approaches to therapy, which will be reviewed in chapter eight, are examples of integrative therapies that incorporate person-centered therapy with contemporary research and practice.

CHRISTIAN CRITIQUE

The debate continues in contemporary Christian theological and psychological literature regarding Carl Rogers as a "friend" or "foe" in his influence on Judeo-Christian thought in the culture and in the church. Thorne (1998), a committed Anglican, emeritus professor and trained person-centered therapist, articulates the challenges of maintaining allegiance to both the church of England and the work of a Rogerian therapist as that of being branded a "liberal heretic doing Lucifer's work" by fellow Christians, and "loss of credibility at best and total rejection at worst" by the psychology community (p.x). Rogers's views of the person, in particular, have influenced the field of pastoral care, the church and the theological anthropology of many Christian thinkers (Browning & Cooper, 2004; Thorne, 1998). In this appraisal of person-centered theory we will draw from a diversity of Christian perspectives to evaluate the congruence of the theory and practice of person-centered therapy with Christian thought.

Philosophical Assumptions

Compared to some traditions, person-centered therapy is commendably explicit about its philosophical presuppositions. Many aspects of these assumptions can be appreciated. The insistence on seeing people holistically and as purposeful, the appreciation of other ways of knowing beyond rationality, and the profound respect of what it means to be a person are all positive in many ways. Rogers reminds us of the uniqueness and wonder of creation, the miracle of being created in the image of God. Thorne (2002), in fact, suggests the presence of a "covert spiritual thread in Rogers's work from the outset" (p.x) and proposes that person-centered sensibilities toward self and others prompt a great appreciation toward and connectedness with others and with creation, that "compassionate engagement with the suffering earth and identification with the beauty of creation become poignant areas for the person-centered therapist's spiritual agenda" as well as "an openness to be surprised by the resourcefulness and beauty of the human being" (p.43).

For the Christian the philosophical presuppositions undergirding person-centered therapy ought also to raise a number of concerns. It would appear that Rogers developed his person-centered approach not only in reaction to the mainstream psychology of the day but also in reaction to (or against) his Christian upbringing and Judeo-Christian assumptions about authority, freedom and human nature. Thus, a reading of Rogers's thought seems oddly familiar, but also disturbing in his reformulation (or outright rejection) of many foundational components of a Christian theological anthropology.

Authority and the self. Person-centered therapy assumes that we are the ultimate force and the sole masters of our own destiny; in other words, all authority is within. We see this in Rogers's clear rejection of all other sources of authority. This is a paradigmatic humanistic approach to psychotherapy in the fullest sense of the word; humanity is the center. This rejection of all authority outside of the self to define truth is reflected in Rogers's life, and central to his decision to leave the ministry and the church to pursue training in psychology.

The self assumes a position of supreme importance in Rogers's person-centered therapy, a notion that can be traced back to the philosophy of idealism and romanticism in the nineteenth century. The strongly experiential, individualistic and relativistic "core assertions" of person-centered therapy unquestionably lead to inflated notions of the self (Vitz, 1977; Myers, 1981).

Certainly we are called as Christians to develop our identities as a matter of good stewardship, but we must also confront the realities of the created order, including the existence of evil both within us and without. Self is not all there is and should not be the center of what is. As Vitz (1977) has said, "To worship one's self (in self-realization) or to worship all humanity is, in Christian terms, simple idolatry operating from the usual motive of unconscious egotism" (p.93). In the Christian tradition, to proclaim oneself to be in control of one's own existence is the ultimate act of rebellion. C.S. Lewis (1968) once remarked that a good functional definition of hell would be the kind of place where all acted as if they were the master of their own lives.

Phenomenology and the self. The emphasis on self is not only a problem for ontology but for epistemology as well. Person-centered therapy boldly states that when one's self-actualizing tendency is in tune with the organismic valuing process, trustworthy self-knowledge is fully obtainable and should take precedence over all else. But to boldly assert the complete trustworthiness of self-knowledge is certainly not within the mainstream of the Christian tradition (cf. Dodgen & McMinn, 1986). The organismic valuing process is not an inerrant guide! No aspect of human nature is untouched by sin and hence inerrant.

Thus the Christian must question Rogers's reliance on self-knowledge as the ultimate authority. The phenomenological approach places great value on subjective experience in discerning truth. Rogers is optimistic about one's experience as the basis of determining truth, but rather pessimistic about the value of culture, dogma, traditions and systems of morality (Roberts, 1993). In contrast, the Christian tradition has always had a high view of divine revelation and the authority of Scripture, as well as the role of the discerning community. Its regard for general revelation, including a deeper understanding of human nature through greater self-awareness and understanding, has been more hesitantly asserted (cf. Roberts, 1985).

Freedom and responsibility. Person-centered therapy is also implicitly a system of ethics. In person-centered therapy, one is ultimately responsible only to oneself. Personal wholeness assumes primacy; it becomes a moral imperative, often at the expense of a proper appreciation of our responsibilities to others. Browning and Cooper (2004) provide an excellent analysis of the moral implications of self-actualization and question the moral philosophy that would propose self-actualization as the objective of the human life and reliable guide for decision making. The authors suggest that humanistic theorists such as Rogers are practicing ethical egoism in their assumption that a pursuit of individual fulfillment, and encouragement of others to do the same, will naturally lead to harmony and altruism in society. In contrast, Browning and Cooper take the position that the individual pursuit of such aims should be in subordination to a social and interpersonal "ethic of justice" by basing moral behavior on what is best for the community. For the ethical egoist a belief in the harmony of nature results in a minimization of the need for individual moral behavior, "The only moral task to be concerned with is one's own growth" (p.80).

Browning and Cooper point out important inconsistencies between the ethical egoist pursuit of self-actualization and the value of mutual and *agape* love in the Christian tradition. Mutual love, they argue, requires a significant degree of obligation and self-transcendence, rather than pursuit of one's own actualization and the assumption that this will harmonize with others who are doing the same.

(Continued in the next Volume)

www.ingramcontent.com/pod-product-compliance
Lightning Source LLC
LaVergne TN
LVHW082021200926
848481LV00010B/2897
* 9 7 8 1 4 5 9 6 6 0 3 1 1 *